NEWS OF THE WORLD

News of the World is the first in-depth study of how television viewers around the world respond to the ever increasing mass of information available from news programs. Researchers from seven countries describe and interpret the type of news available and how it is understood in the context of everyday life.

News of the World develops the tradition of qualitative reception analysis; an approach which is increasingly employed to account for the effect of the media. This study is based on news analysis, individual interviews, and household interviews in seven countries: the United States, India, Mexico, Italy, Denmark, Israel, and Belarus. The contributors examine the flow of news across national borders, and their findings lead to the formulation of a cross-cultural model which offers a framework for further comparative studies of communication.

Contributors: Ann N. Crigler, Nadia V. Efimova, Michael Gurevitch, K.P. Jayasankar, Klaus Bruhn Jensen, Tamar Liebes, Paolo Mancini, Stefania Di Michele, Anjali Monteiro, W. Russell Neuman, Guillermo Orozco, Elena Alemagni Pimpinelli, David L. Swanson.

Editor: Klaus Bruhn Jensen is Associate Professor, University of Copenhagen, and the director of its research program, 'The Visual Construction of Reality.' He is the author of *Making Sense of the News, The Social Semiotics of Mass Communication*, and the co-editor of *A Handbook of Qualitative Methodologies for Mass Communication Research*.

ROUTLEDGE RESEARCH IN CULTURAL
AND MEDIA STUDIES
Series Advisors: David Morley and James Curran

NEWS OF THE WORLD

World cultures look at television news

Edited by Klaus Bruhn Jensen

London and New York

First published 1998
by Routledge
11 New Fetter Lane, London EC4P 4EE

Simultaneously published in the USA and Canada
by Routledge
29 West 35th Street, New York, NY 10001
Reprinted 2000

Routledge is an imprint of the Taylor and Francis Group

©1998 Klaus Bruhn Jensen, selection and editorial matter; individual chapters,
the contributors

Typeset in Galliard by Routledge

Printed and bound in Great Britain by TJI Digital, Padstow, Cornwall.

British Library Cataloguing in Publication Data
A catalogue record for this book is available from the British Library

Library of Congress Cataloguing in Publication Data
News of the world: world cultures look at television news/
edited by Klaus Bruhn Jensen. (Routledge research in cultural and media studies)
Includes bibliographical references and index. 1. Television broadcasting of news.
I. Jensen, Klaus. II. Series.
PN4784. T4N48   1998
97–47559
070.1′95–dc21
CIP

ISBN 0–415 16107 x

CONTENTS

CONTENTS

ILLUSTRATIONS

TABLES

FIGURES

CONTRIBUTORS

Ann N. Crigler is Associate Professor and Director of the Jesse Unruh Institute of Politics at the University of Southern California, USA. She has co-authored *Common Knowledge: News and the Construction of Political Meaning* (1992) and *Crosstalk: Citizens, Candidates, and Media in a Presidential Campaign* (1996) and edited *The Psychology of Political Communication* (1996).

Nadia V. Efimova is Associate Professor in the Department of Sociology, Belarusian State University, and a senior researcher in the Independent Institute of Socio-Economic and Political Studies, Minsk, Belarus.

Michael Gurevitch is Professor at the College of Journalism, University of Maryland, USA. His most recent book is *The Crisis of Public Communication* (1996), co-authored with Jay Blumler. He is also co-author of *Global Newsrooms, Local Audiences* (1996) and co-editor of *Mass Media and Society* (1995).

K. P. Jayasankar is Senior Producer, Unit for Media and Communications, Tata Institute of Social Sciences, Bombay, India, where he is involved in media production, research, and teaching. In addition to journal and book articles on television reception, he has shot and directed (with Anjali Monteiro) many documentaries, including *Identity: The Construction of Selfhood* (1994), *Kahankar – Ahankar* (1995), and *YCP 1997* (1997).

Klaus Bruhn Jensen is Associate Professor in the Department of Film and Media Studies, University of Copenhagen, Denmark, Director of the research program 'The Visual Construction of Reality,' and Adjunct Professor, University of Oslo, Norway. His publications include *Making Sense of the News* (1986), *A Handbook of Qualitative Methodologies for Mass Communication Research* (1991, co-edited with Nick Jankowski, available in Chinese and Spanish), and *The Social Semiotics of Mass Communication* (1995).

Tamar Liebes is the Director of the Smart Institute of Communication and Associate Professor in the Department of Communication and Journalism at the Hebrew University of Jerusalem, Israel. She is the author (with Elihu Katz) of *The Export of Meaning: Cross Cultural Readings of Dallas* (1993) and of *Reporting the Arab-Israeli Conflict: How Hegemony Works* (1997).

Paolo Mancini is Associate Professor at the Istituto di Studi Sociali, Università di Perugia, Italy. His main publications include *Videopolitica. Telegiornali in Italia e in USA* (1985), *Come vincere le elezioni* (1988), *Sussurri e grida dalle camere* (1994), *Politics, Media, and Modern Democracy* (1996, with David Swanson), and *Manuale di comunicazione politica* (1996).

Stefania Di Michele graduated from the Istituto di Discipline della Comunicazione, Università di Bologna, Italy, where she began the research activity that she now carries out with different marketing research institutions.

Anjali Monteiro is Reader and Head, Unit for Media and Communications, Tata Institute of Social Sciences, Bombay, India. Her research interests include ethnographies of media audiences, rethinking development communication, and popular culture, and her work has appeared in edited volumes and journals. She has also collaborated with K. P. Jayasankar on the production of several documentaries.

W. Russell Neuman is the Director of the Information and Society Project at the Annenberg Public Policy Program, and Professor at the Annenberg School for Communication, University of Pennsylvania, USA. His research focuses on information technology and policy, political communications and public opinion.

Guillermo Orozco is Professor of Communication at the Social Communication Studies Department, University of Guadalajara, Mexico. His latest books are *Television y Audiencias: Un Enfoque Cualitativo* (1996) and *La Investigacion de la Comunicacion dentro y fuera de America Latina* (1997).

Elena Alemagni Pimpinelli has spent several years teaching in high school, and is now involved in teaching and research activities at the Istituto di Studi Sociali, Università di Perugia, Italy. With Paolo Mancini, she has published *News of the world. Primi risultati di una ricerca comparativa sulla ricezione dell'informazione televisiva* (1995).

David L. Swanson is Professor and Head of the Department of Speech Communication, University of Illinois at Urbana-Champaign, USA. He is editor-elect of *Political Communication*, an interdisciplinary quarterly journal. His most recent major publication is *Politics, Media, and Modern Democracy* (1996, with Paolo Mancini).

PREFACE

In the streets of Perugia and other Italian cities, one encounters signs with the inscription *senso unico*. While tourists may soon learn the hard way that this means 'one-way street,' to an international conference of communication researchers taking time for a stroll in Perugia in 1992, it summed up the difficulties of discovering how sense is made of signs, both inside the media and outside. Sense is never one-way, hardly ever unified, nor entirely unique. The conference was preparing the study reported in this volume of how television viewers around the world make local sense of global news.

The *News of the World* project dates back to 1989 when Klaus Bruhn Jensen and Paolo Mancini, meeting far from both Perugia and Copenhagen, in Los Angeles, discussed the idea of an international comparative study of the reception of television news. After they had made contact with colleagues in different parts of the world and secured partial funding for the study, Paolo organized its opening conference in 1992, while Klaus coordinated the study itself.

The best way to acknowledge the generous assistance of a large number of individuals and institutions in the course of the project may be to retrace briefly its steps. Morten Giersing, then Chief of the Section of Free Flow of Information and Communication Research at UNESCO in Paris, supported the idea of the study from the outset, and was key to this organization's offer to provide 'seed money.' Cees Hamelink, at the time President of the International Association for Mass Communication Research, which was the formal contractor of the project, gave it a home in the international research community, in addition to friendly and efficient support. The opening conference at Polvese Island, Perugia, 15–19 June 1992, was made possible by additional funding from RAI (Radiotelevisione Italiana), Fininvest, Regione dell'Umbria, Provincia di Perugia, and Università degli Studi di Perugia. At the conference, the planners and participants in the study benefited from the critical, constructive comments of Giovanni Bechelloni, Milly Buonanno, Akiba Cohen, Nicola De Blasi, Francesco Casetti, Federico di Chio, John Fiske, James Lull, David Morley, Gianni Pilo, Renato Porro, Nora Rizza, Kim Christian Schrøder, Celestino Spada, and Mauro Wolf. During the phase of analysis, project participants had the opportunity to present preliminary findings to conferences of the International Association for Mass Communication

xi

Research, the International Communication Association, and the American Political Science Association, as well as at several seminars and symposia. In 1994, the Department of Communication and Journalism at the Hebrew University in Jerusalem graciously hosted a meeting of the research group. The conference travels of some participants were supported, in part, out of funds from the State Media Commission in Denmark. For the quantitative element of the study, coding was done by Lars Andreas Pedersen and Rasmus Helles, and the analyses were conducted by Lars Boesen, consultant to AC Nielsen AIM A/S, Copenhagen. In the first phases of the project, Hans Mathias Kepplinger represented Germany in the study; the other participants gratefully acknowledge his early contributions. Still other colleagues and students, interviewers and transcribers, helped in the countless ways that make empirical research possible. Further acknowledgments are offered in the chapters about individual countries.

Last, but not least, the study was made possible in the first place by the active participation of the anonymous respondents from seven countries. We thank them most of all. The volume proposes to see the world, as represented on television, through their eyes.

Klaus Bruhn Jensen
Copenhagen
October 1997

INTERVIEW TRANSCRIPT
NOTATIONS

All quotations are presented verbatim from the authors' translations made in collabora
tion with the editor. The following notation system has been used:

Questions: SMALL CAPITALS
Answers: standard type
Short pause: . . .
Long pause: —
Interruption by another speaker: /
Words or sentences omitted from present text: (. . .)
Explanatory comments: [in square brackets]
M: male head of household
F: female head of household
B: boy/son (Ba, Bb. . . : first, second, etc.)
G: girl/daughter (Ga, Gb. . . : first, second, etc.)
O: other relative or visitor (Oa, Ob. . . : first, second, etc.)
Numeral following letter: household number (e.g. G9)
Numeral following colon: page number in the original transcripts (e.g. G9: 94)

1

INTRODUCTION

Klaus Bruhn Jensen

The flow of news in the world has been a major issue in international debates at least since the 1970s. The central concern has been a manifest imbalance in the flow of news, from the nations and cultures of the northern hemisphere to those in the southern hemisphere, and, hence, in the representation of the world to itself and the agenda of international politics. Under the heading of a New World Information and Communication Order, UNESCO and other international organizations have addressed the structures and criteria for producing and circulating essential political, economic, and cultural information to citizens around the world. The media themselves have also in some cases been a forum for public debate on access to and balance in the news. In part as a response to the issues raised by public and policy discussions, media research has previously examined the content of foreign news in various settings and, to a degree, the journalistic production of news by international news agencies and by broadcast as well as print media. So far, however, the audience perspective, particularly the culturally specific frames of understanding through which different national audiences decode the news and use it in their respective contexts, has not been examined in similar detail. Addressing the local uses of global news, this volume presents the findings of the first specifically cross-cultural, empirical study of news reception relying on a qualitative, in-depth approach.

By way of introduction, it should be noted that the study was planned and conducted as basic research, emphasizing theory development and the documentation of fundamental processes of media reception in a comparative perspective. Defined negatively, the study was not designed as an empirical evaluation, for example, of the extent to which different audiences may remember news items or learn from particular program formats. Nor was the aim to deduce and test a specific theory, centered around the audience, which might replace the structural, institutional, and textual approaches of a great deal of earlier research. Reception analysis, as reviewed below and employed in the empirical chapters, has sometimes been construed, by advocates as well as opponents, as a wholesale rejection of the critical perspective associated, not least, with the research traditions of international communications and political economy in this area – as a means of confronting the pessimistic thesis of cultural imperialism with a remarkably active and resistant audience. Instead, the present study is premised on the assumption that reception analysis contributes one necessary constituent in a comprehensive understanding of how communication flows across national borders, including a critical potential for assessing audience interests and competences in that process. As such, reception studies of news flow represent one element in a broadening scope of research in this area, from the media themselves as businesses and discourses, to the contexts in which the media participate in economic processes of globalization as well as in localized cultural practices (e.g. Golding and Harris 1997). Also for policy makers, some of the most relevant, realistic information may be forthcoming from basic research. The conclusion in Chapter 9 returns to some of the implications of the present findings for policy as well as for theory development.

The exploratory nature of the study is witnessed both by its qualitative methodology and by the sample of countries studied. The purpose was to examine a wide range of news forms and cultural contexts in order to allow for maximum variation, which might, in turn, facilitate theory development. A total of seven countries were included, representing what has been termed, in the wake of decolonization and the Cold War, the First, Second, and Third Worlds – worlds which currently are in need of a new nomenclature. In addition, the sample comprised two European countries with distinctive national cultures and Israel, being a hybrid culture with a unique history. In each of these countries, television has emerged, albeit at different stages and in varied forms, as a center-piece of the total media environment, a common point of reference for other media and the public alike. The seven countries participating in the study and their media systems are presented with further detail in the respective country chapters, but may here be characterized briefly as follows:

- Belarus – a post-communist country, experiencing the transformation to a market economy and to a relatively open, but still technologically and professionally developing, system of TV and other news media;
- Denmark – a small, homogeneous, northern European welfare state with television news formats which, while rooted in a long public-service tradition, are being challenged by both national and transnational competitors;
- India – a Third World country, with a growing television audience and a government struggling to retain its hold over the medium as transnational and cable networks extend their reach;
- Israel – a complex culture with a troubled history, whose news media serve, not least, as an early-warning system regarding threats to its very existence, and which, at the time of this study, was one of the few remaining countries in the world with only one television channel;
- Italy – a large, heterogeneous, southern European nation, whose television system has undergone major changes over the past decade, in part as a

response to political upheavals in which television and its directors have played an important, direct role;

- Mexico – a major non-aligned, Hispanic country, whose media are poised between market and state, between economic growth and social crisis, and whose news media have played an important role in recent political struggles at regional as well as national levels;
- USA – the remaining super power, whose news media have served as both utopia and dystopia in the cultural and media policy of other nations, old and new, around the world.

The rest of this introductory chapter places the *News of the World* project in the context of previous research on news and audiences, leading up to an account of the elements of the empirical study in the seven countries. While a full review of the relevant literature lies well beyond the scope of the chapter, an overview of selected main contributions may begin to suggest the specific ways in which the news genre enters into, on the one hand, the processes of political democracy and, on the other hand, the practices of everyday life. Audiences for news, across social and cultural contexts, are addressed simultaneously as citizens of a public sphere and as individuals in the privacy of their own homes. First, the following section revisits the large body of work on news and other political communication, tracing the gradual differentiation in the understanding of how news may have an impact on politics. Next, the section on reception studies identifies aspects of the process of communication which, despite such differentiation, remain little understood, focusing on the stages in the process which lend themselves particularly to qualitative methodologies. In the final section of this chapter, the design of the study is outlined and discussed with reference to the contribution that its findings might make to the understanding of some of the most heavily researched issues in the history of media research.

News studies

Classics and basics

The main scholarly, as well as social, justification for the enterprise of media research is, arguably, that the field might serve to establish the consequences of the mass media – broadly speaking, the difference that the modern media of communication make in the lives of their public and to the social structures and cultural processes of which they are a constitutive part. Given the centrality of news in the operation of modern institutions of political and economic power, it is no surprise that the news media have been a center of attention since studies early in this century of public opinion and propaganda (e.g. Delia 1987). And, given the explicit, operational role of audiences in the process of communication and impact, it is hardly surprising that the 'consequences' also of the news media have most commonly been conceptualized as their 'effects' on audiences. Whereas a variety of academic disciplines have contributed to the interdisciplinary study of media following World War II, for a long time the dominant models and methods of research came from the social sciences, not least in research on the mutual influence of political institutions, media, and the audience-public.

A continuous line of this research has been the growing attention given, both in theory development and in empirical projects, to the complex social networks of influence through which news and other political communication can be seen to take effect – in, through, and around the media. While research on the history of the field (e.g. Chaffee and Hochheimer 1985) has shown that early work may have been less committed to a position of direct, massive effects than has frequently been assumed in retrospect, audience studies have gradually come to specify and document several interrelated types and stages of impact. In this development, the *locus classicus* in the published literature remains *The People's Choice* (Lazarsfeld et al. 1944), providing the serendipitous but crucial insight that, to an important degree, the media take effect in stages or steps, which came to be known as the two-step flow of influence, involving direct personal contacts. This suggestion from a study of a US presidential campaign was later supported and elaborated, most famously by *Personal Influence* (Katz and Lazarsfeld 1955), with reference to other forms of communication and culture as well, including marketing and fashion. Whatever impact the media have is further mediated through interpersonal communication and other interaction in the social networks of which their audiences are a part.

More recently, studies of political cognition and socialization have extended this line of research, exploring how news enters into individuals' everyday awareness and readiness to act on political issues (e.g. Gamson 1992; Graber 1984; Neuman, Just, and Crigler 1992). Such studies may be said to uncover some of the conditions of opinion formation and political action by examining the concrete frames of interpretation through which audiences engage political information. The studies have underscored that not only specific opinion changes or voting decisions, but the very construction of people as voters, and indeed as political subjects, are long-term processes of communication with diverse participants both mediated and non-mediated. In methodological terms, these studies have also substantiated the relevance of qualitative approaches, complementing the quantitative approaches which had been predominant in much research since the seminal *The People's Choice*.

The attempt to capture the several aspects of audience responses to the media have generated distinctive research traditions. While these traditions have sometimes been treated as alternative and even antagonistic conceptualizations of media impact, it may be more constructive to treat the major positions as complementary contributions to a comprehensive understanding of the media-audience nexus (Jensen 1995: chap. 4). One of the main challenges for future research will be to explain more specifically how each element in the process of

influence relates to other aspects of influence – as a determination, a preparatory condition, or as an independent circumstance – whether in the immediate
context of media use or at a later point in time. For example, not least studies of
commercial and political communication campaigns have attempted to single
out the audience's responses in terms of their awareness, interest, belief, goal-
oriented action, etc., as it applies to the product or candidate in question (e.g.
Windahl et al. 1991), yet the interrelation of such moments of impact pose an
equal challenge for research on other forms of communication, including daily
newscasts. Too often, for example, in anthologies representing the state of the
art in the field (e.g. Bryant and Zillmann 1994), contributions appear side by
side that seem oblivious to the theoretical and methodological problems which
are posed to their own approaches by those of other contributions within the
same covers. While this may help to reassure each tradition that it is forever
moving forward, such studied ignorance is unlikely to move the field as such
ahead.

Among the research traditions that have crystallized internationally since the
1960s, three may have the most immediate relevance for the present study.
First, the uses-and-gratifications approach has charted the use-values and experi-
ential qualities that audiences associate with different media and genres
(Blumler and Katz 1974; Rosengren, Wenner, and Palmgreen 1985). In part as
a response to the limited impact which other effects research seemed able to
document by the end of the 1950s (Klapper 1960), this tradition began to
restate the central research question, asking – in one capsule formulation – not
so much what media do to people, but rather what people do with media
(Halloran 1970). Uses-and-gratifications research has perhaps been most
successful in identifying at a rather general level the audience's orientation
toward and motivation for media use, what has later come to be referred to as
the 'gratifications sought' from different media (e.g. Katz et al. 1973). Such
research is comparable in many ways to the surveys conducted regularly in many
countries on the perceived quality of different news media. Numerous studies
have found that the news genre lends itself to a variety of uses (see Rubin
1994): as instrumental information, as entertainment or diversion from other
concerns, as an occasion for identity-formation, and as an opportunity for vicarious or 'parasocial' interaction (Horton and Wohl 1956) with people
represented in the medium. Thus, studies have demonstrated the relative open-
ness of media contents to a variety of interpretations and applications depending
on the orientation of the recipient. However, because of its comparative neglect
of the structures of content, uses-and-gratifications research may have overem-
phasized the malleability of that which is being received and hence the
variability of reception, a problem which has also beset later reception studies.
In an apparent attempt to tap some of the more specific qualities of media experience as it relates to particular texts or programs, studies have introduced the
notion of 'gratifications obtained,' as distinct from the gratifications sought.
Still, because of the standardized and decontextualized methodologies also

5

employed for this purpose – largely neglecting media as textual and aesthetic forms as well as the context in which they are consumed – this development of the tradition has produced few insights about the nature and varieties of media experience. (For a critique, see Jensen 1987a.)

Second, one hard and fast way of measuring media impact has been to establish what and how much people remember after being exposed to media. This strategy has been applied particularly to news media, partly because the information transferred (or not) would seem to be easily operationalized, partly also because the audience's recall of news items might serve as one measure of how well the media fulfill their daily task of keeping the citizens of a democracy informed. The large number of studies in this area have almost unanimously concluded that recall is low, although correlated with the respondents' background knowledge and skills of inference, with some studies emphasizing the difficulty of learning from television news (see Robinson and Levy 1986). While representing an important finding in its own right, with implications for the journalistic profession as well as for political theory, this research tradition has left open the question of why, then, a very large proportion of citizens in the several countries studied seem to want news on such a scale and with such regularity.

The third and final tradition of research to be noted here has concluded that, despite such limited recall of specific items of information, and despite the varied gratifications that the news media may give rise to, they serve to focus the public's attention on particular perspectives and issues in the political process – what is referred to as the agenda-setting function of news (McCombs and Shaw 1972). As in the case of uses-and-gratifications research, the distinction between this approach and other effects research has been encapsulated in a formulation: namely, that the media may not tell people *what* to think, but, at least to a degree, they tell us what to think *about*, where to direct our attention, and on which issues to form an explicit opinion. Agenda-setting research has grown since the 1970s to become one of the most influential traditions in political communication research, examining how this process may work for different issues and media and in different national contexts (see Dearing and Rogers 1996). What tends to fall outside the scope of agenda-setting methodologies are some of the fundamental concepts and premises which go into the commonsensical, everyday understanding of politics that equally informs the electorate and which may be seen to underlie many, even most, of the specific agendas that they encounter and engage. Reception studies have begun to show, and this volume elaborates, how audiences may neglect the agendas advanced by established political figures and institutions and disseminated by the media, relying instead on alternative conceptualizations of what social and political issues are all about.

Following this brief overview of some of the basic positions in previous research, it may be worth reiterating the strength of each tradition in its particular domain of relevance – that each of these forms of inquiry have contributed elements toward a better understanding of news media and their audiences. At the same time, the overview has also identified limitations, especially when it comes to documenting and accounting for the processes of interpreting and using news that audiences perform in everyday contexts. After all, for most people most of the time, this is the most immediate interface between institutionalized politics and their own lives. If the field is to arrive at a comprehensive theory of audience activity, there is a special need for a more sustained, cumulative research effort about this moment of reception and its relations with other aspects of media use. Also in studies of news flow, the focus has been placed elsewhere in the process of communication.

Applications and debates

The application of media research to answering particular questions about the international flow of news has drawn on the techniques and models that have been forthcoming from other studies of the three-way interaction of media, their public, and various political institutions. Rather than addressing the specific impact on audiences, however, studies have most commonly focused on the agencies and organizations which are responsible for the production of news and, above all, the type of coverage which is the final product of their activities. This is presumably due, at least in part, to the added methodological complexity of tracing the process of influence across several different political systems and cultural formations. Even more important may be the structural conception of the research issues which have characterized studies of international communication, emphasizing the power relations that are embedded in, and cumulatively enacted through, national as well as transnational institutions of politics and communication. Conclusions about the resulting unequal distribution of resources in the world, including the area of knowledge and information, have been based on organizational and content analyses.

A variety of previous content studies have identified imbalances in terms of the regions and topics covered together with an underlying set of criteria of 'news' which may hold limited relevance for the countries and audiences that are the end users of the information (e.g. MacBride 1980; Sreberny-Mohammadi et al. 1985; Wallis and Baran 1990). Studies have often been large-scale, quantitative, and comparative, proposing to map the world as represented and disseminated in news. One of the most comprehensive studies so far, conducted under the auspices of UNESCO, covered twenty-nine countries (Sreberny-Mohammadi et al. 1985). Among its main findings was, first, that news coverage in any given country tends to be 'regional,' unsurprisingly giving priority to events in neighboring countries and other parts of that geographical region. Second, however, the United States and western Europe came out in the study as the 'consistent newsmakers' also in other parts of the world. In the third instance, the news would focus on the 'hot spots' which are associated with spectacular but singular happenings, drawing intense attention for a short period of time. The study further found that the developing world appeared

7

more often than other regions under this category of trouble spots, while receiving relatively little attention overall. The tendency of news media to give such negative attention to hard news happening in the developing world might be reinforced by the fact that the media systems here, as well, seemed to concentrate on hard news. Nevertheless, the Western news agencies did stand out as key sources of foreign news around the world. And, their practical consequences are probably reinforced by the fact that journalists in different national contexts are being socialized to their particular professional conception of news.

This prototypical study noted the great methodological difficulties, among other things, of tracing items of news content all the way back to their origins (Sreberny-Mohammadi et al. 1985: 50). The implication of this and other comparable studies, however, has been that the flow of news in the world tends to be structured in accordance with the unequal distribution of resources and infrastructure in other areas of life. Another, even larger follow-up study, with participation from between forty and fifty countries is currently in preparation (see http://sunsite.unc.edu/newsflow/), which may provide a broader basis for assessing what types of information are available to audiences in different parts of the world.

Debates on news flow have also targeted the production side of news in an attempt to explain, and perhaps reform, the present role of news in political processes. If the 1980s became the decade studying the audience 'making sense of the news' and of other genres and media, the 1970s had witnessed a variety of projects on journalists and news organizations 'making the news,' noticeably in Anglo-American research (e.g. Epstein 1973; Fishman 1980; Gans 1979; Golding and Elliott 1979; Schlesinger 1978; Sigal 1973; Tuchman 1978). Whereas several of these studies reflect on issues of news flow, the work by Peter Golding and Philip Elliott was a specifically comparative study of news organizations in different cultural contexts (Ireland, Nigeria, Sweden). One important finding of their analyses, reiterating a consensus emerging from other studies, was that the professional routines of journalists and the organizational constraints in terms of time and money constituted more of a determining factor in the selection and preparation of news than either the personal views and ideology of the journalists or the cultural setting of the medium. Based on observations, interviews, and document studies, research on news production has found that journalistic routines tend to result in stories that come across as a sequence of objective events, in effect obscuring the underlying social processes and the more or less hidden structures of power that drive them. The final outcome at the level of the individual news story is a standardized and regularized form of coverage focused around a limited number of entrenched, powerful actors, institutions, and issues. It might even be argued that, paradoxically, the core of news is a set of expected or at least foreseeable events.

Other recent studies have addressed both the shaping influence of technologies (e.g. MacGregor 1997) and the mediating role of international agencies such as the Eurovision News Exchange (e.g. Cohen et al. 1996) in the localized production of news. Whereas the press has always been dependent in many ways on modern technologies, the development of new recording and transmission technologies appears to be changing not only the craft of journalism across different media, but also the expectations of audiences for what will count as a well-crafted, trustworthy, and appealing story. Similarly, at a time when public service and commercial organizations are being reconfigured as part of a more competitive media environment, national television news organizations are trying to attract sufficiently large audiences with the right selection of stories in the right format, in part by relying on news wholesalers on an international market. Cohen et al. (1996), for one, suggests that the raw material of television news may be gradually 'domesticated,' first by newsworkers, later by viewers, both of whom decode the news with a view to their cultural context.

Research on the production and content of news has been fed back into the debates on the world information order, which have remained sites of sometimes intense international conflict, but has also supported various cooperative enterprises, for instance, in the development of regional news services that might provide more, and more relevant, coverage of specific societies and cultures (for overview, see Boyd-Barrett and Thussu 1992). One premise that continues to underlie such political initiatives as well as much research on news is that the general information which is available from media is a decisive resource for the political and cultural action of publics around the world, a notion which has been reemphasized by the widespread understanding of the present epoch as an 'information society,' currently symbolized by the multimedia Internet. Without publication in the broadest sense, and a right of access to the fullest possible range of publications across various media, there could be no public, no citizenship, in the modern sense (Habermas 1989; Schudson 1978). Almost regardless of their background in different normative theories of the press (McQuail 1994: 131–3; Siebert et al. 1956), contemporary political parties, interest groups, and international organizations will refer to an informed public as perhaps the best guarantee against authorities acting in conflict with the interest of the governed, be they a majority or a protected minority, whether in material or symbolic matters.

And yet it remains largely unclear how, in concrete terms, media audiences may engage and employ news as a resource in day-to-day politics. On the one hand, uses-and-gratifications research, as noted above, has shown that surveillance of the environment, both near and far, is an important gratification for audiences, presumably on the assumption that events might call for intervention or other action on the part of the recipient-citizen. On the other hand, the institutional organization of politics under different varieties of representative democracy requires little active participation in, for instance, the form of instrumental uses of news. As noted by Gans (1979: 226), "many people could carry on their lives without national news; and in any event, their need for it is not often urgent. Yet at the same time, people seem to want national news." Some research has suggested that, accordingly, audiences may approach the news genre with a consciousness divided between its central relevance in principle and its peripheral importance in practice (Jensen 1990a). One difficulty of studying this moment of the flow of news is that, in addition to taking effect over a long period of time, the audience's readiness to appropriate information as a potential resource may be largely implicit, being an element of practical consciousness (Giddens 1984). To recall a classic contribution on news audiences, it may be quite possible for respondents to describe 'what missing the newspaper means' (Berelson 1949), but much more difficult to ascertain how this meaning translates into, for example, a mood of uncertainty or specific compensatory activities. And it may be impossible for any respondent to articulate the loss of socialization which might follow from missing all news for an extended period of time in a modern society.

The place of the audience in the international flow of news thus remains under-researched, especially with regard to the decoding and social uses of the information in context as an aspect of citizenship. The recent research tradition of reception studies has proposed a set of interdisciplinary methodologies through which this moment of the flow might be better understood.

Reception studies

Interdisciplinary methodologies

Over the last two decades, reception analysis has offered a new understanding of how the reception, social uses, and impact of mass media may be conceptualized and studied empirically. Whereas reception studies have reiterated some of the founding issues of the field of media research, the classic question of 'effects' has been rearticulated to address broader issues concerning the role that is played by mass media in the production and circulation of 'meanings' in society as well as, significantly, the contribution of audiences to that process. This reorientation of audience studies has involved a convergence between, on the one hand, humanistic studies primarily of media texts and, on the other hand, social-scientific analyses of media audiences. Reception analysis, accordingly, has been developed as a methodology of audience-cum-content analysis which emphasizes qualitative inquiry into the processes of interpreting and applying media contents in everyday social contexts.

The early contributions to what has grown into a heterogeneous international current, with an identifiable Anglo-American 'mainstream,' received their impetus from at least two main sources. First of all, the British tradition of cultural studies (Hall et al. 1980; Hoggart 1957; Williams 1977), in shifting its orientation from art as aesthetic objects to culture as a social practice and from the products to the processes of culture, directed renewed attention also toward the question of how audiences approach media in the context of their everyday cultural practices. The prototypical study of media reception was offered by Morley (1980a) on television news, documenting both that audience decodings of the same manifest content were quite variable, and that the specific decodings had their background in the audience's particular place in the social structure. Media use and interpretation could be understood as an articulation of social interests in a broad sense. At the same time, a variety of projects on different media and genres were forthcoming, including studies of soap operas and other cultural forms which had often been neglected or denigrated in cultural as in literary studies (for overview, see Moores 1993; Nightingale 1996).

By the end of the 1980s, the British tradition of cultural studies, which had itself been dependent on an import of theories especially from France about discourse, subjectivity, and social structure – from Althusser and Foucault, to Barthes and Lacan – had been re-exported to the United States (e.g. Grossberg et al. 1992). Here, cultural studies appeared to provide a common denominator for attempts to create an institutional base – in the form of academic organiza-tions, positions, conferences, and journals for research – which defined itself in contrast to the dominant social-scientific paradigm (Gitlin 1978). In the American context, British cultural studies encountered the home-grown cultur-alism of American communications, as developed most comprehensively in the work of Carey (1989) and comprised of analyses of both mass media and other forms of popular culture. This second source of inspiration for reception ana-lysis has, in turn, made its mark on studies both within and outside the US. Like Morley (1980a), Lull (1980) presented a prototypical study examining family uses of television, which came to inform a range of empirical projects on media use in different social contexts (see Lindlof 1987).

It should be noted that a variety of studies from several national settings have contributed to the 'new' reception studies in international media research. Arising, to a degree, from local research traditions and addressing, like the Anglo-American titles, culturally specific issues, important theoretical and empirical contributions have been published in French (Wolton 1992), German (Baacke and Kübler 1987), Spanish (Gonzalez 1990; Orozco 1992), the Scandinavian languages (Carlsson 1988), and in other contexts. Moreover, the implications of studies about, and from, 'peripheral' cultures for an under-standing of either fundamental processes of communication or of the system of world cultures, may be as salient as studies about and from the center (Gripsrud 1995). In recognizing the merits of the Anglo-American publications cited above, both as early position statements and as scientific achievements in their own right, one should not neglect the fact that they received their circulation and influence, in part, because of a hegemony of Anglo-American research in journals, conferences, and other fora of the field. The field of media research faces its own flow issues.

The theoretical roots of reception studies have, then, been quite diverse. Furthermore, the explanatory frameworks employed in specific studies, have drawn on theories of social class (e.g. Jensen 1986; Morley 1980a), gender (e.g. Ang 1985; Heide 1995; Radway 1984), and ethnicity (e.g. Jhally and Lewis 1992; Press 1991). The studies of the reception of the TV series *Dallas* by Liebes and Katz (1993) represent another example on a relatively large scale of how social-scientific and humanistic approaches may be combined, this time for the purpose of a culturally comparative analysis. As such, reception analysis is not a homogeneous theoretical position, but a form of inquiry whose contributors share certain family resemblances. It may be added that reception analysis has participated actively in dialogues in the area of audience studies across the traditional divide between humanists and social scientists (e.g. Hay, Grossberg, and Wartella 1996). Also outside the emerging tradition of reception analysis, self-reflexive reassessments of the aims and methods of audience research have suggested how the process of communication might be reconceptualized, for example, in work on how media organizations conceive audiences (Ettema and Whitney 1994).

The rearticulation of the field in terms of processes of meaning production has prompted some media research to look much farther afield than to the moment of decoding, and to move further and further into the context of communication, to ethnography (see Drotner 1994; Morley and Silverstone 1991). The turn to various forms of fieldwork about media audiences has generated controversy, especially about the methodological procedures of such research. As argued, for instance, by Lull (1988a), a large proportion of self-labeled 'ethnographic' studies either fall far short of the requirements of ethnography in its originating discipline, anthropology, or instead amount to small interview or textual studies, or, at worst, anecdotal evidence. While a better in-depth understanding of audiences with reference to different aspects of their everyday context, including the several media that they rely on, is clearly of interest, it may be helpful to distinguish between two types of research methodologies in this area. On the one hand, methodologies relying on a multi-method, ethnographic approach can explore how a specific audience group engages several different media and genres as integral elements of their everyday practices. On the other hand, reception methodologies can examine how several different audience groups interpret, experience, and use a specific medium or genre in context. Advocates of more ethnographic studies occasionally seem to imply that reception analysis is a budget version of ethnographic research, that reception studies should ideally become fully-fledged ethnographies. However, the mounting call for ethnographic approaches in media research may be a misguided attempt at a methodological solution to a problem which is, in fact, theoretical. The challenge, not least for qualitative audience studies, would seem to be to devise the criteria for selecting some data – about media, audiences, and their contexts – as evidence, while leaving out most of the potential data, in order to address the research question at hand, rather than amassing data about ever more aspects of the audience's everyday life. Ethnographic research faces a special problem of determining what evidence is *not* relevant. In the end, the explanatory value of the evidence will be decided by theoretical argument and with reference to the theory of science informing qualitative research (see further pp. 195–7).

In sum, reception analysis as employed in the present study is most appropriately understood as a methodology, drawing on both social-scientific and humanistic forms of inquiry in order to explore how audiences make sense of the media and make use of them as resources in everyday life. Whereas the methods of data collection are drawn primarily from the empirical procedures of the social sciences – interview, observation, and document analysis – the methods of data analysis most commonly derive from the broadly hermeneutic approaches of the humanities – discourse studies and thematic textual analysis. In concrete terms, reception methodologies perform a comparative analysis of media discourses and audience discourses, as documented in interviews, observation notes, diaries, and other forms of evidence. While the national segments of the present study refer to several different theoretical frameworks in the analysis and discussion of findings – for example, theories of globalization in Italy, and the work of Michel Foucault in India – the News of the World study can thus be defined as methodology-driven. Before presenting the details of the methodology for the study, this chapter addresses the theoretically, as well as politically, controversial issue of 'the powerful audience.'

Audience powers

If, as underlined by some authors in the field, audiences are both active and resistant *vis-à-vis* the meanings that media offer, then audiences might compensate to some degree for imbalances in the manifest news content, applying the news as it relates to their particular context and constructing their own political agenda. This section first takes a critical, historical look at this notion of a new powerful audience, and then briefly reconsiders the ambiguous concept of power in communication as it relates to news.

An important backdrop to the development of reception studies has been the revaluation of popular culture in academic research as well as in public life since the 1960s. The social and cultural upheaval which had seemingly climaxed in the streets and in the media of the industrialized nations during the 1960s and 1970s, had questioned long accepted standards of taste and behavior. Simultaneously, the social movements of the period had reasserted that culture may express and exercise power, just as culture may be used to talk back at the institutions of power. As part of the resulting redrawing of boundaries between political and cultural issues, and between private and public realms, an extended concept of what might constitute 'texts' and other cultural forms that were worthy of attention gained currency in research as well as in educational systems. The value of any cultural form, be it an artifact or an activity, could be said to reside not in any essence, but in its social and historical position in relation to other cultural forms in a field of contested interests. According to such a more inclusive, anthropological conception of culture, not only the traditions, artifacts, and practices of ordinary people, but also various 'low' forms of the modern media might have real use value for their audiences. The resulting academic interest in media and popular culture manifested itself in several fields, receiving one distinctive formulation in 'cultural studies' with, for example, contributions from feminist (see Moi 1985) and subcultural (e.g. Hebdige 1979) research.

The revaluation of popular culture entailed not just a new legitimation of the pleasure taken by audiences in 'low' culture, but also a questioning of the impact that it might have on them. The critique of media as sources of ideology had, amidst growing theoretical and methodological sophistication, been a unifying force particularly of much European media research from at least Barthes (1973) onwards. Now, the critique of ideology along with contemporary approaches to the political economy of mass communication – from Schiller (1969) onwards, but with long historical roots in the critical theory of the Frankfurt School (Adorno and Horkheimer 1977) – came in for criticism of what might appear as a dystopian politics substantiated by a determinist theory of social life.

It was at this theoretical and political juncture that reception studies came to the fore, providing an approach to exploring empirically how audiences participate in the mediation of culture, with consequences for the quality of their everyday lives and ultimately for the distribution of power in society. Eco (1976: 150) summed up the possible political implications of audience activity in his reference to unanticipated 'oppositional' interpretations as "semiotic 'guerrilla warfare'." Some studies, however, soon ended up celebrating rather than documenting the critical faculties of audiences. Probably the most frequently cited and criticized example has been the work of John Fiske (1987, 1993, 1994), who, in revaluating the aesthetic qualities and use values of popular culture, came to depict audiences as particularly resourceful and, indeed, powerful *vis-à-vis* media. Such claims have been made with reference to limited empirical evidence and with little specification of how single acts of oppositional decoding of media content might serve to question, let alone reform, the wider social context (see further, Jensen 1991). Similar tendencies have been in evidence, for example, in research on fan culture (e.g. Lewis 1991) as well as in other parts of the cultural studies tradition (for critiques, see Lull 1988a; Morris 1990).

Other critics have noted that reception studies seem sometimes to neglect previous research, not only on the structural conditions and social contexts of audience activity, but also on comparable aspects of the audience response within different research traditions (Curran 1990). Representatives of reception studies (Morley 1992) have countered that at the juncture of the late 1970s the dominant textual and institutional research traditions were largely discounting the potential role of audiences as active, even resistant, participants in mass communication. Reception analysis may have been a necessary step in the internal history of European media research in addition to contributing to the differentiation of studies of the process of influence in the American context.

One additional methodological explanation for the celebration of audience activity can be found in the focus of much reception analysis on the decoding of particular texts, rather than on the actions which different media and genres may orient and facilitate for audiences, both within and beyond the immediate context of reception. Moreover, studies have sometimes failed to address basic issues of validity and reliability (see Höijer 1990) and to specify their domain of relevance, implying that resistant reception would be widespread across social classes, genders, age groups, cultures, and time periods. It may have been tempting to take interviews about the somewhat unexpected oppositional decoding of single texts by a relatively few audience members at a particular historical moment as evidence that respondents would also, for instance, resist media agendas in the longer term, perhaps even taking action against them. Like cultural studies, reception analysis has perhaps been informed by a measure of wishful thinking originating in critical politics. If research were able to document audience responses to media which anticipated a reconstruction of social reality, then, equally, the structure of society might be open to major change by this same audience-public, and indeed might already be under transformation. Myopic methodologies informed by relativist theories of society and culture breed political populism.

The distinction between discursive power, as articulated in much interpretation, and social power, as exercised in specific institutionalized contexts of action, may be of particular importance in the area of news media and politics, being key institutions of power in modern societies. Oppositional decodings of, for example, daily television newscasts are not in themselves a manifestation of political opposition to the powers that be in any meaningful sense. It remains for further reception studies and other media research to clarify the relationship between the moments of media use and political action. In the next section, this volume begins to examine these issues with additional reference to recent developments in the broader field of social theory, regarding structure, agency, and meaning.

In conclusion, it should be recognized that reception analysis is in its early stages of development, still accumulating a first generation of evidence about different media and genres while simultaneously seeking to specify its domain of relevance and its complementarity in relation to other forms of audience research. Much empirical work is needed in order to capitalize on the several interdisciplinary contributions from social sciences and humanities to the theory and methodology of the area. Following the presentation of findings from the present study design, Chapter 9 returns to the implications for further research in general and theory development in particular.

Design of the study

Research issues

The News of the World project analyzed the frames of understanding which a small sample of viewers in the seven different countries – Belarus, Denmark,

India, Israel, Italy, Mexico, and the US – brought to bear on the foreign as well as national events that were reported by television news on one particular day, 11 May 1993. While the purpose of this core element of the study was to explore how different national audiences may interpret and apply news within their specific cultural settings, the study also examined the respondents' assessment of the quality of the different available news media and their ranking of the most important events in the world at the time of the study. In addition, a content analysis was conducted of the national news programs in each country during the week leading up to 11 May. Each form of evidence provides a perspective on the meaning of citizenship in an age of global communications as citizenship is reenacted on a daily basis in the interaction between media and audiences.

The news media may be understood as a precondition for the political, economic, and cultural participation of individuals at the local, national, and, in principle, transnational levels. News media can be defined as sources of meaning that help to orient the distributed localized action of citizens which, in the aggregate, constitutes political and other social institutions. In recent social theory, often departing from the work of Giddens (1984), the relationship between such localized action and the aggregated, even global, social systems has been conceptualized with reference to 'structure' and 'agency.' While the twin concepts refer back to the classic foundations of social science, identifying the material and institutional parameters within which humans must act as individuals and groups, recent social theory has reminded scholars that these terms refer to phenomena which are processual and inherently interrelated. Whereas social structure is not merely a set of constraints limiting the activity of individuals, but also a preparatory condition of any complex form of coordinated activity, agency as exercised by individuals equally serves to reproduce and maintain the social structure. It is such a 'duality of structure' which can be seen to underlie the reception and social uses of television news. Mass-mediated information may enable individuals to exercise a share of the agency that serves to reproduce society.

Building on Giddens' (1984, 1990) theory of structuration as it applies to modern and modernizing societies, Thompson (1995), among others, has argued for the centrality of the mass media in the reorganization of time, space, and social agency which characterizes modernity. The argument, in summary, is that modern societies may best be described in terms of their 'time-space distanciation,' that is, the degree to which both material production, social control, and cultural activity may be conducted independently of local time and space. For example, the division of labor is still becoming internationalized through technologies of transportation as well as of communication; computer systems currently enable a gradually more efficient, centralized control with individuals and organizations; and the mass media in general and television in particular offer, more than ever, a vicarious presence by many different national audiences in one place and at the same time. Increasingly, the whole world is becoming

16

both a domain of global activity and a point of reference for the local understanding of self. Conversely, social power, as exercised by multinational corporations and political authorities, may come to appear more remote and opaque.

The seven countries of the present study, though quite different in terms of their distinctive political, economic, and cultural features, have all experienced processes of globalization to varying degrees, as reflected and symbolized by the shared medium of television. Each of the following chapters addresses the respondents' outlook on the world, as articulated in response to television, and their conception of citizenship under these circumstances of globalization. Since the study was exploratory in its aims and qualitative in its methodology, questions concerning the possible decodings and social uses of television news in different cultural contexts were not operationalized as formal hypotheses. Instead, the research issues, as discussed above, can be outlined with reference to the analytical categories and procedures that were employed in collecting each of the three forms of evidence – news contents, individual interviews, and household interviews. These elements of the design are displayed in Figure 1.1.

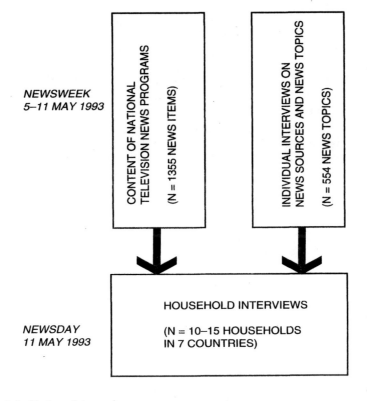

Figure 1.1   Design of the study

News contents

During one week of 1993, 5–11 May, designated as Newsweek, the main evening newscasts on all nationally broadcast television channels in the participating countries were recorded on video and later coded. The purpose was to produce an overview of how the world was presented to viewers in different national settings through television at the time of the qualitative interview study. The findings of the analysis provide a background to interpreting how viewers made sense of selected news items in the household interviews, while disregarding other items. In addition, the findings from the content analysis contain implications for further research on a representative scale about general characteristics of news coverage in these countries, but it must be noted from the outset that the present sample does not justify any such general conclusions.

Details about the design of the content analysis are presented in Appendix A, where the findings are also reported. Some aspects of these findings are noted as part of the analysis and interpretation of audience interviews in the chapters concerning each country.

Individual interviews

Individual interviews were conducted with members of the households that had been recruited for the qualitative interview study. The purpose was to gather information about the respondents' preferred sources of news and about their perception of main topics in the news. As in the case of the analysis of news contents, the individual interviews can be taken as suggestive only since the respondents do not represent a statistical average of each national population. Instead, the findings provide background and supplement to the interpretation of interviews with the households that were examined in depth.

Again, Appendix A presents the design and reports the findings from the individual interviews. In the country chapters, these findings reflect on the accounts of main topics and preferred news sources that were also offered in the household interviews.

Household interviews

The core of the *News of the World* project is contained in the interviews with between ten and fifteen households in each country, conducted on 11 May 1993, designated as Newsday. The design of the qualitative household interviews, including the interview guide which was employed in each of the seven countries, is presented in detail in Appendix B, which also notes the analytical procedures that were applied. The findings are presented in the country-by-country chapters that follow.

As a preface to the country chapters, it may be helpful to introduce the main elements of the household interviews. First, the point of departure for each interview was the respondents' retelling of the main news items on Newsday, as defined by the respondents themselves. The members of the households were encouraged to offer details as well as to discuss stories among themselves. In this respect, the study drew on the seminal work by Morley (1980a) on the decoding of news. Second, the interviews called for a comparative assessment of the different news media which were available to the respondents, as studied on a regular basis in many countries. Third, respondents were asked to give an account of what would typically be happening in the household while the main evening newscast was on. This element of the study drew on Lull's (1980) typology of the social uses of television, and on later research about television in families in different cultural settings (Lull 1988b). Fourth, and finally, respondents were asked to describe any concrete uses of news beyond the immediate context of viewing, for instance, in political activity or as consumer information.

One analytical category calls for further explanation, namely, 'super-themes.' Previous research on the reception of television news has found that viewers may arrive at interpretive themes which are quite different from the journalistic themes that the media might expect audiences to reproduce – 'the viewer's story' may appear to be incompatible with 'the journalists' story.' As originated by Jensen (1988) and developed by Crigler and Jensen (1991) and by Mancini (1990), super-themes are thematic constructs by which viewers may establish links between the world of their everyday lives and the world as represented in television news stories. Super-themes can be seen to mediate between viewer and story by translating a reality that appears complex and distant into simple, general, and personally meaningful terms. Because they tend to be broad and general, super-themes may be distinguished from more specific topical themes that can be identified in the content of particular news stories. At the same time, super-themes may have a concrete quality to them as they depart from specific details in the visuals or commentary of a news item or from the viewer's singular life experiences.

The super-themes are the central analytical category in the following country chapters, which exemplify and discuss the concept further. And, the conclusion in Chapter 9 returns to a comparative analysis and a model of the configuration of super-themes in the present study as a contribution to theory development. Beyond the analysis of super-themes, and of the other main elements of the household interviews, each country chapter provides a thumbnail sketch of the national culture and of the media system in which the production and reception of television news is embedded. The country chapters also consider the content of the television newscasts on Newsday, in the form of listings and thematic analyses, as part of the comparative analysis of media discourses and audience discourses. Reception studies raise a question, not only of what media do to audiences, or what audiences do with media (Halloran 1970), but how media and audiences interact in context as agents of, in semiotic terms (Jensen 1995), the life of signs in society and in the world.

2

BELARUS

Nadia V. Efimova[*]

Political media

A long road to independence

The Republic of Belarus has taken its place among the independent states of eastern Europe only since 1991 – a very short period of relative independence after an age of existing within the borders of other states. During the fourteenth to sixteenth centuries, it was part of the Great Principality of Lithuania and, later, *Rzecz Pospolita* (the union of Poland and the Lithuanian Principality). From the second half of the eighteenth century, Belarus was a component part of the Russian empire, its northwestern province, and with the establishment of Soviet power, it became one of the fifteen USSR republics. The location of Belarus between Poland and Russia for centuries served to shape its culture and the mentality of its people. The fact of being poised between west and east, and of finding both worlds not entirely acceptable, is an important background to the entire history of Belarus. By the late 1990s, however, the Belarusian people put no obstacles in the way of either eastern or western waves of influence, which were rolling over the country and its inhabitants (Abdziralovich 1993).

The Soviet era was a particular period in Belarusian history and culture, and a great deal of the problems currently facing the republic date back to this period. Also the mass media were shaped during the Soviet period. First, the media in Belarus were an organic part of a structure that could not be questioned, namely, the USSR media system. Similar to the state in general, this system was designed according to a hierarchical principle. The dominant position was held by the centrally organized mass media, while the media of each republic took second place, just as the media of oblasts, cities, and regions held

[*] The author gratefully acknowledges the support and valuable advice received from Professor Oleg Manaev, the contributions made by Ms Valentina Erashova and Ms Irina Burina in conducting household interviews and registering news items, and the assistance in transcription and translation given by Ms Kate Ugrinovich.

still lower positions in the hierarchy. Second, the media at each level were subordinate to the power bodies of the corresponding level – central, republican, or local – which were their publishers and funders, and the hierarchy further entailed subordination to the power bodies of the superordinate levels, the Party Committees. The entire system functioned as a single organism, playing within the borders of the country the part of a "collective propagandist, agitator, and organizer" (Lenin 1901: 11).

This situation only changed from the second half of the 1980s, with the advent of *perestroika* and *glasnost*. Within the framework of these policies, the mass media were assigned a special role – that of pioneering reform and accelerating institutional changes in the Soviet political system (Mitzkevitch 1990). This meant a great change in the content of the mass media, which now became much less dependent on the oligarchies of party and government. At the same time, there appeared an alternative press as the expression of new issues and interest groups in social life (Manaev 1991). Liberalization brought with it a greater confidence of the public in the mass media, and brought about an unprecedented increase of interest in the media.

The beginning of the next and current period was marked by the coup in August 1991 and the following disintegration of the USSR as well as of its unified media system. The independent states – the former USSR republics – now formed their own national mass media. According to surveys of the Belarusian public, carried out by the Independent Institute of Socio-Economic and Political Research (IISEPS) in 1994–95, this period has been marked by a redistribution of public interest, away from the formerly central, Russian media and toward Belarusian media, both locally and at the level of the republic. This took place against the background of a marked reduction in the consumption of media information. Before the events of 1991, Russian newspapers were read by 57 percent of the Belarusian audience, the republic's own newspapers only by 24 percent. With the independence of Belarus, the number of readers of the Russian press was reduced to a fifth of its original figure, while those reading Belarusian newspapers on a regular basis rose by about one and a half times the earlier figure.

It must be added, however, that this shift applies mostly to the printed press, and least of all to television. The same surveys found that 91 percent of Belarusian viewers prefer watching the news programs of the First Russian Channel; the Belarusian programs are watched by 25 percent of viewers. The major reason for this choice is the quality of programs. The viewers interviewed for the present study named as the most important drawbacks of the Belarusian newscasts, and of Belarusian TV in general: a lower level of professionalism compared to Russian television; a lack of bright individuals among the newscasters; the established tradition on Belarusian TV of announcers reading the author's text rather than being newscasters with a deeper knowledge of the subject themselves; and the lack both of a diversity of viewpoints and of independent assessments.

21

Belarusian TV

The relatively low professional and technological level of contemporary Belarusian TV (BTV) is easily explained. BTV was created in the 1960s as part of the broadcast television system of the USSR. The role of 'national' TV – for the immense and tremendously diverse country – was played by the Central TV of Moscow. From a linguistic and cultural point of view, Central TV was, without a doubt, Russian. This was not understood as a form of discrimination or a limitation of access to the media for one or another group of the population. On the contrary, it was considered an achievement of the new society whose aim was the creation of a new nation – 'the Soviet people' with a common language and culture. Along with television in other Soviet republics, BTV was to be a regional, and hence subordinate, station. Consequently, for many years it was not sufficiently funded or equipped.

As a result of the disintegration of the USSR, BTV was transformed – in a matter of days – from a regional into a national television of a new state, even though it was not quite ready for such a change of status. The reconstruction of TV – being part of the complex process of the cultural and politico-economic formation of Belarus as a sovereign nation – is still in its early stages (Vashkevich 1993).

Elected in 1994, the first Belarusian president began pursuing a policy of restoring socialism, including tight control over the economy and ideological matters. The dissolution of parliament in 1996 marked the climax of this policy, leading to the international isolation of Belarus and to a reinstatement of a dictatorial regime. Also the mass media, which had gained independence during the period of reforms, were the target of a most prejudiced attitude on the part of authorities. The state monopoly with, and control over, especially the electronic media was in fact intensified (Manaev 1996). In one of his first decrees, the president subordinated national television to the state and further delegated to national television the right to exercise control over local and regional television on the territory of the republic.

As of 1997, there was only one national TV channel (BTV), which is state-owned. Nevertheless, non-state television and radio have been developing since the early 1990s. Some private companies united in the Belarusian Association of Non-State TV (BANT). Such an association was a necessity for the development of other broadcasting, dictated by the interests of survival under the conditions of an economic crisis, by an underdeveloped legislative basis, and by state ownership of transmitters, relay lines, as well as of other means of producing and disseminating information. The plans of BANT originally included the founding of a second national, non-state television channel. However, at the time of writing, there was much talk of a second such channel which would also be state-owned.

Satellite television has been spread rather widely in Belarus; citizens of the republic can watch more than ten channels originating in the west, although only about 10 percent of the population watch satellite programs regularly. The main reason for this has been a sharp decrease in living standards owing to the deep economic crisis afflicting the country. Satellite TV is simply unaffordable for most (Efimova 1994).

The only real alternatives to the state-owned Belarusian TV throughout the republic are therefore the Russian TV channels. It seems ironic that in a situation where Belarusian authorities are tightening control over the mass media and suppressing alternative voices, Russian TV has come to perform the same role with respect to Belarus as did Western radio stations previously with respect to the Soviet Union. The Belarusian audience now expects to receive authentic information and unbiased analyses of domestic political events from the Russian news programs rather than from Belarusian TV. It may be no surprise that the level of confidence which audiences express with regard to the mass media has been constantly falling. According to IISEPS, during 1993–6 the proportion of the audience trusting BTV was reduced by 13.6 percent, just as the proportion trusting Belarusian radio was reduced by 12.1 percent (Efimova 1996).

National news programs

BTV broadcasts four to five news programs daily, depending on the day of the week. The main program is the evening newscast which lasts forty minutes, the others having a duration of between ten and fifteen minutes. Newsday was typical for BTV newscasts from the point of view of both composition and content. Out of forty-seven news items broadcast on that day, thirteen were devoted either to the decisions and activities of the highest bodies of power within the state – the Council of Ministers and the Supreme Soviet of Belarus – or they reflected the official political stand on such basic issues as the economy, foreign policy, or ethnic relations. The fact that the broadcaster considered these topics very important is suggested by their being placed early in the program (among the first three to five topics), and by their being repeated at least twice during the day.

By these two criteria – top placement and repetition – the most important topic on Newsday was the official visit of a Belarusian government delegation, headed by the prime minister, to the United Arab Emirates (UAE). This information opened three out of the four newscasts, including the main evening program. Its obvious importance becomes clear in the light of Belarus's efforts at consolidating itself as an independent 'subject' with international relations. The key sentence of the news item was: "The first visit in the history of the interrelations of the two countries is to mark the beginning of a mutually beneficial cooperation between Belarus and the UAE." This implies that the history of the international links of the USSR (from where visits to the UAE had taken place previously) has nothing in common with those of Belarus. The republic begins from scratch, as a new state. An important idea is conveyed by the phrase saying that the Belarusian delegation hopes to establish trade relations with the UAE. Though the content of these relations was not revealed in the news text,

23

many of our respondents interpreted that phrase as an allusion to buying oil from the UAE and therefore to taking another step toward independence from Russia.

Another example of news of supreme importance was an item dealing with the Congress of the Belarusians of the World. Its significance is that it illustrates the government's policy of a national renaissance. As in the previous case, the independent status of Belarus is emphasized, but the style is, moreover, elevated and solemn: "Belarus, being now an independent country, calls up its sons and daughters. History gave us a unique chance to revive Belarusian statehood, language, and culture."

The third example of important news topics was the conversion to civilian production at a military factory. Real independence can be asserted by economic independence, along with non-participation in military blocs, and a policy of neutrality was declared by the government in power in 1993. One of the ways to realize this policy is converting military factories to producing consumer goods. In the story, conversion is described as consolidating the economy and bringing immediate benefits to consumers: goods which had previously been imported from Russia and other countries, can now be produced at domestic enterprises; high-tech equipment, previously working for a military purpose, can be used to improve the quality of peaceful production; and, thanks to conversion, the consumer goods market will become richer.

All these topics, representing state political guidelines and the activities of the highest bodies of power, contain neither comments from experts, politicians, or citizens, nor opinions or assessments of events that do not coincide with the official stand. This is evidently a consequence of the state monopoly over the national TV channel, something which is pretty well understood by viewers. In the course of the interviews, many made critical remarks on that score. At the same time, some respondents offered arguments to justify such a manner of narrating the news: for one thing, a formal way of presenting news is a tradition with television as they know it; for another, the state supports television and has a right to demand that TV express and defend its interests. Some of the respondents further associated a uniformity of opinions and assessments on television with order and concord within the state. For example, "It's better to have one newspaper telling the truth" (M1: 3). And, "It's the honesty and truthfulness of the mass media that matters and not a plurality of views" (M7: 88).

Another group of items on Newsday represents a counterpoint to the reports on the official stands and fruitful activities of the republic's leadership, comprising such topics as 'the milkmaid's confession' (pp. 30–1) and a complaint from the residents of run-down housing. Both stories are critical, and both contain the views of common people speaking of their problems and hardships caused by authority actions. These topics were not singled out by the broadcaster, but during the interviews, viewers would repeatedly refer to them, and considered them most important and exciting. Therefore, this group of items may be said to constitute a second highlight of the news programs.

The main part of the newscasts on Newsday described events in Belarus. Other news items were of two types, regarding events in the former Soviet republics, the so-called 'near-abroad' region, and regarding events in 'far-abroad' areas. The 'near-abroad' news items constituted the largest part of foreign news on Belarusian TV. Traditionally, only 'far-abroad' news items have been entitled 'international.' Thus, international events, regardless of their world importance, such as the war in Bosnia, were interpreted briefly. (The short duration of a relatively substantial number of such items may help to explain the seeming attention given to foreign news in Belarus during Newsweek (see Appendix A).) It was only in the evening program that international events received any substantial attention, and then for only about four minutes of the forty-minute program. In addition, the form of narration is remarkable: world news is prepared by CNN and presented with no comment, explanation, or assessment of the events from Belarusian reporters. Since 1993, excluding the international element, the essential part of BTV news programs has been produced locally. Up to the time of writing, BTV has had no correspondents of its own abroad; instead it disseminates, with minimal comments, material that has been prepared by various news agencies. This is probably not just due to a lack of professionalism or insufficient technological facilities and financing, but more importantly because BTV – although the national television of a new sovereign state – has retained the mentality and style of work typical of a regional television station. The overall picture of current events is available from Russian TV, which is, as noted, very popular with the Belarusian audience, while BTV can add some local news.

Sources of news

Most of the respondents from our selected households said that they prefer television as a source of political news, a suggestion confirmed by numerous surveys. Up to 80 percent of the public in Belarus learn about the latest events from television news. TV is attractive to viewers because it is able to create an integral presentation of the event and to produce an overall emotional impression, something that may be considered even more important than the speed of conveying world news (M5, M7, F7, M8).

Such an impression can be a powerful prompter for searching out additional information revealing details of the events and giving an analysis. The individual interviews suggested the printed press as the second most important news source. Because TV does not give a diversity of viewpoints or interpretations of current events, but applies a particular set of rules and makes people see the world with its eyes, viewers may 'set themselves free' only by switching to another channel, making up a news program according to their own taste – "his own mosaic of the events taking place" (M6: 80). Still, everyone is said to have his or her own newspaper, whose opinion is respected and shared. In addition to having a free choice of reporter, interpreter, or expert, readers – in contrast to viewers – can keep their own pace and rhythm in the communicative process.

Radio comes in third place according to these respondents, offering in the morning what television provides in the evening. Both news media were described as a habit, satisfying a need to put a frame around every day. "In the evening I have the time and wish to watch on TV the course of events. In the morning the news is better understood by ear" (M8: 99). The ideal form of radio news may be short precise messages "on everything in the world" (G6: 79). They may be memorized better than television news as one listens to them in the car or at home before going to work. But, the need for a deeper analysis of news after listening to the radio will again draw the respondents to newspapers, weeklies, and magazines.

Indeed, television, radio, newspapers, other periodicals, as well as communication with colleagues, family members, and acquaintances can be seen to form an integral information field. The respondents suggested that they will use most of these sources to find out about ongoing events and to form their own opinion. In any given case, the structure and intensity of media consumption may depend both on relatively constant factors such as the social and psychological features of the public or the quality of the available sources, and on the specific situation in which news can inform action.

The context of viewing

In Belarus, as in many other countries, television viewing will accompany everyday family life, and is interlaced with the numerous activities and troubles of family members. At certain moments, a TV program can focus the attention of all present, while at other times it will serve as a backdrop to more important business.

In eight of the twelve families visited by interviewers, a television set was placed either in the kitchen or in the living-room – in those places where family members meet and spend a great deal of their time. Four families had two sets, and the rule seemed to be that the old set would go into the kitchen, the other one into the living-room. One family had three sets – one in the grandparents' room, the second in the room of their son and his wife, and the third one in his sister's room.

However, even if there is only one set in a household, which might unite the family and involve its members in discussion, in reality this appears not to happen very often. Only one married couple of pensioners answered definitely that they would regularly watch television together, in particular news programs (Household 1). Families of workers and farmers told the interviewers that, as a rule, they did not have an opportunity to watch together because they worked at different times of the day. "Now that the children are small, this situation suits their parents well as they can look after the children for the whole of the day" (F9: 111). All the women who were employed outside the home, noted that they had very little time for bringing up their children and doing their homework, and older children would be busy doing their homework in the evening.

Nevertheless, TV programs are watched and discussed to a degree by the whole family, even if not often and not for long. The interviews suggest that purely political news was less of a topic of discussion than economic news. The year of 1993 may have witnessed the lowest point of interest in political news among the Belarusian public for the past ten years. At the beginning of *perestroika* there was a boom of interest in politics as such and in political information in the mass media. Consuming a certain measure of news could be considered a political act, and discussions of the unusual and shocking events of the period, conveyed by the media in abundance, would continue at home, at work, and in public places. By 1993, the overall enthusiasm had given place to weariness.

By contrast, economic news was mentioned as being more frequently debated by the family in front of the TV set. Two interrelated explanations suggest themselves. First, the social practice of economic activity was changing, suggesting variants to the sole activity of the past – namely, hired labor for the state. Second, people were now less alienated from economic information itself, which no longer merely spoke of fulfilling the plan at the plant or harvesting the crops on the collective farm, but also addressed the issues of shares, stocks, currency rates, real estate, and other useful topics.

"The country we want to live in": super themes

In December of 1991, after the denouncement of the Union Treaty of 1922, the USSR disappeared from the political map of the world, and the territories of the former union republics emerged as new independent states. The deep-rooted causes of the ruin of the communist system lie in the economic field. A deepening economic crisis was the background of centrifugal tendencies, which, in turn, were reinforced by a democratic movement that opposed the central party and state structures serving as the main support of the conservative forces in the country. Yet, in the majority of the republics, including Belarus, the idea of separating from the Soviet Union was not very popular in the broad population. Sovereignty was implemented mainly through the efforts of the powers that be, in the interest of self-preservation, as this made it possible to deviate from the wave of democratic reforms initiated in Russia and to lay claim to leadership in the new state.

Accordingly, the policy pursued by the authorities of sovereign Belarus did not allow the country to take proper advantage of sovereignty. This policy has been characterized by counteracting the beginnings of market reforms, by attempts to retain bureaucratic control over the economy, and by suppressing entrepreneurial activity while accepting large-scale corruption. The result has been a drop in living standards and a further deepening of the crisis. In order to develop sovereign Belarus in the interest of its citizens, and not in the interests of old and new nomenclatures, a qualitatively new form of state may be needed, free of relapses to the Soviet system. In their choice of words, respondents suggested that they belong to a 'nation' – the Belarusian people – and this is sometimes associated with the 'state' – the Republic of Belarus. A primary relation of the state remains its political ties with Russia. However, the respondents assessed their government's policy with reference to its contribution to nation-building, approving its actions when they consolidate the position of the nation-state (e.g., above, the delegation visiting the United Arab Emirates) and criticizing inadequate initiatives (e.g., in the references to the army below).

The problem of putting their new country in order is highly topical to respondents, as indicated by their references to the most important items in the news program. A man from the countryside pointed to the information about the activities of government:

> M10: 126: The item about the visit of the government delegation to the United Arab Emirates is the most important for me among other news. The fact is important for me as it is important for Belarus. I am sure our delegation went to the United Arab Emirates to ask for oil though it was not directly announced on TV. Our economy is now in a bad state . . . in a crisis. The main reason is that we have problems with Russia.
> WHICH PROBLEMS DO YOU MEAN?
> M10: Russia used to give us oil and now it does not want to. If Arab countries supply oil to Belarus we'll become an independent state and if not . . . well, then I don't know . . . maybe we'll appeal to Russia again.

The thoughts expressed in Household 10 about independence with regard to oil as a guarantee of sovereignty are widespread in Belarusian society, among politicians as well as rank-and-file citizens. This explains why the news item about the visit of the government delegation to the UAE, a brief message without comments and not accompanied by video coverage, was noted by several respondents in four households:

> B4: 47: (. . .) There is no petrol now . . . those having a car feel how difficult the situation is. If our government took money for oil transit on the territory of Belarus, we should be treated in a different manner. But, perhaps, our Government is afraid to raise this question in such a way. Maybe in the Arab Emirates, Kebich [then Prime Minister, Chairman of the Council of Ministers of the Republic of Belarus] will get the oil. There is no sovereignty without oil.

The meaning of oil as a crucial condition of independence is a distinctive stereotype in the public consciousness (Kostenko 1993). It was formed during the years of the Soviet super power, which existed for many years in isolation from the rest of the world, relying mainly on its domestic reserves, the most important being mineral resources and natural conditions. This idea is here extrapolated to quite a different situation, and now a different country. Earlier experience participates actively in the process of conceptualizing current information (Crigler and Jensen 1991).

Another widespread stereotype with similar origins is the decisive importance of a strong army in the creation of an independent state. A middle-aged man expressed his viewpoint on a news item about military maneuvers on the territory of Belarus thus:

> M8: 91–92: (. . .) The army has different problems today. No money, no modern equipment . . . living conditions of officers are not good . . . poor conditions, I mean (. . .) If we don't take every measure to support the army, we'll be helpless in two years (. . .). We'd like to live in the independent Belarus — so, well . . . it is necessary to support the army.
> YOU MEAN IT IS THE MAIN FACTOR OF THE STATE'S POWER AND INDEPENDENCE?
> M8: The army is the main factor of the state's power. Our authorities are not clever enough to realize this. They do everything for themselves — not for people, not for the state.

A similarly critical attitude toward the authorities was expressed by another man in connection with information about eight opposition parties that had made a protest against the military union with Russia:

> O12: 149: (. . .) Many people approve of such a union [a military union with Russia], especially our government. They think: "There is not such a strong army in Belarus as it had been in the Soviet Union, and somebody has to guard the country. So let the Russian soldiers protect us." But in such a way we may get involved in war . . . in Central Asia, in the Caucasus. They will not defend us, they will defend themselves — with our help. It would be better to create our own Belarusian army since it could not be worse than the Russian army. The fact is that there is no petrol for the army's airplanes now.

Thus, the respondents' identification of nation and state – according to the formula: a strong army plus oil equals the Republic of Belarus – reproduced on a smaller scale the Soviet model of a sovereign state, with reference to the main factors constituting its system. The other conception of nation and state in the respondents' discourse took aim at a consolidation of the very name of the nation (Belarus) and a renaissance of national culture – that is, at creating their state on the basis of purely national values. Next is a comment made by a

woman working as a lecturer in the University of Culture on a news item
dealing with the upcoming Congress of the Belarusians of the World:

> G7: 85–86: Of course, I heard on the radio and read in the newspapers
> that the Congress of the Belarusians of the World would be held. But
> television introduced its sponsors, the organizing committee of the
> Congress, told us some new details (. . .). There are not so many
> Belarusians in the world. Some of them emigrated and there, abroad,
> forgot that they had been Belarusians. Others forgot that they are
> Belarusians living in their native country . . . they forgot their language
> and culture. We could have disappeared as a nation if the USSR had
> existed several decades longer. It is good to have an opportunity to
> meet our countrymen now, it is possible that we could do something
> useful together. There will be no country without this — the country
> we want to live in.

Neither the first nor the second conception of the country involves the
economic component as a basic prerequisite for establishing Belarus as a state.
This, however, does not mean that the issue of the economy was not mentioned
by respondents. Instead, it was referred to in one context only – the crisis.

Economic crisis

Inflation, a drop in incomes, a loss of jobs and social guarantees – all these are
economic realities that are encountered directly by the majority of the population of Belarus. People's accepted standards of economic behavior have proved
inadequate for a changed economic reality. As for new models of behavior, they
seem to have been assimilated by few people so far – time and a minimal
stability are needed. A large part of the population, especially elderly people,
may feel that they are not wanted in this new life. Essential aspects of the
economic processes can be seen to have destructive consequences for the life
and well-being of the common people.

The news item that might be called 'the milkmaid's confession' found a
broad response in several families. It was pointed out as important, impressive,
exciting, and, in particular, typical of or similar to many people's lives. This is
how one respondent interpreted the item:

> M5: 58–60: The woman, a collective-farm milkmaid, gave all her life
> to work. Just think, she has nothing but her work: at dawn she had to
> go to the farm to milk the cows, in the evening — again to the
> farm . . . not to her own one but to the collective farm. But, perhaps,
> she did not even think about it (. . .). Nevertheless, she had some
> satisfaction from her work: money, respect . . . she became a Hero of
> Socialist Labor, the deputy of the regional Soviet. And now . . . she has

lost everything. Payment for labor is not satisfactory — all employees get the same small sum, those who work and the people not working. Generally speaking, our life seems irreparable (. . .). Our parents have had a similar life — they worked in their youth and mature years for the state, and now they live from hand to mouth.

WHAT IS — IN YOUR OPINION — THE KEY MOMENT OF THE ITEM?

M5: I think it is the emotional state of a laborer, her psychological frame of mind. The euphoria of the first years of *perestroika* has gone, and we are left alone with our bitter thoughts. We don't know what to do and who is to be blamed that we worked much and honestly for many years, but the society or politicians or, perhaps, history deceived us.

In the life of the elderly, hard-working woman who is no better off than before the changes, the respondents saw a symbolic expression of their own lives and of the lives of those near and dear to them. We may speak of an emotional-cognitive process of unconscious identification with another subject, when a link is established between the viewing subject and the reflected object, the character on TV news, and the viewer thus experiences identity with the 'object' (Semyonov 1979).

Realizing the crisis in the national economy as a whole, people may look for their own way out of the situation, or at least for a chance to somehow get used to it. A woman with no job – the enterprise she worked at was closed down – considered a news item on 'women and business' very useful:

F8: 101: I lost my job and I just don't know what to do. The profession I know, that I studied at the Institute is no longer popular . . . nobody is interested in it (. . .) I can do some more things: sew, knit, etc. But I never took it seriously. Though it is quite possible to earn money in this way. The most difficult thing is to find customers, suppliers, to organize advertising for your business, your products. This is called to start one's own business. Nobody taught us this, neither at school nor in the family. If I could finish some business school or if somebody helped me, give some advice. . .

The other way out of a hard economic situation – for an entire plant, not for the single person – was described by the man who took note of the item about the conversion of military plants:

M3: 34: (. . .) It was one of the most powerful military plants. And after *perestroika* it stopped working. Many jobless among workers (. . .). Unfortunately, only my son will see 'diamond skies,' not me. Isn't it so?

Economic disaster, with terrible consequences for individuals, their personality and well-being, as well as for their confidence in the future, was ascribed in the respondents' discourse to supra-personal factors – the actions of 'authorities', 'politicians,' and, even more globally and abstractly, 'economic laws,' 'historical fate.' The image is almost of a natural calamity in which individuals inevitably become the victims. Still, hope remains. According to these respondents, it comes from relying on one's own strength, one's entrepreneurial activity. Significantly, this hope is not supported by some positive experience – none of those who made conclusions about the necessity to be more active, or to use one's brains, was an entrepreneur, or had their own business. The hope is based on negative experience: the state that used to give people everything – a job, an apartment, and all the rest – has gone bankrupt and is unable to help. You can survive only by relying on yourself.

War

War came out as one of the most important topics of news for the Belarusian respondents. And, the reference was not only to the war in the former Yugoslavia, which drew the respondents' attention in western Europe and some other countries. In Belarus, there was also mention of the wars in Nagorno-Karabakh, Tajikistan, and Georgia, the Checheno-Ingush and North Ossetian conflicts, and the tension between Russia and the Ukraine over Crimea. The war in the former Yugoslavia was understood as a continuation of this chain, a phenomenon similar to other wars in the more immediate neighborhood. The story about the measures taken by Russia, Turkey, and the US to settle the conflict in Nagorno-Karabakh was commented on by an elderly collective farmer:

> M10: 124: (. . .) We are already surrounded by wars from everywhere: there is war, over there is war. We live like islanders. Different countries try to influence those who are at war, to stop bloodshed, but with no result. There has been war in Karabakh for seven years . . . and there is no end to it. God forbid something like this should happen in Belarus, to us. But I don't think it could happen . . . even if everywhere in the world people start shooting, Belarus will be the last to do it.

The peaceful life in Belarus, against the backdrop of more and more wars and conflicts, is here understood not as mere chance, but rather as a regularity that can be explained by the peculiarities of national character.

Further, a female scientist commented on a news item about the war in Georgia and the Ukraine's initiative to settle the conflict between Georgia and Abkhazia.

> F5: 55: (. . .) The Ukraine wanted to be a peacemaker in Georgia earlier than Russia . . . did you hear that? . . . I'd call it "hurrying to hell leaving one's father behind." In general, I believe, Ukrainians are too ambitious: we Belarusians, are not so ambitious. We are quiet,

peaceful, friendly people. We shall wait until hard times are over, we shall not interfere in other people's affairs, neither in a war, nor in a conflict. Let them fight . . . and we could secure a decent life thanks to our patience, hard work, little by little. What do you think of it?

However, the key to a comprehension of 'war' may be given by a middle-aged engineer:

M3: 39–40: (. . .) I remember seeing an old American film, *They Shoot Horses, Don't They?* The story is as follows: in America in the depression period, dance marathons were organized. The pairs danced until they were exhausted, some fainted — they participated to get the prize . . . money. And the crowds gathered to look at them. What did they gather for? They wanted to see people more miserable than themselves. Maybe seeing this, seeing that you are not in the worst possible situation gave them some consolation . . . maybe they again wanted to live, they found in their hearts the desire to live. You see, when I hear or watch on TV that in Russia, in the Caucasus, in the former Soviet republics there is war, of course, I sympathize with people. But at the same time I think: 'we are lucky, we have a peaceful life.' Though it is difficult to live, but we have no war. Though the danger of war and the threat to human life is hanging over our heads, we are happy that it is not our problem.

TV news, building a bridge between the respondents' experience of a peaceful Belarus and the information from the former USSR regions that are now at war, may lead to this conclusion.

Those who suffer and those who threaten common people and people with power

The theme of injustices done to ordinary people, as well as the theme of violence or threats, are commonly present in news programs. People become the victims of terrorism, catastrophes, accidents, but also, even to a similar degree, of the routines of bureaucratic mechanisms. A respondent interpreted the item about the inhabitants of a house in need of emergency repairs as depicting victims of the indifference of bureaucrats:

M6: 72–73: (. . .) Building development blocked up several streets. It created a lot of problems for the people who live in the locality. The people live in houses in need of emergency repairs. It is high time they moved to other houses. And these shocking things are going on for three years but the authorities are not going to help the people . . . though the people wrote complaints and went to the chairman of the

city council. As usual, the situation is irreparable for ordinary people, and the authorities are indifferent to their troubles.
WHAT WERE YOU THINKING WHILE WATCHING THIS ITEM?
M6: I thought that I saw similar slums many times in Minsk when I was a child. The well-being of the authorities does not depend on ordinary people, that is how their indifference can be explained. People are on one hand, the authorities — on the other.

In a similar perspective, M6 interpreted quite a different item, about the conversion at the military plant:

M6: 68: (...) It is not important for the chief engineer what to produce and at what price ... the main thing is that the machines run and the authorities are satisfied. It is essential that the accent is placed on fulfilling the plan, plan, plan, not on manufacturing the products that people need. As ever, the plan is more important than a man (...) with such kinds of leaders our life will remain the same. You can find such leaders everywhere throughout the country.

News is understood as an important means of realizing the new political reality in which viewers exist. The remarks about ordinary people being 'the victims' of 'the system' that is working in its own interests, not in the interests of citizens, suggest that nothing has changed radically in the new country of the post-Soviet period. In matching the situation 'here and now' against the recent past, respondents point to a stable feature that has not changed – the dependent, wretched state of the individual, who can do nothing about the violence of the state. In talking about state or government, the respondents frequently substituted a single name for the institution: Stalin, Yeltsin, Kebich, etc. State power is still embodied in a certain individual, and the government is identified with its head.

This theme of state violence became more urgent in interpretations of news about the consequences of the Chernobyl nuclear-plant disaster. A woman commented on an item about Germany's assistance to Belarus in overcoming these consequences:

F2: 23: Germany is giving us a helping hand. Thanks to this, there is an opportunity to send children from the radioactive zone to Germany for treatment and recreation. A lot of children from the Chernobyl zone really need it (...). Many thanks to Germany ... let the children get good medical treatment (...). We are all ill after the Chernobyl disaster ... we all got a high dose of radiation in 1986. I think of my child (...). He also needs treatment (...). Our government must do everything for the sake of the children's health. Not only Germany but our Belarusian government as well because the children's health means the nation's health (. . .). They speak about money, that they have no opportunity to do this. As usual, we think only of the present day, not of tomorrow. But then we have no future.

The theme of violence and its victims was also discussed in connection with a rise in crime. Household 6 offered their interpretation of a story about an assault on a Uniat Church priest:

G6: 77: The danger of burglaries and assaults is rising. If somebody rings at the door, you are afraid to open it even in the daytime – there behind the door may be a burglar, a killer. The burglars burst into the priest's apartment in the daytime, tied him . . . he could even have been killed. Criminals become impudent because they are not punished properly, the crimes are rarely revealed. I think if somebody sticks me up in the street or steals something from me, nobody will stand up for me and there will be no militiaman nearby. You may cry for help. Everybody is afraid to do something. Perhaps, there is only one way out – to study karate or judo and to take a gas can or even a gun with you.
M6: And you see, the priest was attacked by people who came from the Caucasus. We are in a difficult situation, and those people are aggravating it still more.
WHAT IS YOUR OPINION, CAN ANYTHING BE DONE IN THIS SITUATION?
M6: Maybe it is necessary to adopt a law against Caucasians or simply forbid them to come to Belarus (. . .) because they arrive here only to make money and to rob.

The recently announced democracy may be associated with total freedom of action, including freedom for criminals. This is in contrast to the totalitarian regime which was strict to everybody, also thieves and gangsters. Such an analogy was made by the male head of Household 1, speaking about a story of the assassination of an entrepreneur from Minsk, the president of a private bank:

M1: 8: There have always been crimes and murders . . . but I hadn't heard that somebody could employ the killer. This is already a profession, a great profit — never before did I hear about such things. Maybe in America it was always a common practice. As regards us, before *perestroika*, especially under Stalin, there was order. Can we say that it is freedom if people are shot dead in the street? We do not need such freedom.

A shared feature in the discussions about these different forms of violence is the appeal to the state – to change its attitude to citizens, to protect them from danger. However, in certain cases, such as the last one (M1), wishing to do away with violence may lead people to want to do away with freedom as such and to reestablish the order that had existed in the country for seventy years.

A resource for a new reality

The social uses of news were motivated by the Belarusian respondents with reference to a need for general orientation – adequately comprehending and assessing events, and forming attitudes. This need is premised on the equally general assumption that individuals facing an unfamiliar situation will be uncomfortable until they orientate themselves, emphatically so in a context of national and social crisis. While the public can turn to news media as a resource for such orientation (McCombs 1994), media use may be limited: first, because of the individual's own previous life experiences and, second, because of the existence of social institutions other than the media which have at their disposal more and better information – for instance, on the economy – for subsequent use by citizens also.

A major aspect of the current 'cultural crisis' in Belarus is explained by the fact that the news media have grown considerably in importance as means of social orientation, while the two other sources – life experiences and other social institutions – have become less prominent. Again, the background is the radically changed situation in which citizens find themselves – politically, with the Republic replacing the USSR; economically, with the transition from a planned economy to a market economy; and socially, with an altered structure of society and the formation of new classes and other social groups. The personal experience of people, especially that of the older age groups formed in a different historical era, has come to appear inadequate for orientation in a new reality. In addition, a large number of social institutions have either stopped functioning or have lost their former power, trustworthiness, and informative value.

Under these circumstances the mass media may become a universal source of information, orienting individuals in relation to all aspects of the present situation. This helps to explain why the Belarusian respondents gave paramount importance to the content of news compared to its form. It is a short step from their immediate comprehension of an event to its inclusion into an existential personal context. For example, the usual criticism of BTV professionalism does not present an obstacle to viewers' choosing or using the topics that appear meaningful to them.

The analysis of the interview discourses suggests that, whereas the news media provide audiences with a variety of resources for orientation and for realizing their different projects, one of them may merit special attention. Any social activity may serve as a psychological resource, generating a feeling of confidence and security. This is due not only to a certain content or form of, in this case, mass media, but also to the regularity with which, for instance, the news program appears on the screen. Conversely, unexpected intervals in news programs or cancellations may be interpreted as a sign of danger, causing anxiety or alarm. "If you switch on the TV and watch the program announced," said one woman, "I know that everything is OK in the world on the whole and I have nothing to worry about. And if the news program does not begin in due time or the program stops all of a sudden – this means something has happened. Such things happened when [former General Secretary of the Central Committee Leonid] Brezhnev died" (F1: 10).

News media give audiences resources for orientation and activity in the economic field, as already noted. The practical interest of viewers in economic information is that, under the conditions of market reform, individuals become 'subjects' along with state institutions. The idea that personal well-being depends on one's own enterprise is clearly attractive even if the concrete ways of realizing this are not always so clear to respondents. In the news media, people can seek information about models of behavior in a market economy:

> F6: 82: I took the information on the shares I should buy, where money should be invested to reduce losses from inflation, how to make use of privatization cheques. Nowadays it is very important in our life.

In view of the general crisis of the country, personal activity in the economic sphere presents not only an attractive opportunity, but a vital necessity. Unemployment and dissatisfaction with their conditions of labor or wages, make people turn to the news media in search of practically useful information: "If you are unemployed, TV can help you and show what other people do in similar situations" (F8: 109). Finally, basic information on prices, inflation rates, advertisements on vacancies, and the like, regularly televised in news programs, was noted by respondents as valuable information which they can use in their everyday activities (F6, B7, G7, F8).

The further social uses of political information seem to be more limited. None of the respondents found that they would somehow use information from news programs in their party, trade-union, or other such activities. It is interesting to note that, according to surveys taken before *perestroika*, the political activity of audience members as propagandists, political informants, or active workers in the Party and Komsomol, was the main area of social uses of mass media information at that time (Manaev 1986). In these 1993 interviews, the respondents rather noted spontaneous discussions with family members, colleagues, or acquaintances as the only actual social use of political information (M11, O8).

Conclusion

The radical restructuring of the political, economic, and social conditions of life in Belarus since 1991 has inevitably also influenced the characteristic social uses of the news media. For example, the shift of emphasis toward economic information and the changes in the conception of political news correspond to new needs of orientation as viewers adapt to a new reality.

The scale of change has been such that the Belarusian respondents may be especially prone to abstract, general explanations of the course of events. They used such terms as "economic laws," "natural laws," "the pace of history," or simply "fate" to denote the powerful who fatally oppose the people's efforts, turning them into helpless victims. The Chernobyl accident, wars, the crisis – all these are not just the authorities' fault. Events are thought of as a manifestation of fate. Even though fate brings misfortunes to people, such misfortunes may be considered a form of punishment for their own actions: "We were committing violence on nature for so many years that it had to teach us a lesson" (F11: 136 – about Chernobyl); "We have the inflation because we neglected economic laws" (M2: 27 – on the crisis).

3

DENMARK

Klaus Bruhn Jensen[*]

Introduction

In 1992, a tiny majority of the Danish electorate voted against full membership in the European Union. This happened in spite of the fact that almost the entire Danish political establishment and practically all Danish news media supported the European Union. A year later, in a second referendum, a somewhat larger, but still quite small majority voted for the Union, provoking, among other responses, unprecedented riots in the streets of Copenhagen when the result was reported as news. For once, Denmark thus made it into the headlines of major news media in other countries, and even live coverage of the riots on CNN.

During the early 1990s, the wider European public witnessed, again through the news media, several other even more spectacular and profound developments that might equally be difficult to account for. In eastern Europe and the former Soviet Union, political, economic, and military unions of the past dissolved. This happened in spite of the fact that powerful interests, both within the countries and in international political-economic cooperation, and both inside and outside the media, seemed to prefer the existing framework supporting business, trade, and a generally peaceful social life, at least during an interim period. Concurrently, cultural, ethnic, and religious sentiments reappeared on the surface of society, having been 'forgotten' for ages, at least in many political circles, media, and, to a degree, in research.

These historical developments can be taken as pieces of evidence that a significant aspect of the phenomenon which news media, politicians, and researchers commonly refer to as the formation of public opinion goes unnoticed in the

[*] The author wishes to thank Karen Bredegaard, Helle Fritze Holm, Mimi Olsen, Ib Poulsen, Kim Christian Schrøder, Tine Stampe, and the students in the 1993 graduate seminar on television news reception, Department of Film and Media Studies, University of Copenhagen, for their assistance in conducting the household and individual interviews for the study. The transcription of interviews was funded by the TV Research Department of Danmarks Radio, and carried out by Helle Fritze Holm and Mimi Olsen. A longer report of the findings in Danish, *Verdensnyheder* (1994), is available from Danmarks Radio.

media. In certain cases, the undercurrents of communication and interaction in society apparently accumulate to produce momentous change. The News of the World project may throw light on some of the everyday processes of interpretation which enter into and orient such change, even while focusing on the immediate encounter between viewer and news discourse.

Following an overview of the structure of Danish media, this chapter first considers the conception of what was considered as 'news' by Danish viewers, including their comparison of different news sources and their assessment of how new media forms may be changing the concept of news. Next, the place that the respondents assign to television in the home setting and as a part of their everyday activities is examined briefly. As a preface to the analysis of the four main super-themes that can be seen to orient reception for the Danish respondents, the content of the news that they addressed on Newsday is described in terms of its priorities and topics. Besides a discussion of each super-theme, this section reconsiders the special importance of visuals in television news from the viewer's perspective. The final section of the chapter assesses the potential role of television news as a resource for viewers in politics as well as in their everyday lives.

Danish mass media: an overview

Denmark is a small, prosperous, and homogeneous nation, far from most centers of conflict in the world, but also relatively far from most international centers of influence. Being small, Denmark has depended historically on political and military alliances with the larger European nations, and there exist strong cultural ties with the rest of the Scandinavian and Nordic countries – Finland, Iceland, Norway, and Sweden. Being prosperous, Danes enjoy a generally high standard of living, one of the best social and medical systems in the world, and a democratic educational system without tuition fees through to the university level. Being homogeneous, with small regional differences and only a small immigrant population, Denmark has experienced few fundamental conflicts since its occupation by Nazi Germany 1940–45. While the past two decades have witnessed a succession of Social Democratic and liberal-conservative coalition governments, the deep-structural agenda remains a commitment to the welfare state, being the product of a century of political reforms, labor union activity, and of an institutionalized commitment to popular enlightenment through lifelong education. Denmark is a member of both the European Union and NATO.

The modern press in Denmark dates from the period of the first democratic constitution in 1849, which established freedom of expression and of the press. The newspaper press developed as a set of platforms for the major political parties to a point where, at the turn of the century, a four-party press system was in place in most cities. At the same time, a strong undercurrent of popular papers addressed the needs and interests of readers in events outside, and from the underside of, official public life. During the twentieth century, especially from 1945, the locally organized political press has gradually lost ground especially to national newspapers catering to a wider political spectrum as part of a process coupling economic concentration and political mainstreaming. Not least, the tabloid press has held its own against the challenge from other media. Whereas about 75 percent of Danes still read at least one daily newspaper, that figure is decreasing, particularly among the young.

The Danish electronic mass media have traditionally been organized in accordance with welfare-state principles of universal availability, quality, and diversity, without being state-controlled institutions (see further Petersen and Siune 1992). Danish broadcasting began in 1926 with the establishment of Danmarks Radio (DR), a public-service radio monopoly financed through license fees. With the addition of more radio channels, and of television from 1951, DR developed into a full-scale modern media institution. As in other European countries, this position was challenged during the 1980s by the simultaneous introduction of transnational technologies, particularly communication satellites, and of deregulatory policies in telecommunications generally. Partly as a response to such external challenges, a political compromise served to establish a second Danish television channel, TV2, in 1988. Being financed by a combination of license fees and commercial breaks between programs, TV2 is a lightweight organization that subcontracts most of its production to other companies and which, in addition, comprises a series of regional entities. Within two years, the new channel managed to attract a share of 50 percent of the viewing audience with a more popular, commercial profile than that of DR. In addition, local television and especially local radio stations have challenged DR since their introduction in 1983, initially as an experiment in public access to the media.

By 1993, then, a new media system was in place in Denmark. While the full range of satellite channels from other European and international broadcasters is available to Danish viewers, by an overwhelming margin they spend most of their television time on viewing DR and TV2, although increasingly also on the Scandinavian competitor, TV3. TV is commonly perceived as the central medium of the media environment as a whole, also in terms of political communication, with radio and newspapers offering updates and background respectively to the public. Within this political communication system, the main evening newscasts of DR and TV2, broadcast at separate times, constitute points of reference and agenda-setters for public debate and for the political process. These programs, which were the points of departure for the *News of the World* interviews, both attracted an average rating of approximately 19 percent during the period of the study.

The worlds of different news media

What is news?

Although the respondents were not asked directly to define 'news,' in the

41

course of the interviews they referred to a specific set of features which amount to an indirect definition – a common denominator and a premise for their other arguments about the news media. News includes both domestic and foreign events, and both the events and issues covered should be current. Coverage must be fair, in the sense of giving 'both sides' a hearing, and it should follow up on major events. Most important perhaps, news is expected to cover developments which have 'consequences,' for the public at large or least for a significant group of the population, or which carry implications, for instance, for political principles and cultural traditions beyond the single event.

Criticisms, moreover, offer indications of what news is, or ought to be. A variety of criticisms came under a heading of a lack of coherence or continuity, from day to day and between the world of news and the viewer's world of everyday life. One young woman, for example, noted, with reference to the Gulf War (1991), "all those oil wells burning down in, ah, Kuwait," that "Okay, we heard a lot about it when things were happening, but what does it look like now?" (G5: 60). The respondents' criticism seemed to intensify when they spoke of the news visuals, with frustrations being voiced at the recycling of the exact same images and of "boring footage" suggesting a particular type of incident. Alternatively, one respondent argued, this audiovisual medium might be used differently to tell the story:

> M11: 28: You might experience a program, that is, if there was something about Yugoslavia, if they had an hour-long program, where it would just be images and perhaps music or something like that which could create associations. That might be just as telling, but the problem is that they have so little time, you know.

The issues raised concerning follow-up information and the recycling of images, point toward a more general issue of how to weigh overview and background. On the one hand, some respondents demanded a brief, clear, and concise overview of major events. One elderly man talked at length and with passion against what he saw as irrelevant 'talk':

> M3: 1: (. . .) I'm annoyed daily when they bring you news, and then they give you a long talk about something. And then all of a sudden, there's a few more news items. Instead of taking all there is of news first.

On the other hand, some of the respondents who called for an overview also placed special emphasis on longer in-depth coverage of selected items. With reference to the relations between Israel and Syria mentioned in coverage of peace negotiations about the Golan Heights, a respondent criticized the lack of depth and the absence of interviews with representatives from both sides, concluding that it might be preferable to leave out the item altogether: "Or else they had damn well better wait and present it on another occasion" (M10: 27). Assuming that the basic daily news bulletin addresses everybody, one way of satisfying both groups of viewers and their different requirements might be a differentiated form, distinguishing more clearly between overview and background as part of an overall communicative strategy.

Denmark 1, Denmark 2

Differences and similarities between the news programs of the two national television channels in Denmark – the original public-service channel established in 1951 (Danmarks Radio – DR) and the semi-commercial newcomer from 1988 (TV2) – were given a great deal of attention by the respondents. And yet the two programs were seen above all as the same 'product' in a different packaging. For example, no major differences in terms of selection and news criteria were mentioned, and the fierce debates over (especially left-wing) political bias which had been prominent in Danmarks Radio and other European public-service institutions during the 1970s and into the 1980s, as well as in public debate, were not articulated in the interviews. The difference between the stations, in the eyes of their viewers, is apparently a matter of style, profile – the 'way' of the two stations.

In a historical perspective, it is interesting to note the changes that viewers perceived in the news programs of DR and which they described as a form of product development. The format now has more "colors," is "smarter," and leaves scope for the personality of the individual anchors and journalists who are appreciated as persons with a look, a style in clothing, and an occasional off-the-cuff comment. As one woman said, "The curls are now in place" (F5:78). She specifically mentioned seeing news clips from seven or eight years ago, or older, "and then you think to yourself, my God! But that's the way things were back then" (F5: 81).

Old media, new media

Compared to newspapers and radio, television news was described as the pivot of the entire media environment – the central medium of political communication. However, it is important to note that also the Danish respondents conceived the news media as a mix or package of different sources, all of which are available for selective and combinatory use (Appendix A).

Newspapers were said, not surprisingly, to offer the background that is often missing on television. 'Background' implies both the availability of further nuances and the opportunity to read again, recall, and feel reassured that one is truly well-informed. Newspapers were also associated with more credible final information, even though the news visuals were mostly considered a reliable representation of reality by Danish respondents. And newspapers were said to allow the readers to become the 'director' of their own news consumption rather than following the predefined sequence of television news.

43

It remains clear, nevertheless, that television has replaced newspapers, to a degree, as the respondents' interface with society. One young man mentioned that "in the old days (. . .) you would sit down and read the newspaper from A to Z to stay informed," whereas today he will skim the paper for something of interest, or something that complements what he heard earlier in other media. Television has the further advantage, he noted, that the visuals make it an efficient, attention-holding medium, so that "biologically, naturally, it sinks in better, uh, when there are visuals to go with it" (M1: 61–2). Consequently, another respondent concluded, if one has little time, television offers "a high information value about some central issues in an easily accessible way" (M11: 77).

Radio news, like television news, was said to offer an overview – in addition to sometimes providing inspiration to also watch the events on television. In some references to radio and newspapers, it appears to be a hidden assumption that these media are somehow more serious than television – the latter is labeled by one respondent as "a bad habit" (M10: 35), given that the same information is available through radio. Still, the visuals were considered a decisive if 'fatal' attraction that may distract attention from the overall message of a news item, as remarked by one young woman:

G5: 4: The visuals are incredibly important. As if there were, uh, background music, you know. (. . .) It's the visuals. Mostly. So I fail to listen a little bit. Yeah, it's the visuals, I think. (. . .) That's what [*makes a hissing sound*] carries you off.

Transnational news

The foreign television channels that are available in Denmark, either from neighboring countries or via satellite, offer examples of what a national news program might alternatively look like. Whereas programs from both Germany and Sweden were said to provide examples of news formats that would differentiate more clearly between overview and background, it was CNN International which attracted most attention as a distinctive alternative and as a possible sign of things to come. One respondent found that, at least in certain respects, the news program of the semi-commercial TV2 resembled the image that CNN was trying to project of itself in its self-promotion as the omnipresent live broadcaster mirroring the world to itself. It is striking that the Danish respondents reproduced this image of constant live transmission, well-suited for a quick update and overview, without much reflection. (Research conducted shortly before this study suggests that a very small percentage of the ordinary daily flow on CNN International is in fact broadcast live, in addition to a substantial proportion of items being recycled. See Bredegaard and Davidsen-Nielsen 1992.) An elderly man recounted the live experience:

M3: 97–8: One day, uh, we were watching, uh, it was CNN, and then, uh, all of a sudden they break, we had been told that one of those hurricanes was heading for the coast of Florida (. . .) And our boy has been to America, and the second youngest of the kids lives in Florida (. . .) and then, uh, as we're watching, I mean, hearing that, you know, sitting, and CNN is telling you, and then all of a sudden CNN interrupts its program, and then we see how it hits (. . .) the coast at a certain place in Florida (. . .) and how it just moves like a bulldozer through the whole thing, and the cameraman who was recording it, he had to hold on, so the camera was going like this (. . .) it was almost impossible (. . .) but he had tied himself to something (. . .) to be able to watch it. And it was, the clock was precise, I mean, we could see (. . .) it was happening here and now.

The 'advocates' and 'opponents' of CNN among the Danish respondents were divided according to their conception and evaluation of overview and background. On the one hand, some respondents who would criticize too much talk in the ordinary Danish newscasts took a position as 'advocates' of CNN and wished that "we would do something like that sometimes here in Denmark. When there's a very important event just coming in" (F3: 99). Indeed, the members of this household called for more news breaks between the other programs rather than full-length newscasts, thus spreading the news across the flow of television.

On the other hand, the 'opponents' singled out the style of CNN for criticism, comparing the channel to tabloid newspapers with little substance. Reference was also made to the journalists on-screen as being too sure of themselves, and CNN was said to exploit "visuals and effects and all those kinds of things" (M4: 37).

CNN, thus, came to symbolize the challenge that Danish and some other European national news programs were, and are, facing. CNN offers quite a different type of brief and accessible form of news for those calling for an overview. But CNN also, in principle and in some of its actual magazine formats, allows for a more differentiated programming within an interminable sequence of programs – for the benefit of viewers demanding background. The challenge for national broadcasters may be one of combining these two elements within a new form of addressing viewers which they understand as meaningful.

The world in front of the box

The home setting is a decisive mediator of political communication in prefiguring particular conversational and other contextual uses of news, but also in suggesting selective attention and specific interpretive procedures for a given news item. Notwithstanding some cultural criticism and public debate which, with regular intervals, seems to suggest that television rules the lives of its viewers (e.g. Postman 1985), the everyday comes before television. This becomes evident, for example, when respondents describe how the different daily rhythms that are associated with the changing seasons may decide which specific news program will be watched in the household. And, even minor changes in the television schedule can be felt as a disruption of a finely tuned accommodation of the medium within the everyday setting. Timing is of the essence, since television is associated with particular times of day and the accompanying moods. Television news, in particular, may serve as a boundary ritual, mediating between different time periods and between private and public spaces of the everyday structure (Scannell 1988).

Television news was found to contribute to the ongoing reflexive structuration (Giddens 1984) of everyday life in at least two distinctive ways in Denmark. The findings are compatible with Lull's (1980) typology of 'structural' and 'relational' uses of television in general, but serve to specify the particular social uses of the news genre. First, like other media, television lends structure to many daily activities. Mealtimes and bedtimes can be conceived in relation to the television schedule, and the question of whether to eat the evening meal in front of the box was said to be among the most hotly debated issues among the Danish respondents. Moreover, television has different roles to play, depending on the age of children in the household: television viewing may be a practical impossibility, a substitute babysitter, a common point of reference for the family group, or something that 'the old man and woman' will do. Special importance and prestige seemed to be attributed to news compared to other television genres. Being a recurring link between the political process and the everyday, newsviewing may be defined as an obligation for the viewer-citizen, something that ought not be missed. Even so, the Danish respondents noted that their attention would frequently be divided between the news and other activities, from cooking and reading to conversation.

Second, television news provides many frames of reference for reinter-preting everyday events and for drawing a variety of parallels to the respondents' own lives, thus facilitating interaction in the family and sustaining its social relations. In one household, the woman was an employee at an institution caring for the elderly and, according to her husband, this affected their viewing decisively since his wife would comment extensively on stories relating to that sector:

F3: 131–32: I hadn't thought about that. Do I really?
M3: If there's something on the care sector, then I may as well as give up watching the rest of /
F3: / Is that true? I start going on about the job?
M3: Then you talk, well, no, it's not so much the job, uh, the topic (...). Because then there's something you just must tell me. . .

The world in the news

Table 3.1 presents the line-up of stories on the main evening newscasts of the two national television channels in Denmark on Newsday, which were the point of departure for the household interviews. In addition to the opening labor dispute that carried major implications for the relations between rank-and-file workers and their unions, which have historically been central to Danish politics and social life, priority was given to two other stories, namely, the continued hostilities in Bosnia and the upcoming second Danish referendum regarding the European Union. This is suggested by the several interrelated items on each of these stories in the two programs. Other domestic stories addressed recurring concerns such as the level of taxation and street violence, and international items took up developments within familiar topics such as the Middle East conflict and a political transition in one of Denmark's EU partners, Spain. Both programs also included coverage of the fire in a toy factory in Thailand which, apart from the Bosnian crisis, was one of the stories relayed in several countries. It may be particularly noticeable that the two programs provided substantial coverage on various soft cultural items, including one item on DR about video art, and as many as three features on TV2 covering a new dissertation, bees, and a Third World soccer team supported by Denmark. This was on top of the two 'upbeat' segments at the end – on the first strawberries of the season and a parade – found in newscasts in many countries. While the number of these items on Newsday was probably unusual, it was and is common to find such an element of cultural coverage in television newscasts in Denmark.

The form and narrative of the news items followed familiar patterns which have been established in much previous research on news texts and their viewers (for example, in Denmark, see Jensen (1988), and in the United States, see Jensen (1987b)), and which were found to recur in several countries in the present study. Briefly, in particular, domestic stories are repeatedly structured around the maneuvering of political parties and social interest groups, as expressed in interview statements and as clarified by reporters with reference to earlier developments or economic consequences. International stories will in certain cases follow similar lines, often with additional attention given to the institutions and procedures which may put an end to the mutual maneuvering of parties to a dispute, and which may thus arrive at solutions to conflicts with international ramifications. It should be added that Danish newscasts will also take the standpoint of viewers as consumers or citizens – as, for instance, suggested in the Newsday programs by the items on street violence, the taxation of vans, and, perhaps, if the strike in the meat industry would continue and cut off supplies. To some degree, this is reflected below in the respondents' interpretation of stories from their own perspectives. But while the treatment of ordinary citizens as 'experts on consequences' of whatever events are reported in the news was pronounced on Danish television during the 1980s, this form of address has given way to other strategies during the 1990s as the competition between channels has intensified.

Table 3.1   Danish national news story line-up, 11 May 1993

Nyhederne (The News), TV2 19:00–19:25

1 Labor strike in the Danish meat-processing industry: compromise turned down by workers.

2 OVERVIEW OF STORIES COMING UP.

3 Effects of meat-industry strike on farmers.

4 Unrelated labor strike at Danish electronics plant.

5 Compensation given to 15-year-old victim of street violence.

6 Continued Croat offensive around Bosnian town of Mostar.

7 Muslims in Bosnia defending themselves with primitively produced weapons.

8 Major fire in toy factory in Thailand.

9 Announcement of general election in Spain following allegations of corruption.

10 Update on campaign before Danish referendum regarding the European Union: questions over legality of TV spots.

11 New dissertation on deceased Danish politician, written by his nephew.

12 Research project on the behavior of bees.

13 Danish development aid to Zambian soccer following the death of its entire national team in plane crash.

14 Weather forecast.

15 First strawberries of the season in Denmark.

TV-Avisen (The Television News[-paper]), DR, 20:30–21:00

1 OVERVIEW OF STORIES COMING UP.

2 Labor strike in the Danish meat-processing industry: compromise turned down by workers.

3 Local environmental dispute over natural gas vs. recycling.

4 High taxation of vans.

5 NEWS IN BRIEF: more restrictive domestic regulation of alternative therapy; major fire disaster in Thailand; action against Italian mafia fails.

6 US–European disagreement on arms aid to Bosnian Muslims – in context of Danish Prime Minister's meeting with US President Clinton.

7 Croats attacking Muslims around Mostar.

8 Peace negotiations on the Middle East in the US.

9 Swedish perspectives on the Danish EU referendum.

10 International press interest in Danish EU referendum.

11 Video art.

12 Weather forecast.

13 Parade from squatter settlement addressing the EU referendum.

Regardless of attempts by the news organizations to address and orient viewers along particular lines of interpretation, and regardless of the many nuances of daily political tactics that were offered for contemplation, the respondents would consistently and studiedly introduce their own interpretive constructs – the super-themes – in order to make relevant sense of the news. What comes out in the following section on the four super-themes that were identified in the Danish interviews is not so much a preference for the softer items, which in fact attracted little commentary overall, it is rather that viewers recast the central dimensions of news in ways that go against the grain of professional journalism. In doing so, they engage both major international conflicts and momentous decisions such as the EU referendum.

'The world in the head'

Our little corner of the world

Denmark was a center of international press attention in the days leading up to the second referendum concerning the European Union, to the degree that the number of visiting foreign journalists proved too great for the size of the press headquarters at the Danish parliament. This was taken by some respondents as a literal indication of the modest size of Denmark and its institutions, but also more generally as a symbol of Denmark being a small self-satisfied country. On the one hand, the outcome of the Danish referendum, at least in principle, would decide the future of Europe, since a rejection of the treaty by one country would result in a renegotiation of the entire treaty. On the other hand, respondents felt unsure whether this would in fact be the outcome, speculating that in such a case the larger nations would probably feel justified in making alternative plans. One respondent even suggested that the emphasis which was placed by press and public on the decisiveness of the Danish position was evidence of a national megalomania, an "egotrip (. . .), us Danes, we're damned good, you know" (M8: 53).

A similar perspective was developed with reference to coverage of a visit by the Danish prime minister to the US. While the prime minister met President Clinton in his capacity as chair of the European Community during the first six months of 1993, some respondents underscored that he was there on behalf of somebody else, here voicing a feeling that Denmark might be less than an international political authority. One respondent summed up this feeling in a reference to "visiting the big bears" (M1: 26).

In connection with some other stories, the coverage of minor events, especially human-interest or cultural domestic issues, was taken as an indication that nothing major seems to be happening in 'our little corner of the world,' certainly when measured on an international perspective. Repeated use was made of a widespread notion in Denmark of living at 'the duck's farm' or 'the duck's pond,' in part with reference to a familiar fairy tale by Hans Christian

Andersen about "The Ugly Duckling." Even though the duckling appears ugly and is put down by the other inhabitants of the duck's farm, it turns out in the end that it was really a beautiful swan in the making who later rejoins the other swans. The common use of this notion implies criticism of the self-sufficient attitude of a group or nation, in the present case denouncing both a tendency in Danish news to cover minor domestic news and various references to Denmark playing an independent role in an international context. Along with the news media, certain individuals, such as politicians, drew criticism from respondents for their self-sufficiency.

Less attention is normally given in the media and conversation to the eventual transformation of the duckling in the fairy tale into a swan, which represents the more positive, hopeful moral to the story. Though such a negative line of thinking may stop short of a national inferiority complex, these respondents also suggest that they experience pronounced difficulties in attempting to define their place in the world. Another major theme of Danish culture resonates with the feelings of uncertainty or inferiority. A familiar work by the Danish-Norwegian author Aksel Sandemose (1936) refers to the Law of the town of Jante (*Janteloven*) that preaches, in essence, "Don't think you're as good as us!" and "Don't think you're anybody!". *Janteloven* is a well-known term in everyday talk as well as in public debate in Denmark. The eagerness with which the respondents displayed their ability to deconstruct their arguably self-centered culture may be a circumspect way of reasserting their identity against the odds: in recognizing the limitations of their national point of departure, the respondents might be able, after all, to demonstrate their personal competence and insight into the world, thus in effect leaving the duck's farm behind.

The prominence of the super-theme concerning 'our little corner of the world' might be explained, in part, by the events of European politics at the time, which in certain countries, including Denmark, entailed something like a national identity crisis. That historical juncture, may have reemphasized a cultural characteristic. It also seems likely that such a perspective on the world may be shared by the Danish public with the public of other small countries. This first interpretive construct among the Danish respondents suggests that super-themes are not merely abstract cognitive categories, but are rooted in a specific cultural and historical context as well as in particular events in the news thematizing this context.

War

The diametrical opposite to 'our little corner of the world,' in some respects, is the super-theme of 'war.' It is significant that the reference was commonly made to *the* war, in definite, yet general terms. The respondents' accounts of several stories suggested an experience of a vague but real threat to them as individuals. This threat was normally said to originate far away – 'down there' – but had come close enough to create concrete worries, specifically in the case of the crisis in the former Yugoslavia, which might ultimately involve these Danish respondents. While an earlier study of Danish television newsviewers (Jensen 1988) also identified a super-theme of 'war' – referring to hostilities in remote locations and to the then still chilly war between East and West – the present set of interviews expressed a much more acute feeling of powerlessness, shamefulness, even dread in the face of events which were now seen to occur in 'our' corner of the world. In the words of one elderly man describing the nature of the conflict, "I wouldn't call it being shot, because they are simply being murdered" (M3: 22). For viewers with a certain historical background knowledge, Sarajevo became a symbol of the recurrence of such threats to ordinary people, being the place where the shots providing the occasion for World War I were fired, and where the continued shelling might set off World War III (M10: 6).

Some respondents speculated on the implications of the conflict for the future of democracy in Denmark, Europe, and the world. As one young man said:

> M8: 11: I do feel a bit ashamed, being part of a, being in the European Community, being in one the European countries, that can't seem to do anything sensible about this. Really. We have so many hundreds of thousands of politicians, or at least hundreds of politicians sitting around both at home and in the EC and all over the place, and they can't seem to do a darn thing about it! (. . .) I really think we need to begin to address this point fundamentally, and then find out what can be done in a situation like that.

The statement serves to suggest that, despite the sense of urgency which respondents expressed at the hostilities, they were much more hesitant or ambivalent when it came to ways of solving the conflict. One respondent found that other nations ought perhaps to intervene, but "not directly with weapons" (M3: 24). Several were concerned that the result of armed intervention might be another Korean or Vietnam war with protracted hostilities. And one young woman expressed the need to do something because she felt that the Yugoslavian conflict was not only closer, but also more violent compared to, for example, the Gulf War of 1991. (An assessment that was affected, no doubt, by the different types of reporting from the two contexts and by the tight control of the press during the Gulf War.) The young woman went on to characterize the deliberations among politicians and in the media about whether to intervene as "a conflict within ourselves" (F11: 15), and her husband added that the experience of urgency was greater in the case of this culturally close crisis, compared to, for instance, the coverage of hunger in the developing world.

Despite the various expressions of urgency, then, the Danish respondents also articulated a feeling of distance from such violent events, partly by labeling them as 'more of the same,' partly by expressly limiting their engagement with the events. Faced with different kinds of disaster and trouble, some respondents developed an argument to the effect that it is quite legitimate to be primarily concerned about one's own affairs:

> F1: 17: But of course you shut it out, you know. Because we do have, you know, we do have our own everyday, our own life to be involved in. If we had to constantly ponder and be affected by what's happening around the world, we couldn't find time for anything else, I would say.

War and disasters serve to remind Danish viewers that they are comfortable in their little corner of the world. While the exposure to such news may end up in a commonsensical acceptance of the general state of things, that the good life must go on, the news also provoked other, mixed feelings among the respondents – on the one hand, a bad conscience at not being able to share their prosperity with the rest of the world and, on the other hand, a sense of obligation to at least contribute to relief campaigns for the victims of events in the news. The world of the familiar everyday is experienced as comfortable, but limited; the world beyond the nation, and sometimes even beyond the home, represents a threat, but also an obligation for the viewer-citizen; and the news creates an occasion for mediating between the two worlds. If this mediation becomes too over-whelming, viewers may turn down their engagement and distance themselves – for example, by reference to the peripheral role of Denmark in world affairs or by reasserting their right to live their own good lives.

Those who take the rap

A third super-theme centered on the victims of events in the news, broadly speaking, not only wars and conflicts elsewhere, but also decisions and develop-ments in 'our little corner of the world.' Current television news, to varying degrees, features interviews with ordinary citizens who are supposed to be experts regarding the consequences of news events, and who in this respect resemble and represent the ordinary viewer. This does not imply that the respondents necessarily see themselves as the impotent and innocent victims of a merciless world, but the different possible consequences of events do constitute a measure of their news value for respondents as well as a frame for their inter-pretation of specific stories. Also in stories that were singled out for their global significance, the personal consequences could be brought in as an important perspective. For example, discussing the events in the former Yugoslavia, an elderly man noted that the eventual rebuilding of that region would have to be paid for by somebody: "And who is going to pay for it? We are — the three, four of us sitting here" (M3: 24). In such cases, viewers would be among those affected, 'those who take the rap.'

Violence on a different scale to war affects the victims of 'meaningless' street violence, who potentially include everybody. It is noteworthy that whereas some respondents were critical of the tabloid coverage of this area which is sometimes also found on television, they simultaneously displayed a keen interest in, as well as a detailed knowledge of, specific recent cases. The principled discussion of violence in society thus coexisted side by side with comments on the case of a boy, crippled by street violence, who was interviewed on the TV2 channel on Newsday, saying, among other things, that he wanted a puppy for himself. Also the coverage of violence of this type and on this scale can be said to monitor for viewers one of a variety of threats, far and near, potential and actual, to their personal safety.

Innocent third parties were singled out as those who may be affected most often by violence as well as by other types of conflicts in society. This became clear, for example, in the coverage on both national channels of a major labor conflict in the Danish meat-packing industry. However, different respondents, depending on their political-ideological position, described the farmers, the workers, the consumers, or the animals as the innocent third party. Parallels were also drawn to other conflicts, such as that in the public transportation system which had affected passengers in buses and on trains, suggesting that such disruption may be more of a rule than an exception in modern everyday life. In a complex, interconnected social structure, actions in one location cannot but affect third parties throughout the structure.

Accordingly, a substantial segment of the public, even the majority, may be seen to take the rap when, for example, the consequences and burdens of collective decisions are to be distributed. With reference to the meat-industry conflict, the son in one household mentioned that his immediate response was a question of whether there would be any ham for his ham-and-cheese toast, and a young woman noted that the story helped to explain why she had been unable to find a particular kind of meat at the supermarket. More significantly, perhaps, above and beyond the day's news item on the taxation of vans on the DR channel, taxes were brought up as a generalized consequence for citizens, either of external pressures on, or internal imbalances within, the social system. For instance, that not only may the European countries have to pay for the rebuilding of the former Yugoslavia, but that the European Union may eventually include some or most of the eastern European countries, which will probably require massive subsidies from other members if the eastern European countries are to become actual partners in the economic and political community. One young man had heard a reference on radio news to eastern Europe as he was driving along in his truck:

M9: 29: (. . .) I almost fell out of the truck. (. . .) Because that's gonna cost real money. (. . .) And I think we have a very, a nice high standard of living in this country, you know, but we damn well don't wanna lose any of it. (. . .) And we will lose part of it, you know. (. . .) That's the simple fact of the matter. No matter how the hell they figure it, it's us, we will be the ones footing the bill.

Moreover, such skepticism regarding the consequences of events in the news on individual citizens was directed not merely toward international developments, but also toward the effects of, for example, the meat-industry conflict on consumers, or a tax reform, debated around the time of the study, on tax-payers. One middle-aged woman summed up the sentiment:

> F4: 12: I've been a taxpayer in this country for twenty-two years, and I've been told eighteen times that now there will be a tax reform, and I'm damned if I ever, no! (. . .) I've never seen a reform that meant things became any different than they were. Then they'll call it something other than a tax.

Those who are in charge

The question of who takes the rap, predictably, is linked to the question of who makes the decisions that have consequences for the viewer's everyday life. Authorities – 'those who are in charge' – constitute the fourth and final super-theme in the Danish context. While most of the stories on Danish television news that respondents addressed in the interviews on Newsday examined issues of power in national and international politics, rather than several recent scandals in banking and elsewhere in the private sector, it was clear that the very notion of power being exercised through impersonal but effective hierar-chies was central to the respondents' experience of news. The organization of Danish society as a welfare state also helps to explain the prominence of the state in the respondents' references to 'those who are in charge.' An earlier comparative study of the conceptualization of politics among respondents in Denmark and the US has suggested that whereas Americans would emphasize the role of the market and private initiatives in shaping the social system overall, Danes would refer in this respect to the state as a super-theme (Crigler and Jensen 1991). The Danish respondents in the present study pursued the criticism of taxation and public subsidy one step further with reference to a rather vague entity of 'the powers that be,' arguing, for instance, that "those who are working must work more and more, and pay more and more taxes, you know. (. . .) Somehow they're tormenting us more all the time, you know" (M9: 8).

The distance between the top and bottom of social organizations was central to the respondents' thematizations of the story about the conflict in the meat industry. The news angle of that particular day was that a settlement between management and labor which had been agreed to by union officials was rejected by a large majority of their membership. One respondent, having suggested that the union officials were too far removed from the rank-and-file members, drew a parallel to the way the political system works, noting that most of the parties in the Danish parliament:

> F6: 3–4: are totally convinced that we should be in the EC [European Community], or that we should vote 'yes' to this Union agreement (. . .) But still there are so many, at least, probably close to 50 percent that are still going to vote 'no.' (. . .) And I think that's serious (. . .) and almost regardless of the particular issues being talked of, there's this enormous gap between those who, who, how should I say, who [*sighs*], it sounds so tough saying 'those in power,' but who do have some sort of influence, and those on whom the influence is taken out (. . .).

At least for certain of these respondents, the fact that some ordinary citizens would still oppose decisions that had been made centrally, such as the meat-industry compromise, was an encouraging sign. These ordinary citizens "get up and fight," which is "admirable" (F6: 5).

Whether it may in fact be possible for citizens to affect a course of events will depend, of course, on the circumstances of each case, and also on the scale of the economic and legal considerations it involves. Some respondents suggested that 'the system,' rather than any concrete assessment of the pros and cons of a case, might make certain decisions inevitable, referring, for example, to a local conflict over the introduction of a natural-gas scheme backed by the state in an area that seemed to be well-served by an already existing system of recycling and energy conservation. Both national, long-term planning and various vested interests may be seen as trumping ecological ideals and local initiatives.

Also in an international perspective, the respondents found evidence not only that the vested interests would prevail in the end, but also that power corrupts those who are in charge. The TV2 broadcast on Newsday included an example of corruption in Spanish politics, and the respondents volunteered similar cases from Italy, Germany, and France, as well as a historic case in Denmark where a former minister of justice was impeached for mismanaging immigration legislation. Interestingly, a respondent argued that power corrupts regardless of the political color of the people involved. Another worry for some was that when, presumably, there will be a further concentration of power within the European Union, this will place "small groups" at a disadvantage generally:

> M9: 32–3: You may twist and turn it any way you like, you know. (. . .) I mean, when it becomes a great power, there will always be a greater chance that some small groups are shunted aside, you know. (. . .) Many times they are the ones who damn well make things go around, you know.

It should be added that the news media themselves were included among the powerful institutions in society which represent particular interests and, hence, call for a measure of skepticism on the part of viewers. Referring to the story about the taxation of vans, a middle-aged man suggested, half-jokingly but insistently, that an auto dealer might have bribed the journalist in order to make him show the brand name of the vans clearly in the visuals. And a young man argued that this particular story really did not raise any general perspectives the way the news should. Instead, it might have been selected as part of an ongoing confrontation between politicians and news media that may attract viewers. The journalists simply wanted to expose "legislators making a dumb decision" (M11: 41).

Images in the head

In addition to the four super-themes that helped to frame the Danish respondents' interpretations, the news images call for a brief analysis. The visuals of television news provide some measure of insight into locations which are far removed from the local place and time of the viewers. The visual aspect of newscasts is also important in shaping the viewers' basic comprehension and experience of the information offered, as well as their further deliberations about the events covered (e.g. Höijer 1990; Jensen 1988). Nevertheless, it is a familiar experience – for newsviewers, journalists, and researchers alike – that quite often the images are not integrated into the narrative of television news. Rather, the norm in many countries may still be a structure in which the spoken commentary by anchors and journalists carries the story line, as supplemented by interviews and other statements, as well as by graphics and still images, whereas the moving images can be said to illustrate various aspects of an event or issue.

The findings from the present study suggest that there are both problems and potentials in the various ways of telling the story by showing it. Visuals may encourage the form of generalized interpretations, far removed from journalistic and political–scientific conceptions of news, which are also suggested by the super-themes; visuals may also offer an interface between 'the journalists' news' and 'the viewers' news.' From the viewers' perspective, it was possible to identify at least three types of images.

At one end of the spectrum there are 'stereotypes.' All television viewers know such images – of a politician or expert behind a desk, of a burnt village in a war zone, or of a starving child covered with flies. One problem with the stereotypical images is that they appear to produce a form of 'noise' which may interfere with or even silence the main point of a story. As noted by one middle-aged man regarding the story about natural gas, a person being interviewed in front of a typical government building "does not tell us very much about the sort of 'green' energy that may be used" (M4: 9). Such images may even come to contradict the main point of a news item, as noted by some respondents with reference to the coverage of the meat-industry conflict where the visuals would show meat being cut up and packed despite the fact that this was exactly what was *not* happening during the conflict.

At the opposite end of the spectrum, one finds 'autonomous images' – that is, images which appear to have been cut loose from their context and which may create streams of associations in the respondents' interpretations. As a result, viewers might lose themselves in the scenery of foreign countries or in the looks of an anchorperson or interviewee. While news visuals inevitably contain information in their own right, such autonomous images counteract the communicative, journalistic purpose of news, as do the stereotypes.

It is one of the challenges in the production of television news to navigate between these two extremes. When a middle ground is found, one can speak of 'eye-openers.' First, an integrated discourse of verbal and visual elements can lead to a better comprehension by viewers, as suggested by previous research on the recall of news (p. 6). One example of such integration is the frequent use of graphics to explain economic developments. Second, images which are simultaneously striking and to the point can contribute to what might be called a 'sensuous presence' of viewers in the universe of news. In the interviews with the Danish households, such an experience was related in their retelling of the meat-industry story, with specific reference to the animals which, because of the strike, could not be brought to the slaughterhouse, but had to be herded on overcrowded farms, eventually to be buried in mass graves. These images affected several respondents deeply, even to the point where some declared themselves willing to deviate from their stated political positions and principles. Commenting on the fact that the animals were killed in the context of a labor struggle, one young man found that although "I consider myself a socialist" (M10: 2), this treatment of animals was unacceptable to him. A common denominator for these and some other images which affected the respondents – for example, close-ups of the young victim of street violence – was that they came very close to the body of either humans or animals which we tend to compare ourselves to.

A third type of 'eye-opener' may have special, practical implications for the discursive, narrative construction of news. In several stories, both domestic and foreign, the visuals came to serve viewers as a 'concrete symbol' of what was at stake in the event. In the coverage of the former Yugoslavia, some "rather peaceful" images of people "just trotting along" on a road were singled out as producing greater empathy than images of death and destruction (F11: 16). Also in the coverage of this conflict, two video sequences that had been juxtaposed in one news item depicting buildings in the town of Mostar before and after the devastation vividly brought home the scope of the intervening events. In domestic coverage of the meat-industry conflict, a dual interview confronting a farmer and a worker provided a concrete illustration of the positions and principles of the case by bringing the two together and depicting them in the same time and space. Contrary to the stereotypes, the 'eye-opening' images had symbolic implications which were noted by respondents; contrary to the autonomous images, the 'eye-opening' images had been integrated with the journalistic text as part of a communicative strategy. In themselves, such concrete visual symbols do not provide much information beyond the generalized level of the super-themes, but the 'eye-openers' may become a point of access to, and a means of processing, the audiovisual story as a whole from the viewer's perspective.

News as a resource in the world

Following the news, to a degree, the information stays with the audience as part of their awareness of the world and may become a resource for action beyond the immediate context of viewing in front of the screen. The possible uses of the information help to explain why special importance was attached to the news, compared to other television genres, by the respondents:

> M2: 47: (. . .) we want to be well-informed and, about our society, I mean, we want to be well-informed about what's going on in the world, we want to be well-informed about what's going on in Denmark. And if you want to be well-informed, then you have to read a newspaper a day, and then you have to watch a news program a day.

Even though most viewers could presumably get through their day without news (Gans 1979; see also pp. 9–10), the respondents articulated a need for generally 'keeping up.' Furthermore, a distinction was made between short-term and long-term uses. In the short term, the specific uses were considered to be limited, apart from conversation: "It's more like information about what's going on than really something about what concretely I can do" (F7: 20). Of course, farmers among the respondents would find the weather report of special interest, and a teacher in the sample mentioned that he would often use examples from the news in class.

References to long-term uses were formulated in rather unclear terms and supported with few examples. When pressed for an answer, though, the respondents would refer broadly to the political process in which they have a constitutive role as citizens, voters, and, potentially, activists. Having determined that oneself, one's family, one's community, one's country – one's 'significant others' (Mead 1934) – are not in danger, since 'nothing major' has happened, one may begin to establish links between the news and the political public sphere (Habermas 1989). Conversation also emerged in these interviews as a central, mediating aspect of the social production of meaning, disseminating and explaining information further to others, including members of the household, as well as initiating discussion of world events and national issues. While contributing in the long term to setting a public agenda (McCombs and Shaw 1972), in the short term the news serves as a source of arguments for interpersonal debate.

It is significant, however, that such debate was characterized as brief, and often not very serious, being part of quips, teasing colleagues, or other casual interaction. As suggested by earlier studies in different national settings (e.g.

Jensen 1986; Nordenstreng 1972), viewers may conceive of themselves as audiences surveying their social environment at a distance through television and other news media without intervening as citizens in public debate or political activity to any significant extent. Whereas this is in keeping with the Danish respondents' assessment that the news does not affect their political positions, it contradicts a widespread participatory conception of citizenship that these respondents also appear to presuppose – for example, in the remarkable emphasis that they place on the importance of constantly keeping up. Instead, their political participation may be enacted primarily in the consumption of news.

Other areas of coverage, such as the economy, were referred to with a similar ambivalence regarding principle and practice. In principle, economic information could become a basis of intervening politically, making investments, or planning one's personal economy. In practice, the respondents noted, economic news may have its relevance in more delimited areas such as consumer spending and, even in such cases, any information with specific implications for action would be likely to reach them through other channels first – for instance, their bank. Again, if the news genre has a limited use value, this may be due not merely to its forms of presentation or to restrictions on the information which is made available by the key economic and political institutions of society, but as much to a lack of precedent on both sides of the screen for conceiving the news as a resource for action in social life.

Conclusion

Like a number of other reception studies, this analysis has found that mass media audiences are able to identify, interpret, and appreciate 'hidden realities' with personal relevance behind the surface discourse of news. It is this ability in particular which has led some previous research to characterize audiences as sophisticated and critical users of the media to a point where all reception might seem equal. In conclusion, it should be specified that the Danish respondents demonstrated two different ways of approaching such hidden realities that amount to two modes of reception, and which are not equal, either in their type or in their degree of sophistication and criticism. While the two modes of reception can be related to the respondents' social background, the present study only documents the occurrence of the two different modes and their relationship to the super-themes, leaving a description of their distribution across social groups and contexts of media use for further research.

The first mode of reception, as articulated by a group of respondents with a relatively shorter education, was characterized by two features. First, these respondents referred to a specific hidden reality underlying television news, in the sense that certain 'conspiracies' might explain what was reported. Such illegal or illegitimate arrangements were seen to underlie both events reported in the news and the fact that certain events received coverage – even though references to a specific manipulation of the news were not widespread. One example in this respect was the item on the taxation of vans which clearly showed vehicles of a particular make, perhaps by agreement between the journalist and the automobile dealer. Other examples included the developments in the meat industry which might be accounted for as a conspiracy between the industry and the supermarkets marketing their products against the best interests of both workers and consumers. Second, this group of respondents found it difficult, in their re-telling of news items, to go beyond the super-themes so as to specify the agendas, issues, decisions, and implications of a particular story. From their perspective, a large proportion of news might be grasped through the super-themes only. In socio-demographic terms, the group of respondents who articulated this mode of reception had up to four years of studies following basic schooling of ten years.

The second group of respondents can be said to represent an educational elite, primarily with a longer professional or university education. First, whereas these respondents made references to the same super-themes as the other group, and while they appeared to reproduce a similar mental mapping of the world in their interview discourses, they were able to move beyond the super-themes in discussing, for example, both the details of the issues in the meat-industry conflict and its social implications arising from the gap between the top and the bottom of the union movement. Second, regarding the existence of a hidden reality, these well-educated respondents rather suggested that the news bears witness to a double reality whose elements they were able to distinguish. Underneath the day-to-day politics reported by television and other news media, they identified fundamental impersonal structures of society, rather than individuals or particular organizations conspiring, as the factors determining the decisions and developments which ultimately affect the ordinary viewer.

In sum, the super-themes and their configuration in the Danish context begin to suggest an interpretive framework which, in different articulations, may structure the reception and social uses of television news. In addition, the findings concerning the respondents' assessment of different news media identify certain criteria which might make news both more comprehensible and relevant to viewers in an everyday context. At the same time, the interviews suggest the difficulties that viewers experience in approaching news as a resource for political and other social action. The super-themes may make up a two-edged sword, facilitating the making of sense, but discriminating against those who are not able to reflect and act on their sense.

4

INDIA

*K. P. Jayasankar and Anjali Monteiro**

The news of the state and the state of the news

This chapter attempts to conceptualize how 'spectator' identities are negotiated within networks of power and resistance (Foucault 1984: 93) as a specific group of viewers – ten families in the city of Bombay, India – encounters the discourses of the state, as represented by news from Doordarshan, Indian state television. The authors draw on Foucault's formulation of the state as a new distribution and organization of an old power technique, originating in the Church, namely, pastoral power (Foucault 1986: 213). The state, accordingly, becomes a "structure in which individuals can be integrated, under one condition, that this individuality would be shaped in a new form and submitted to a set of very specific patterns" (ibid.: 214). The state's power is thus both individualizing and totalizing, and works toward the constitution of subjects as spectators.

The first part of this chapter, "The news of the state," contains a broad overview of television in India, and situates the notion of crisis that emerged as a dominant theme in the viewers' responses. The second part, "The nation-state and the other," examines, in the context of this sense of crisis, the construction of national and ethnic identities *vis-à-vis* the discourses of news. The negotiation of viewer identity appears to involve the invocation of various 'others,' an issue which is also explored in that section. The concluding part, "The spectator, the state, and the other," delineates the flows of power and resistance that emerge from the interpretation of viewer discourses.

* The authors gratefully acknowledge the contribution of Dr Nasreen Fazalbhoy and Dr Lakshmi Lingam in conducting four of the household interviews; Ms Vanmala Hiranandani for transcription, translations, and research support; Ms Sheela Rajendra for secretarial assistance; and the ten families for their wholehearted participation in the study. The authors also thank Dr Klaus Bruhn Jensen for his support.

The news of the state

> M3: 1 (. . .) TV amounts to a medium for government propa-
> ganda. What else is it? There's nothing called news in it . . .

The Indian television network, Doordarshan, is entirely state owned and controlled, and its programming is in consonance with a state agenda; it is impossible to separate television news in India from the state. At the time of this study, there was only one channel available to the bulk of the viewers. Channel 2 (the Metro channel) and the other three state-owned, satellite channels were restricted either to the major cities or to a small segment with access to cable networks. The main daily news programs were on Channel 1 on Doordarshan.

For Indian viewers, the news is inextricably tied up with their identities as citizens, their stance towards the news bearing within it a stance towards the state. This became apparent in the responses about news programs:

> F4: 11 (Daughter-in-law): (. . .) TV is government controlled . . . it is but natural they will use the media to voice their opinion. I wouldn't be surprised . . . tomorrow if any other party comes to power – they will do the same . . .

All the Indian respondents acknowledged this relationship in their interpretation of news, even while drawing varied inferences from this perceived nexus. Some viewers thought it was inevitable:

> B6: 16: (. . .) any government which comes to power will use the media for their own weightage . . . [advantage]
> YOU THINK IT IS INEVITABLE?
> B6: To some extent, it is inevitable because after all . . . the state has its own life, it has to exist . . . I think any government in the world will do it.

An analysis of the news items on Doordarshan during Newsweek (Table 4.1) bears out the conclusion that the bulk of the items were related to the state and its machinery. Of the 143 stories recorded, about 35 percent were reports on the activities of the state (whether of its executive, legislative, or judicial arms). If one adds the items concerning foreign relations and terrorism, which directly involve the state, an overwhelming close to 60 percent of stories reported the news of the state.

One noteworthy feature of viewers' discussions is that they digressed from the specific news stories of the days (several days, for practical reasons) when the interviews were conducted (11, 12, 13 May 1993) (see Table 4.2) to a range of other issues. The discussions tended to focus on events of the recent past and on TV as a medium. India, as a nation, has witnessed widespread communal and ethnic violence in recent years. These incidents find their way to viewers'

Table 4.1 Classification of Doordarshan news programs, 5–11 May 1993

Topic	N
Govt. – Executive	34
Govt. – Legislature	12
Govt. – Judiciary	5
Terrorism	21
Foreign Relations	12
Bosnia	3
Accidents	3
Economy	2
Misc. Political	3
Misc. Foreign	16
Misc. Domestic	16
Sports	16
Total	143

Note: N = number of news items

accounts of the various facets of news reception. The bland newscasts consisting mainly of reports of parliamentary proceedings and ritualistic government programs were quite imaginatively short-circuited by viewers to discuss general issues related to the nation-state, the body-politic, the role of television – in short, their world. To facilitate a more detailed discussion of these issues in later sections of this chapter, a brief overview of the development of television in India follows.

Television in India**

Doordarshan (DD) was instituted in the 1960s in the context of media policies informed by modernization theory – specifically, the communication approach to development (Krippendorff 1979). In a country characterized by a bewildering linguistic and cultural diversity, where less than a quarter of the population are native speakers of the national language, Hindi, an ambitious agenda was set for the media, the attempt being to foster a pan-Indian identity based on secularism (see Madan 1987; Nandy 1988).

** Portions of this section are taken from Monteiro and Jayasankar (1994). For a historical overview of Doordarshan, see Mitra (1993).

Table 4.2 Lead stories on Doordarshan news programs, 11–13 May 1993

Date	Item No.	Topic
11 May	1	Parliamentary debate on impeachment of Supreme Court Judge
	2	Supreme Court cancels bye-election to Haryana State Assembly
	3	India and Tanzania hold high-level talks 4 Botswanian delegation calls on Indian President
12 May	1	Lower House of Indian parliament approves extension of President's rule in four states
	2	Ruling party abstains from voting in impeachment motion
	3	Leader of Opposition condemns ruling party's stance
	4	Impeachment motion (May 11) fails
13 May	1	Parliament approves extension of President's rule in four states
	2	Prime Minister exhorts police and intelligence service to break terrorist-drug mafia nexus
	3	India asks Pakistan to hand over bomb-blast suspects
	4	USA accuses Pakistan of drug smuggling

The growth of television in India can be broadly divided into three phases, the first phase consisting of the period up to 1980. It was during this time that the Satellite Instructional Television Experiment (SITE) was conducted – in 1975–6 – in order to arrive at a relevant prototype for the use of television in development. SITE covered 2,330 villages in six states and was geared to the rural audience, being disseminated through community television sets. The production of programs was undertaken under the aegis of a state-run development communication organization, and the thrust was primarily on educational and information-based programs in the areas of agriculture, health, and family planning. The structure and content of SITE reflected the dominant national credo of the 1960s and early 1970s: self-reliance, 'socialism,' and progress through technological input.

Up to the early 1980s, television in India had a negligible viewership. In 1983, while the reach was 210 million (28 percent of the population), the viewership was only 30 million (4 percent of the population) (Singhal and Rogers 1989: 66). The introduction of color television, the liberalization of television imports, and the installation of the satellite Insat 1-B marked a qualitative change in both state policy and the structure of television viewing. With this, one sees an abandoning of the old development paradigm in favor of a more commercial variant with marketing techniques and commercial sponsorship of programs being invoked to sell development. This new approach to development involved changes at the level of production structures, programming, as well as in the modes of reception. With the introduction of commercial sponsorship of TV serials in 1980 and of private software production in 1984, and with the shift in emphasis from community television sets to a proliferation of individually owned sets, the stage was set for a new, second phase of television.

The state's strategy of going commercial with television has been regarded by many researchers as a dilution of its development goals (Chowla 1985). However, it is precisely this strategy that has made possible the entry of the state into the familial space and, in the process, redefining the viewers' relationship to both the public and private spheres. The marketing approach used for development communication was also extended to the political arena where, for the first time in the 1984 general elections, the Indian National Congress and other parties relied heavily on media campaigns designed by advertising agencies.

Starting from the decade of the 1990s, a third phase has been marked by the emergence of transnational networks such as CNN, STAR, BBC, etc. Private cable networks bring these programs to many households, in cities and small towns, at a nominal cost. These networks have made considerable inroads into Doordarshan's viewership in a city like Bombay. With the growth of cable television and multinational satellite networks, DD has intensified its strategy of going commercial. The change in programming – with more time being allotted to feature films and entertainment serials and the number of programming hours being increased, as well as the leasing of the Metro channel to private sponsors – has been seen as inevitable if DD is to survive the competition from its new challengers.

Subsequent to this study, DD has gone on to augment its services to include a Movie Club channel and several regional satellite channels. It has also changed its formats for news presentation, including more varied camera angles, a larger number of newscasters, and an increased use of on-location reporting, trying to model itself along BBC lines. Since 1996, major transnational networks such as Star Plus, BBC, and Zee TV have started national newscasts in Hindi and/or English. Though figures are not available, from the commercial sponsorship that these newscasts have been able to attract, they appear to command an elite viewership. These programs have extensive live reporting and exclusive interviews and teleconferences with political leaders. The weather forecast, which had been a drab affair with DD, has been transformed into a spectacle by Star Plus with slick graphics and an attractive anchor. In a country where the weather has never been a topic of conversation due to its predictability and constancy, it is striking that this forecast has become a popular attraction and, hence, an arena for marketing with sponsorship from multinational automobile and air-conditioning giants.

At the time of the study, cable television was relatively new, but had already considerably reduced news-watching. Previously, in most households, the TV set would be switched on to the main Doordarshan channel at 7:30 or 8.00 pm, and kept on until 10 pm or later. News was watched as a part of this flow, often only by the male members of the household. However, with the proliferation of cable channels, the viewership of the national network has been eroded, with the Metro channel (now a film-based entertainment channel in the place of a channel in regional languages) and Zee TV constituting a serious threat. Perhaps the program to be affected most by the multiplicity of channels is the national network news in Hindi and English. DD audience research ratings for the week of 29 May to 14 June 1994 indicated a 16 percent viewership share for the English news, as opposed to 50–60 percent for Metro channel serials (*The Times of India*, 26 June 1994). When selecting households for the present study, it was difficult in fact to locate households where the national network news was watched as a regular feature. Even households without a cable connection would prefer the Metro channel to Doordarshan news on the main channel.

The news of the crisis

> G1: 8: (...) In our own lifetime ... everything is getting split ...

The major super-themes that inform viewers' discourses are those of 'crisis' and 'identity,' as examined further below. The constitution of identity involves "dividing practices" (Foucault 1986: 208) that invoke an 'us' versus 'them.' The viewer identity, invoked by all respondents, thus relates to contested concepts of nationhood and the state. In this study, the two super-themes come out as interrelated.

The super-theme of crisis sets the horizon for a number of the viewers' accounts of the news, though there was no news item directly pertaining to the crisis that most viewers nevertheless chose to speak about. The intensity with which the super-theme of crisis informs the viewers' accounts is related to the specific conjuncture described below, and it would no doubt be articulated differently if the interviews were to be done in, say, 1997. However, the strategies that viewers deploy in order to define their identities would hardly be different (Monteiro and Jayasankar, forthcoming).

During the six months prior to this study, Bombay witnessed the most savage and prolonged violence in the post-independence period. In December of 1992, proponents of *Hindutva* (Hindu-ness), represented by political parties such as the Bharatiya Janata Party and the Shiv Sena, and by organizations such as the Rashtriya Svayamsevak Sangh and the Bajjrang Dal, demolished the centuries-old Babari mosque in the town of Ayodhya on the grounds that the mosque was built over a temple marking the birthplace of the Hindu deity Ram. The government remained a mute spectator to the demolition, perhaps because of the possible effects at upcoming elections of antagonizing pro-Hindu sections of the population. Arson and clashes broke out all over the city, lasting for about a week. There was a fresh upsurge of communal violence in early January of 1993. During this phase, *Hindutva* supporters systematically targeted Muslim households, business establishments, and localities, ostensibly to revenge alleged attacks on individuals of their community by the Muslims. This was followed in March by a series of bomb blasts in public places, leaving hundreds dead and injured. These blasts were allegedly engineered by Dawood Ibrahim, a Muslim mafia don, in retaliation for the attacks on Muslims during the riots. This series of events dealt a blow to the identity of the city as a cosmopolitan melting pot, a thriving commercial center, untouched by the ethnic strife that has affected other parts of the country:

> M4: 16: (. . .) over there [Punjab and Kashmir] life is so . . . that way, we are lucky in Bombay . . . we are safe and . . . but after this bomb blast thing, the position has reversed, now, now, our life is more in danger and their life has become safe now . . .

It seems as if terrorism or ethnic violence, which had hitherto been an 'object,' suddenly transformed itself in to a 'subject' (Masselos 1993). When an event was seen as an object, "apparent meaning was imposed on what was happening, according to the perceptions and viewpoints of those who made the ascriptions (. . .) The terminology linked it into other occasions and sets of ideas – and engendered a variety of connotations outside the originating situation and suggested appropriate behavior as a result of those connotations" (Masselos 1993: 183). As opposed to this, the event as subject evokes a reaction that perhaps makes it resistant to reification: it poses itself as an 'active text' that needs to be negotiated immediately:

> M10: 18: Yeah, but it's like only when Bombay was rocked by the riots and bomb blast that Bombayites woke up and said, "Oh, we never thought that would happen to us." We heard about it happening in Delhi, but how many Bombayites got up and spoke up. No one. Only when it happens to you immediately, that you are going to speak . . .

In the transformation from object to subject, certain issues that once were distant had become immediate. This transformation, in turn, spawned various other objects that were to influence the production and circulation of news, myths, rumors, and stereotypes. Most of the interview responses in this study merit the status of objects that were generated subsequent to the riots.

The riots brought to the fore the assertion of communal and national identities, leading to a hardening of divides and a breakdown of trust between communities. For instance, for one Indian family, an upper-class Muslim household living in downtown Bombay, their sudden vulnerability during the riots brought home to them their Muslim-ness, which for them had perhaps never been a crucial marker of their identity prior to the riots:

> F9: 20: Like, we [though Muslims] have more friends in the Hindu

community than our own community but now, you know, the situation is also such that we hesitate. Things have changed now.

YEAH, IT MAKES YOU MORE CONSCIOUS ...

F9: Yes, it does make you conscious and it makes you feel, are you secure and safe now in this own country of yours (...) It was like, we used to eat from one plate, one hearth, but now, we hesitate. (...) The people who used to sit down and share the same table as us — they are the ones who are doing this to us. So you feel a little ...

All sections of the population appear to experience feelings of insecurity and threat, including communities not immediately affected, as the following excerpt from a discussion with a South Indian Christian family indicates:

M8: 8: (...) Now this bomb blast is happening everywhere ... nobody knows where it may happen ... anytime, anywhere, without any prior notice, it is happening ... so there is no safety in Bombay ... it is becoming a miserable place to live ... so even we are feeling to shift [thinking of moving] from Bombay ...

For several of those belonging to the Muslim community, however, the post-riots situation was experienced as one where their basic rights as citizens of a democratic country were in question:

F9: 10–11: Because even freedom of writing ... nowadays ... everything is censored. You have to think ten times before you put down in writing, ten times before you say anything (...) the rights of a democratic country ... you can do whatever you want ... you can say whatever you want ... those rights have ...

THAT YOU THINK HAS HAPPENED BECAUSE OF THE EVENTS OF THE LAST THREE MONTHS?

F9: No, it has been gradually ... gradually ... and more after the riots.

The feeling of crisis extends to other spheres of life, as well. For instance, breakdown of morality, law, and order is another recurrent theme. In Household 1, the father, in response to an item on the proposed impeachment of a Supreme Court Justice on grounds of corruption, felt that he could not take a stand on the issue because, in the public domain, there was no longer any way of separating true from false:

M1: 2: And, nowadays, it is like that ... in work matters, honesty becomes dishonesty ... with one's brains one can implicate any man ... if this can happen to such an important man — then what becomes of small people ...

The husband in Household 3 strongly articulated the pervasive sense of disenchantment with the functioning of the state machinery, and its implications for public order:

> M3: 4: (...) People have lost faith in law. If today someone says that Sharad Pawar [the chief Minister of the Indian state of Maharashtra, whose capital is Bombay] was also involved in the bomb blast, people won't get a shock. People are so fed up.

The same person went on to characterize the malfunctioning of the state as the main cause of the crisis facing the country today:

> M3: 9–10: (...) So, our rules and regulations have become such a jungle that if a police officer wants to do something he is asked whether something else will be destroyed. That's why no government officer wants to put himself into a problem. That's why he does not do any work. They tell the common man, this is according to the law. What is the law, nobody knows ...

Still other manifestations of crisis, mentioned by the father in Household 1, are the increasing impersonality of city life and the spiraling cost of living. The predominant stances that appear to emerge in the course of the discussions are not those of victimhood or passive subjection, but more an assertion of anger, outrage, and surprise. Even where viewers regarded their lives as being under threat, they still articulated the need to speak out, to do something about this situation.

The nation-state and the 'other'

> G9: 20: I think it is war between the politicians into which the common man has been pulled, and from all sections of society, be it a Hindu, Muslim, or Christian. Everyone is being pulled into it.

At the core of the present crisis gripping the Indian nation-state is the question of national identity. The construction of identity, in the context of the modern nation-state, involves the creation of communities imagined through language (Anderson 1983) and a "new imagination: a new vision of calendrical time (linear teleological history), a limited but generalized space, occupied by homogeneous and equal 'citizens,' who are the protagonists of this new drama of the 'movement of history' " (Smith 1986: 169). Paradoxically, however, the new sensibilities of national identity are built up on a premodern ethnic core of myth, memory, symbol, and value.

In a multi-ethnic country such as India, the process of forging a homogeneous national identity is fraught with tension: Which of these identities gets represented in the 'national' identity? Which alternative traditions and local cultures get suppressed? For instance, the nationalist movement in India owed much of its populist appeal to the invocation of Hindu myths and symbols. The contradictions of a secular India, built on a mass base of *Hindu Rashtra* (Hindu Nationhood), continue to bedevil the polity as bitter ethnic battles are waged over the reinvention of history and definitions of national identity. The present resurgence of *Hindutva* sees the past solely in terms of the golden age of pre-Muslim India and, conversely, the barbarity of the subsequent period of Muslim rule. In the popular reconstruction of history, the Muslim appears as the proselytizing invader who desecrated the shrines of other religions (Pandey 1993).

There were no news reports on any of the days of interviewing that related to religious or ethnic issues. Despite this fact, the construction of 'others' along religious divides figured prominently in viewer discourses. Doordarshan has an almost absurd way of skirting references to religious groups. To cite a purely hypothetical instance, it would not be altogether unusual to find a news item on the lines of, "In Bombay, members of two communities clashed after a shrine belonging to a particular community was set afire by miscreants . . . " In some instances, the euphemisms adopted are 'minority' and 'majority' communities, to refer to Muslims and Hindus respectively. The euphemism of 'minority' does not appear to include other non-Hindu religious groups. After the riots and blasts in Bombay, there was a tendency, even among other religious minorities, to constitute the Muslims as the 'other.' It seems amazing that a South Indian Christian (M8) chooses to interpret the demolition of a mosque by Hindu religious fanatics as proof of the basic aggressive nature of Indian Muslims in general:

> M8: 9: As such, our church or Hindu religion, specially our Christian community, we adopt peaceful methods. Whenever anything happens, our leaders think over it . . . and give the message to the people to be peaceful . . . don't enter into violence . . . they tell the people . . . also they keep the people in the pocket in a silent manner, which keeps us [Christians] silent . . . that activities are there . . . that has a direct effect . . . for example, this Ayodhya issue took place . . . Muslims were more aggressive . . . at a certain time they lost their freedom in India . . . so they were afraid of their position . . . so they were also taking violence in their hand to make others to fear . . . one day [in the Mughal era, early sixteenth century AD], it was [a] temple, tomorrow they may spoil some other thing . . . so they are actually opposing . . . to restrict it . . . whereas our community, we [Christians] remained impartial . . .

There is also a class dimension to this portrayal of Muslims as *lumpen*, uneducated, and "not so much refined":

> M8: 9: (. . .) But these people are taking the message of the Almighty

in their own language which is being interpreted by their own . . . so the value that is going into them is [of] their quality . . . their values are being reduced to the human state . . . so these values are not so much refined.

While constructing Hindus as basically tolerant and nonviolent, Hindu nationalism upholds the myth of the intolerant Muslim aggressor. This definition is applied to create a stereotype of Muslims in India today as fanatical, aggressive, and anti-national. The opposition to this is the 'secular' Hindus:

M6: 2: Yes, communalism has to be rooted out, because secularism is very much required in the country, because I think in our country, people of so many religions, caste, and creed are living together . . . secularism is very much essential for our country.

The movement for the Hindu nation equates nationalism with an upper-caste, homogenized, and modernized version of Hindu culture (Nandy 1993b: 17), in which Ram becomes not merely a Hindu deity, but a national hero, and reverence to Ram a condition for Indian citizenship. The destruction of the Babari Masjid at Ayodhya was aimed at recreating the lost glory of the Hindu nation as well as at settling scores with the Muslims (the 'other') and showing them their place in the Hindu order of things. Holding Muslim politics responsible for the partition of the original colonial territory into India and Pakistan, the Hindu fundamentalist view cannot but see all Indian Muslims as Pakistanis at heart, unless proved otherwise. Both the Muslim families interviewed for this study (Households 9 and 10), appeared to be aware of this collective onus to demonstrate their Indian-ness and their secular credentials. They regarded the sanitized euphemism of 'majority' and 'minority' communities as loaded and objectionable:

G9: 19: India is a secular state first . . .
M9: We know we [though from the Muslim minority community] are first Indians. So we are all equal, so why do they keep saying minority community and majority community?

Household 10 further contested the exclusive claim of the proponents of *Hindutva* to represent true nationalism. M10 pointed to the regional chauvinism of Shiv Sena, a political party which, until recently, claimed to represent the aspirations of people from the state of Maharashtra (with the capital of Bombay) and had targeted even Hindus from other Indian states for their attack:

M10: (. . .) We [as Muslims] do feel we are Indian and we have given up going to Pakistan at the time of partition. We have personally opted for India. What I feel is that there are a number of people who hardly feel anything for India as a whole. They may feel, "we are Maharashtrians or this thing," . . . not doing anything for integration.

Even international political relationships get refracted and rarefied by this discourse of Muslims/Pakistan as the 'other'. For instance, referring to the issue of ethnic strife in Bosnia, M2 remarked that even there, the Hindus and Muslims are fighting each other! The following excerpts frame the news of Bosnia in surprisingly different ways. M6 is a retired railway employee, a Hindu who had to flee Pakistan at the time of the partition in 1947, and B10 belongs to the Muslim community:

M6: 8: Yes, I think Bosnia is [important] international news, because the major reason is Yugoslavia is no more . . . now they are all different states now, who are fighting among one another . . . the Muslims of the [Yugoslavian] states are aided by other Muslim states . . . they are sending mercenaries.

BUT WHY DO YOU THINK BOSNIA IS IMPORTANT?
B10: 4: If you look at it — we are not communal or anything like that. But the entire media all over the world is controlled by the Christian, Christian world basically. Right now, this Islamic revivalism and funda-mentalism and a break-up of Russia. I think these people really fear this revivalism. So you find a lot of emphasis being given to the things happening in Islamic countries and probably, the negative aspects are brought out more, and this might also be getting reflected in our TV . . . I don't know . . .

In the present study, also apart from Hindus and Muslims, minorities and majorities, secularists and communalists, the authors encountered many an 'other' (see also Crigler and Jensen 1991, on 'powerful others'), employed strategically to constitute various multi-layered spectator identities. The anti-thetical pairs included: India/Pakistan, Citizens/Terrorists, Friends/Enemies, Big People/Small People, Politicians/Common People, Doordarshan/Cable, and National/International. They are examined further below for their relations to the super-themes of crisis and identity, as well as to the respondents' percep-tions of different media and political factions.

India/Pakistan : citizens/terrorists : friends/enemies

The discourse of Doordarshan on terrorism was exemplified by three items in the English and Hindi newscasts of 13 May 1993 (see Table 4.2):

• The Prime Minister, while addressing a conference of high-ranking police functionaries of the country, calls on the police and intelligence agencies to break the terrorist-drug mafia nexus. He also commends the role of the police in curbing terrorism in Punjab;

- India again asks Pakistan to hand over the Memon brothers, prime suspects in the Bombay bomb blast case. India accuses Pakistan of aiding and abetting terrorism in Jammu and Kashmir;
- The US accuses Pakistan of smuggling heroin into the US through Pakistan International Airline (PIA) flights, threatening to cancel all PIA flights into the US.

These items bear witness to the "home-brewed, hard state-oriented 'theory' of political terrorism" (Nandy 1993a: 38) which Doordarshan has been producing and circulating in recent years. This theory is built around the myth of the powerful modern nation-state – modelled after global powers such as the US – which privileges the totalizing abstraction of a nation over the lives of its citizens, a myth which may be accepted by citizens and viewers:

> M1: 3: So, we feel that . . . this Indian government has so much of a burden on it . . . because of the terrorism (. . .) some solution to this should be found.

This type of 'pastoral' power allows for the annihilation of the enemies of the state for the collective good of its majority. The aspirations of smaller orders that form this nation-state, are seen as illegitimate, insofar as they do not fulfill the agenda of the state. Terrorists are constructed as mercenary professionals, using sophisticated technology, backed by the 'foreign hand,' mainly Pakistan, which is held responsible for the current crisis in Punjab and Jammu and Kashmir:

> M8: 2–3: (. . .) something that is affecting our country . . . now terrorism is spread all over . . . it is causing destruction. As such there is no clear solution. We used to analyze who is doing this, whether Pakistan is involved . . . whether Pakistan is getting any international help . . . and why are they doing . . . as such our India is a poor country . . . it is a developing country . . . so, our development even with all these constraints is quite rapid . . . our technological developments and all is quite rapid (. . .) So, they [Pakistan] may be more jealous . . . so they may be trying all these things . . . or they may be having memories of Partition, or they may be thinking their state is not developed, or some individual persons in their personal capacity might be getting money . . .

Such an interpretation, however, elides the fact that most insurgency movements in the country have started as something like popular resistance to the state's power, but have been gradually and conveniently branded as terrorism and forced to live up to this name by the excesses of counter-terrorist measures of the state. This threat to the nation-state, in a widely held myth, can only be eliminated by the use of high-tech counter-terrorist initiatives of the law-and-order machinery (Nandy 1993a):

> B6: 1: These stories are very important, because terrorism is the biggest enemy, as it is said, of the democratic structure of the country, therefore, whatever the Prime Minister has said to the police and the intelligence bureau is very important. Second thing, [the stories are important] because peaceful co-existence of the country is important for the economic development of the country (. . .) I feel so long as the country is ruled peacefully and there's no strikes and such like things . . . destruction in the country . . . then the possibility of advancement of the country . . .

The mass consumption of these myths through the media has certainly increased because of the immediacy of ethnic violence in the lives of many in the city of Bombay, as suggested also by the respondents. The riots and blasts as 'subjects' have created many 'objects' and 'others':

> M8:1: (. . .) But this terrorism is the existing subject. That seems to be more important, and that too is an external creation . . . It is not created by our own people . . . or a momentary, spontaneous happening . . . it is most important.

The analysis of the interviews found only one account that was critical of the theme of police-as-defenders-of-the-nation, in an interpretation of the ceremony awarding the police for its role in Punjab:

> F7: 4: Yeah, because when there were riots and all, what did they [the police] do . . . they are not able to handle things properly and then are getting awards for what? When there are riots, they can't handle it and the army is called in.

The syntactic arrangements of the three news items on terrorism, mentioned above, are noteworthy: the law-and-order machinery is exhorted to fight the terrorist-drug mafia nexus; Pakistan is requested by India to extradite the bomb-blast suspects, and also accused of aiding terrorism in Jammu and Kashmir; and Pakistan is accused by the US of smuggling heroin. Put together, the three items construct Pakistan as a deviant terrorist state that breaks the law in every way, not only the laws of India, but also the laws of its friend, the US. Its opposite is the normal, law-abiding Indian state which follows legitimate protocols to combat terrorism. Viewers can unambiguously position themselves as citizens of this normal state. As in the televisual portrayal of the Gulf War of 1991, the human costs of this process of eliminating terrorists may be lost in an abstraction akin to a video game. Here, good triumphs over evil "through the 'right' kind of media coverage provid[ing] the Indian middle classes with the slight, delectable touch of nervousness which thrills but does not kill, especially at a distance from the places where the action is" (Nandy 1993a: 37).

The three respondents of Household 4 (of the Parsi or Zoroastrian community, a micro-minority, settled largely in Western India) are interesting for their different interpretations of this battle between good and evil, with varying degrees of understanding. F4 is a social worker/teacher who has done extensive work in the area of substance-abuse counseling and rehabilitation. She foregrounded the issue of drug dependence in her account:

> F4: 1: Drug abuse, however invisible it may be . . . because we don't go out much where the abuse is, but it is there . . . I think drugs at that national level are . . . and all of us are aware that much of the terrorist activities in the country are funded out of the money earned by drugs smuggled into the country, and I think it is of great national importance.

F4 went on to add that "(. . .) somewhere inside I said, 'very good, they [Pakistan] have really been culprits for so,' . . . I mean . . . I think Pakistan also hasn't been spared." She quickly went on to qualify her statement: "I am not happy that Pakistan is being banned, but happy that at the international level, now people are coming together to do something about it" (F4: 2).

In contrast, B4, the husband in the family, was more categorical about the need to take stern action against Pakistan, bringing together the themes of drug trafficking, terrorism, and bomb blasts:

> M4: 3: (. . .) Pakistan drug trafficking and all that, because Pakistan is playing a very important role in it on the borders. And secondly, even in the Bombay bomb blast also it has been proved that Pakistan hand was there — they were involved — so I think, some step should be taken against them.

And G4, in her account, linked up the bad things being perpetrated by Pakistan with the most traumatic event of Indian history, the Partition. She sees the drug trafficking as a plot by Pakistan to destabilize the Indian state:

> G4: 3: That Pakistan thing . . . means first Pakistan was with India. After becoming separate they are doing all bad things with India, means they are smuggling drugs . . . it is very bad thing for the generations of India as well as Pakistan . . . if they continue to do this, it is bad for both India and Pakistan . . . no . . . and they do bomb blast and all in

India and so the population of India is also decreasing . . . so many people are dying . . . there is so much unrest is there . . .

In this battle between good and evil, the side taken by other countries, particularly the US – Pakistan's 'friend' – becomes crucial:

B6: 7: From the point of view of India's stability, we are more concerned or we are more exposed to Pakistan's involvement in various issues in India . . . it has been highlighted . . . and I am directly concerned because it concerns Pakistan and USA, USA and India . . . so the interests of all the three countries are involved . . .

This positioning also sets up lists of friends and enemies globally. Any item related to international affairs tends to be interpreted in terms of its implications for the India–Pakistan relationship: "(. . .) the Queen of England [referring to former Prime Minister Margaret Thatcher], like she has said — that they [the UK] are also enemies of terrorism like India — so like this, we get support from outside . . . " (M1: 5), and from Russia that is "India's friend" (G9: 3).

Viewers who may have been situated earlier in 'our little corner of the world', now find themselves at the hub of events, which were previously mere 'objects,' but underwent a transformation into 'subjects.' The rest of the world becomes significant insofar as it impinges on what is happening to 'us.' The interpretation of events ranging from Bosnia to US–Pakistan relations, comes within the ambit of this transformation:

M8: 5: Normally we are conscious about the American developments . . . for example, what is happening with Pakistan . . .. Now, these Clinton . . . if any Clinton news is there, we watch that consciously . . . what is his reaction to Pakistan and other neighboring countries . . . because it affects us . . . and our country also . . . or what is his reaction to India or these Gulf countries . . . what is happening there . . . Iran, Iraq, and other countries. So that is of importance to us . . . so we watch that and store that information in mind and see that next day what development has taken place, we talk about it and analyze.

Responses that would not agree with such generalizations about friends and enemies, or which see the portrayal of Pakistan as a construction, run the risk of getting branded as anti-national, perhaps particularly when they come from a Muslim:

B10: 5: Similarly, the other two news, there were 2–3 times that they showed about Pakistan /
G10: PIA [Pakistan airline] /
B10: PIA was most irrelevant in terms of /

G10: It was like a smear campaign against Pakistan. But it is relevant from the point of view of Pakistan, from the angle of the United Nations declaring Pakistan as a terrorist state. So USA is banning trade with them and threatening them. They can't do without USA.

Immediacy/credibility : television/newspaper : Doordarshan/cable : national/international : illiterate/educated

M1: 9: (. . .) the meaning of news is that, despite everything, things remain as they are . . . so we think, forget the item . . . let's go on . . . all this . . . the problem of terrorism, problem of inflation, what can a man do?

The feeling of crisis and the emergence of ethnic violence (as an immediate 'subject' and its documentation and impact as 'objects,' discussed in earlier sections) apparently have changed the viewers' relationship with the news. News no longer represents distant stories of terrorism and violence from Punjab and Jammu and Kashmir, but is a means to fathom the immediacy of these events in one's own life, something that "affects our very lifestyle . . . " (M8: 8). Paradoxically, however, the frequency of regular newsviewing in the country has been reduced considerably. Also most of these respondents would watch news only 'when something happens.'

When it comes to credibility, television as a medium was preferred over newspapers by the Indian respondents. The argument was that the visuals make television unambiguous: "(. . .) On TV, everything can be clearly shown (. . .) everything can be seen" (G1: 9). Stories in newspapers, in contrast, can be constructed, making them opaque to spontaneous and active reading. TV cannot easily accomplish this, for the spectator can actively witness the event to arrive at independent interpretations. Moreover, with television, since most viewers rely on Doordarshan's newscasts, they do not have to confront conflicting versions. Most respondents agreed with this generalizing assessment of the univocality of TV, in contradistinction to the possibility of multiple interpretations associated with the newspapers:

O2 (Daughter-in-law): 6: However many newspapers are there, it is different in them — all the newspapers don't give the same news — on TV, the news in English and Hindi is the same. But in case of newspapers — if you read many papers — it is different in each one of them — so one can't have faith in that (. . .) on TV, we see with our own eyes, so we have more faith that such a thing is happening — in the paper they give incorrect news also.

One reason given for this preference, then, is the presence of video images in TV newscasts. Other interpretations, however, regard the visuals as entirely superfluous:

F4: 6: (...) the TV visuals take away our attention from what they are actually saying ... and that is one disadvantage of TV throughout turned elsewhere (...) I think people become more insensitive ... at least I did not see CNN, but people who watched the Gulf War on CNN said ... they ... after some time, it becomes like watching any other serial [soap opera] ...

These generalizing assessments of television as a medium do not necessarily hold true for Doordarshan – here the opinions were more diffuse. The fact that it is controlled by the state was seen by some as the major obstacle to DD's credibility:

G9: 10: So that's why whatever is of benefit to the government, they show only that ... it is a propaganda of the government. What is happening behind, that they don't show — only the good side of the government, they want to show.

DD is also seen to represent the interests of the ruling party:

M2: 6: They [Doordarshan] have been bought — the lies of big people are presented as true — different parties hide the facts about themselves.

On the other hand, state control, to some respondents, imbues DD with a ring of credibility:

M6: 5: TV is more able or it is [an] authority.
WHY DO YOU SAY THAT?
M6: Because it is controlled by the government, they're responsible for that ... they have to answer for that.
BUT DON'T YOU THINK THERE IS A DANGER OF THE GOVERNMENT TRYING TO USE THE MEDIUM FOR ITS OWN ADVANTAGE?
M6: The danger is ... but because of the structure of the country which is democratic ... people have the right to ask anyone while utilizing that ... so they are answerable to the public ... but the newspapers are not answerable to the general public ... the public cannot do anything against the paper.

The discourses invoked here relate to the place and role of the public sector, and of private enterprise, in the country at the present juncture. These discourses have gained a lot of currency in the country due to structural adjustment programs, economic liberalization, free markets, and the proposed privatization of many public-sector undertakings. Popular conceptions about the public sector hold that it is inefficient, poorly managed, and easy on its employees, resulting in low productivity and quality. At the same time, it is seen as serving the valuable social functions of generating employment and providing subsidized services without the sole motive of profit as well as providing job security to their employees. Given this image, government-controlled institutions are seen as impervious to petty motives of furthering their own interests, which, even if they wanted, their inefficiency would render it difficult to achieve:

YOU FEEL DOORDARSHAN IS MORE RESPONSIBLE?
B10: 12: I don't know about being more responsible, but maybe because Doordarshan doesn't have the time and space to go on and on. They stick to certain norms and just report the main . . .
M10: They don't have so many colorations.
WITHOUT TOO MUCH COLORATIONS, WHICH MEANS IT IS OBJECTIVE . . . ?
B10: I think so . . . because the newspapers can very easily be biased according to who is publishing it . . .

In comparison, the sole motive of the private sector is to generate as much profit as possible. This motive makes it imperative to have tougher production control mechanisms, incentives for efficiency, and higher levels of automation. DD represents the unwieldy yet friendly 'neighborhood' public sector, while cable TV and newspapers stand for the efficient private sector. In contradistinction to DD, other networks and newspapers have to sell themselves to survive and, hence, some respondents felt that this leads to sensationalism in their news coverage:

B6: 16: (. . .) I find that other than BBC, I would say a lot of unnecessary thrill is put in the news which I don't approve. If an accident has taken place somewhere, then you will send your reporters to the maximum possible extent and get the person's views, even if he is dying and you put him on the television . . . even if the person dies after two months or two days and you don't bother about it . . . you have used him. That kind of thing is more in commercial privatized kind of thing than in Doordarshan.
BBC . . . ?
B6: BBC, I would rate a little better but . . . I would say, yes, it covers quite details, but again in BBC, I have seen the weightage given or the order of the news depends again on the importance of the news in connection with . . . not necessary the international this thing . . . but they want to fairly highlight, expose and use the item for their own benefit . . . I think that way only . . . in the public sector like Doordarshan, this kind of thing is much less . . .

Further, the portrayal of India by transnational networks was regarded by F4 as stereotyping the Third World and as an affront to the national pride of an Indian:

> F4: 16: Because abroad the tendency is to show droughts and famines in India, poor people begging in India, elephants walking on the roads ... they [transnational networks] do not show good things about India ...

Still, the perceptions of BBC by B6 and F4 were not shared by many respondents. They instead regarded 'private' networks like BBC and CNN to have changed the viewers' expectations of news, making them more critical of the fare being dished out by DD:

> M5: 5: The definition of news has changed ... as it is happening in CNN or BBC ... they show while it is happening, but here [on DD] they don't show ... they will censor something ... whatever is convenient for the ... only that part they will show in an encapsulated form.

The transnational networks were seen by most of these respondents to have more credibility ("more realistic than our news," M8: 2) and professionalism than DD:

> M9: 11: (...) there was a cartoon by Laxman in *The Times of India* sometime back that a minister is sitting in his office and there is a demonstration, by some people, outside. So the minister asks his secretary to switch on the BBC to know what is happening outside his office. He himself does not know! (...) there is no question of comparing DD with BBC or CNN. BBC and CNN are free. They have no restrictions, they can show anything. Whereas here, whatever news they get, first it is censored.

However, the fact that the cable networks are transnational may deprive them of immediacy. They seem unable to present relevant news, except during moments of crisis, when India appears on their agenda, and when the issue of credibility and the possibility of knowing what exactly happened impel people to turn to these networks in preference to DD:

> F3: 5: (...) Their visuals are nice, they [BBC] show interviews on the telephone and they have all the modern techniques, but India does not have prominence in their news, unless something very important happens, like the bomb blast, which means if it is of importance from their viewpoint only, then they show it. So, as an Indian, I do not get the news that I am looking forward to every day. First about my Bombay, then about Maharashtra, then about India, and then about

the world, this is my priority which BBC etcetera can never fulfill.

M8: 1: It [international news] is not of much importance to us. It is not directly affecting us. It is a secondary part of the news. If it is directly affecting our country . . . then we will be more conscious . . . because the problems are internal . . . like terrorism and all that . . . this is just information for us.

There is also the belief that BBC and CNN are for the elite ("I think the educated class do not watch the Doordarshan. They will always prefer BBC," F9: 11), setting up yet another 'other', who may not be able to handle the truth. In M8's account, there is an implicit assumption that these "mass[es] in a mobile condition" can and do cause riots, hence justifying censorship of news by the state:

M8: 2: (. . .) Because all people are not aware, some are not bothered, some are indifferent, some are more careful, some are least concerned . . . some are more conscious, some are more aggressive. If all the news are [sic] given . . . the mass will be in a more mobile condition. Because if all news is given . . . everybody's interpretation will be dangerous. That may spoil the peace . . . there might be destruction. To avoid disturbance, normal learned people may react differently.

Given its national character, DD has the potential to achieve immediacy, but appears unable to do so because of various factors ("Doordarshan has become very 'Door' [far] !," M9: 14). One of the reasons cited was the control over it by politicians in power:

M7: 9: (. . .) they were showing Sharad Pawar and Narasimha Rao visiting the blast sites. But I am not interested in seeing their faces. What I would like to see is the families of those who have died, their agony, you know, how many have died . . . such things . . . I am not interested in seeing the politicians making their rounds!

DD's definitions of newsworthiness were equally questioned by several respondents:

B10: 9: In fact, I think that the news is very stunted.
M10: Frankly, I mean, all these things are there. They are not world-shaking news, as such!
No, THEY ARE NOT NEWS . . . ?
F10: They are just filling in the time . . .

There is also the suspicion that the newscasts of DD are outdated, as in the case of its reporting during the riots all over the country. DD is commonly accused of dragging its feet and of being way behind international news agencies. The reason given is that DD officialdom and the political mandarins are not sure of people's ability to stomach controversial and traumatic news. But as witnessed during the Bombay riots, this only led to an erosion of DD's credibility. In the absence of credible news, rumors ruled the roost:

> M3: 4: There is so much of frustration and they [Doordarshan] show all false things, that's why people don't have any faith in them. They think they can fool the public, but it doesn't happen that way. Because of such factors, people resort to riots, the reason is only this.

> G9: 11: (...) when BBC and CNN give news, Doordarshan proclaims that it is a wrong kind of news, specially where the figures of death toll are concerned. They are always accusing BBC. So basically there is always a conflict, they are trying to prove something, and BBC is giving us some other news.

The suppression of video coverage of sensitive events like the demolition of Babari Masjid, which in any case was shown by BBC, is a case in point. F4 felt that there was an overdose of such visuals on BBC, and felt that such repetition was not called for as it desensitizes people:

> F4: 6: BBC showed the same thing again and again. Advani [Hindu rightwing leader] is being interviewed as he is coming down the staircase and he says the government is going to fall.

In contrast, M3 set up such reporting as an ideal toward which DD should strive:

> M3: 2: (...) Though TV is a visual medium, they don't use TV with the idea that TV is a visual medium. That they don't understand (...) it has more of talking rather than showing. They should show news on TV news, and for that they should collect news. Wherever it is, they should reach there ... that does not happen, that's why on STAR TV, the BBC, and CNN, news that they show is watched even by people in Dharavi [a large slum area in Bombay] who cannot even understand English.

According to M5, rather than trying to learn from its first encounter with the transnational networks, DD is struggling to retain its hold by imitating them, in terms of increasing its film-based and entertainment-oriented programming:

M5: 15: This [cable networks] is called cultural invasion. When there is this kind of invasion, these people [Doordarshan] are imitating them rather than facing them. Just similar kind of stuff. But more degenerative kind of stuff, that is what they [DD] are doing.

Politicians/common people : big people/small people

The most virulent critique of politicians and of the political machinery came from M7: 4: "(. . .) Given a chance, [I] would like to shoot all those [political] leaders," so as to escape the fate of seeing them constantly hogging the limelight in the newscasts of DD. Other comments common to almost all the respondents, though less vituperative, constructed the politician as the most loathsome 'other':

F9: 2: (. . .) You know, the politicians which are always there (. . .) the focus is on them . . . whether it is the Prime Minister or the Chief Minister or Finance Minister or the Home Minister . . .
M9: (. . .) We feel there should be nothing by the name of politics. I think even if this thing [impeachment of the Supreme Court Justice Ramaswamy] comes in front of the common man or a small child also, even that person will be able to understand that all these things are just to save the person's chair. Everyone is involved in saving their own chair — and in that, they harm each other.

This state of affairs of DD news is, according to M5, an indicator of the larger malaise affecting the country – an amoral and opportunistic political milieu. No political party is an exception to this, whatever the ideology it espouses. He regarded the present ethnic crisis in the country as exacerbated by these very forces:

M5: 3: The entire political culture here is such that . . . no matter whatever its label, you know, [every party] tries to get a political mileage out of it [communal sentiments] — they do not view any issue in a broader perspective, in a national interest (. . .) See, the degree of this thing may differ, but when the crux of the matter is this, they work in the same fashion . . . and no party is an exception to this (. . .) whenever it is convenient for them . . . they play these cards, whether it is caste, communal, or anything . . . which suits them.

Many of these respondents were cynical of the goings-on in the name of legislature, perceiving it as a game played by the ruling and opposition parties:

G9: 4: I think Doordarshan was trying to show that the opposition is playing its role as an opposer as usual.

THAT THE OPPOSITION IS PLAYING THE ROLE OF AN OPPOSER?
G9: That's their basic ideology.
F9: The opposition is always opposing ! [*F9 and G9 laugh*]

This leaves no space for issues related to the common man. Several viewers felt that DD news did not touch on their everyday lives:

> M1: 14: Yes, like . . . they show everything about important people, but there is no voice at all of poor people (. . .) Like if anything happens to poor people's hutments . . . they don't show anything. When the whole world burns, then they show it . . . and like you said . . . if any small thing happens to big people, they show it.

Conclusion: the spectator, the state, and the 'other'

The viewers in the present study adopted various strategies for constructing their identities as spectators, at the site of the discourses of news. These constructions assign varied uses to news and its place in everyday life. For M7, the uses of news ranged from personal safety and security, to budget planning, to its use in conversation with friends. He constituted himself as a discerning viewer who interprets news in the light of his past experiences and opinions:

> M7: 2: (. . .) Like there is a riot and it is affecting the peace in the neighbourhood, then definitely there is interaction in the house . . . between us . . . that such and such a thing has happened . . . what we should do, what we should not do . . . to take better care of ourselves, meet friends or people living close by, then we happen to talk about it. Or in case of money matters . . . if there is a budget then we think of how to use our money accordingly . . . in planning our budget. (. . .) I know whom to keep . . . who are the good apples, who are the bad apples . . . so certain opinions are formed in my mind . . . by seeing what is happening around, reading newspapers, at least, in my personal capacity, opinions get framed . . . and there are interactions with people, we discuss things . . .

To M10, the very act of watching news was linked to his status as a citizen of the country:

> M10: 17: I think it makes you conscious of your status as an Indian citizen by the fact that you are watching the news . . . means you are interested in the affairs of the country.

Several respondents – for instance, G1, M1, and M3 – felt that the news in its present form does not have much use, first, because as a viewer, one is powerless to influence the course of events and, second, because DD newscasts focus on useless information such as government ceremonies and the visits of dignitaries from abroad. M3 also pointed out that while the news talks about various government schemes, in practice, the average viewer would be unable to access these schemes due to a lack of detailed information and to bureaucratic obstacles. In terms of the uses of news in the immediate context of viewing in the family, only F4 referred specifically to newswatching as a family occasion that takes place around the evening meal and becomes a source for dinner-table discussions.

The viewer as critic appears as a recurrent theme in M5's accounts of the news. As opposed, for instance, to M6, cited later, who regards the news as educative and his own identity as a spectator as unproblematic, M5 foregrounded the assertion of his identity as a critical viewer – this element appears to be more significant than the news as such:

> M5: 11: (. . .) we normally . . . we have the ability . . . it gives a certain level of intellectual satisfaction . . . because we tend to view some things critically . . . with a critical view . . . and when things are happening at a high level, we definitely look at them critically, you know . . . and discuss it with friends . . . and from your own point of view . . . you are already holding certain views and opinions . . . from that point of view . . . definitely find it interesting.

M8 adopted yet another subject position. While he accepted the objectivity of the news and of the state, the visual element of news made him aware of his position as a privileged spectator, giving him a sense of mastery over the news as object:

> M8: 3: (. . .) By seeing this picture we are seeing as if the original at that time . . . we are understanding . . . that feeling is there . . . when we see something, there is something to recount it later . . . so it [TV news] is more interactive . . . that is a practice of our intelligence or our mind.

Summing up, the identity of Indian 'spectators' *vis-à-vis* news is mediated in flows of power, related to the state and the 'other' (see further the model in Chapter 9, Figure 9.1). The relationship with the state appears to be primary – news is the news of the state. The stance of viewers *vis-à-vis* the news becomes, in effect, a stance towards the state. Thus, for instance, viewers who regarded Doordarshan news as neutral and transparent would also construct the state as the guarantor of truth and security. M6, for instance, saw a potential for education and awareness through newsviewing:

> M6: 10: When I watch the news, what I am looking for is a striking point, an educative point. If the news is striking or educative, if

anything is new to me, I keep it in mind and make whatever use of it I can. The general news, that is of no use to me . . . that I can't store within me. My idea is simply to know the things that are unknown to me . . . so far as I come to know new things, it is good!

At the same time, the same respondent appeared to be oblivious of the role of news-related discourses in constructing his own identity as a citizen:

M6: 12: Television doesn't give me more for identifying myself as a citizen of this country . . . citizen of this country, I am already there, then I was a citizen of this country . . .

In contrast to M6's reading, M5 adopted a stance of resistance towards the news and the state. This resistance is expressed in categories of credibility and of immediacy (in the sense of Foucault, with resistance being directed at the most immediate power flows). News is a representative of the state:

M5: 15: No, the way they present news . . . there is so much of resent-ment . . . You get more conscious as a citizen . . . because you get more critical . . . [*laughs*]

Such resistant readings would not be uncommon among the educated, upper-class urban Indians as also among, for example, minorities who perceive themselves as being marginalized by the state (Monteiro 1993: 256).

The relationship with the 'other' is, by definition, a relation of exclusion and resistance. The self is a construction opposed to the various 'others' invoked. And, the specific relationship of the spectator to the state also emerges in the relations of the 'other' to the state. To cite examples, when the 'other' is terrorism, the spectator's relation with the state is one of identification, for the state is also against the terrorist. When the 'other' is politicians, the resistance is directed towards the state as well as the 'other' – the state can be seen as a guild of political power. When the transnational networks become an 'other', the spectator assumes the identity of a loyal citizen. Conversely, when DD is regarded as the 'other', the state is simultaneously resisted.

These positions in relation to the state/'other' are not necessarily consistent. In other words, the same respondent may assume differing stances *vis-à-vis* the state, depending on the 'other' being invoked. There are modes of "contradictory interpellations" of the subject within discourses, thus pointing to the "unstable, provisional and dynamic properties of positioning" of subjects (Morley 1980b: 166). M1, for instance, in speaking about terrorism, sympa-thized with the burden on the Indian government, but would see himself as small, being pitted against the 'other' of big people, who are in league with the state.

In the Indian context, then, it appears almost impossible for viewers to problematize television news without problematizing the state – the stance adopted towards news is congruent with the stance taken towards the state. When the relationship of the 'other' to the state was one of resistance or antagonism, these viewers would identify with the state. Conversely, when the interests of the 'other' and the state were seen to coalesce, the viewer's resistance could be directed towards both. The news, particularly its credibility, comes out as one of the most immediate points of resistance to, or identification with, the state.

5

ISRAEL

Tamar Liebes[*]

Media in Israel

Television came to the People of the Book (Katz 1971; Liebes 1997) only in 1968, under heavy suspicion that it might personalize Israel's highly politicized party system and de-ideologize its politics. Until that time, Israel had fought its stormy political debates on the pages of its printed press and, to a lesser extent, on its public radio.

The Hebrew press preceded the founding of the state itself, operating in the service of the Zionist movement in its fight against the British mandatory government. The various newspapers also gave voice to the tactical and strategic debate among the various Zionist parties within the Jewish community. With the winning of independence, the party press gradually gave way to a largely commercial press, some of which retains a journalistic sense of mission.

Television, the latecomer, was founded in the wake of the Six Day War in 1967, with the naive hope of facilitating the occupation of conquered territories, by inoculating the newly occupied Palestinians against 'enemy propaganda.' Joined with the radio which preceded it, it was incorporated into a BBC-like, independent authority, financed by a license fee. Its aims, as defined by law, included providing a fair and objective coverage of the news; carrying out social tasks such as reflecting the plurality of voices in Israel – ethnic, cultural, and religious; teaching each of these traditions about the cultural heritage of the others; and providing a stage for the advancement of Israeli art and culture.

Two developments in the beginning of the 1990s constituted no less than a communication revolution in Israel, dramatically transforming consumption patterns for the electronic media. In the fall of 1993 (following data collection for the present study), a second ITV-like television channel, publicly controlled

* The author wishes to thank Elihu Katz for his insightful comments on a first draft of this chapter. Gali Gold, Hadaya Ben-David, and Michal Marmari were indispensable in finding the families, carrying out the interviews, and registering the news items.

but commercially financed, was introduced. At the same time, a network of cable television was established throughout the country, offering a number of Israeli-edited channels and dozens of foreign satellite channels, and privately owned regional radio stations have also been established. The tradition of professional journalism which addresses the entire body politic was also threatened by the growing segmentation of society into religious and ethnic enclaves. This development has given rise to numerous intra-community radio channels, further dividing the various groups of Israeli society (Liebes and Peri, 1998).

If the commercialization of the press and electronic media threatens the continuation of a professional journalism working in the interest of the public, this risk is exacerbated by a concentration of ownership. As of 1997, three families each own one of the three most widely read newspapers, and each of these families also controls a chain of local papers, in addition to holding shares in the TV companies which constitute Channel 2, as well as in the cable companies (Caspi and Limor 1992). Thus, ironically, at the very time when the power of military censorship and government control over the press has waned, there is a threat, familiar from Europe and the US, to the independence of the press and other media from the motives of capitalist owners, augmented by an increasing tendency toward monopoly and cross-ownership.

TV news – the focus of prime time

In Israel's highly politicized society, the news – in newspapers and on radio and television – has always occupied center stage. News production exhausted most of television's financial resources, and has been labeled the most popular drama series in the history of Israel. That no other drama could ever compete with the drama of news, is often cited as an excuse for not producing any local drama series for television.

Prior to the introduction of the second channel, the main evening news, *Mabat* (Viewpoint), was broadcast during prime time on Israel's only television channel, and watched nightly by around 70 percent of Israelis, typically on the family set (Liebes 1992). The reason for the centrality of news was, and still is, the political, even existential, uncertainty of Israelis, in a country which has been in a state of war since its founding. 'War,' as referred to in several other chapters in this volume, is not identified with Bosnia, as is the case for European viewers: Bosnia may seem too close for comfort, but is still far from being an actual threat. For Israelis, war means a son or a husband doing army duty in Lebanon, an imminent confrontation with Syria in case negotiations fail, or a nuclear attack by countries as far away as Iran or Iraq. The classic functionalist definition of news as surveillance (Wright 1960) takes on an acute meaning for news viewers in Israel.

As everybody would watch the news, viewing meant belonging to society. Conversation at work the next day presumed the shared experience of having viewed *Mabat*. Thus, the evening schedule of Israelis would take account of the news: dinner had to be over in time for viewing; telephone conversations were postponed; and people were invited socially only 'after the news.'

Interestingly, although the news constituted a shared agenda for conversation – a genuine forum for discussing public issues – it did not cause a convergence of political ideologies. Apparently, television news supplied both 'dovish' and 'hawkish' camps (*vis-à-vis* the Arab–Israeli conflict) with ammunition for their own positions (Liebes and Ribak 1991; Liebes 1992). Arab citizens of Israel also considered this main TV news reliable. It is true that hawks may have had, and still have, an easier time in drawing on the portrayal of violence, such as *intifada* incidents (relating to Palestinians' violent demonstrations) and Palestinian terrorist acts, whereas doves could be more comfortable when the benefit of compromise became evident in the peace process. Still, society continued to be divided around a shared image of the conflict. The continued vitality of these two ideological players argues against any easy equation of the idea of a multiplicity of TV channels with a pluralism of opinion (Keane 1991). Israel's monopoly television news did not repress public debate, but rather constituted its public space.

Ironically, again, instead of adding a further voice to public debate, the competing newscast on the new, commercial, Second Channel, ended the centrality of television news. In less than a year, news viewing (the total number of viewers on both channels) dropped to 30 percent (from 70 percent), with people abandoning TV news altogether. Such a dramatic change could not be due only to the change of time (*Mabat* moved from 9 pm to 8 pm, the second channel news time), but suggests that the very offer of choice (between news programs) "abolished the norm of viewing TV news" (Katz and Haas 1994). By a nice coincidence, this study during May of 1993 provided a last chance to study news reception in Israel before its 'normalization' to the dominant pattern in other Western countries, where news is marginalized in the programming schedule, and viewing is diffused across several channels.

The context of family viewing

News viewing in Israel is typically a family affair. This means that viewing is active and lively, characterized by parasocial interaction (Horton and Wohl 1956) between family members and characters on the screen as well as by conversation among family members about the screen characters, with TV presenters and politicians serving as 'third persons' to gossip about, to evaluate, and to give good or bad marks.

Nine families took part in the *News of the World* project in Israel. Participant observation was conducted at their homes during viewing, followed by household interviews as well as individual interviews. Evidence of active viewing comes particularly from the observation of interaction during news viewing. Such interaction has a special status in terms of the overall design, as it can be assumed to be closest to the 'natural,' everyday conversation that takes place in the normal viewing context. Although the presence of an observer will change the definition of this situation, it may be argued that the change is negligible. First of all, family members were not given other assignments during viewing. Moreover, the presence of their usual co-viewers may have ensured that they would not risk the embarrassment of too radical a change in their style of conversation, which might be sneered at as a performance for the benefit of the observer. The indication that interchanges during viewing resembled everyday interaction is supported by the observed ease of the interchanges, by references to past conversation, and by the often 'telegraphic,' implicit character of the comments. (This shortcut style of interaction also makes salient the limitations of the researchers' interpretation. The ethnographer may only guess at some – perhaps the most superficial – meanings of comments that are embedded in a long series of daily conversations about recurring news themes, and closely connected with family history, shared culture, and the dynamics of gender/power relations (Ang and Hermes 1991: 308).)

Although we have distinguished analytically between two types of interaction – 'parasocial' interaction with characters or announcers and 'real' interaction among family members relating to the screen – it is not always easy to distinguish between the two empirically. The personal and the political are inseparable in casual, sometimes intimate, comments addressed to well-known politicians: a Government Minister was reprimanded for putting on weight; an announcement on economic policy by the Prime Minister was received skeptically with a raised eyebrow (M3: 23); a religious Member of Parliament who was putting on airs ("let's sit down before we begin") was booed (F5: 47).

More common were comments, intended for the benefit of co-viewers, which consist in giving bad and sometimes good 'grades' to well-known politicians and to ordinary people for breaking or upholding social norms. Thus, Members of Parliament were admonished for not keeping the rules ("what a mess", Ga1: 3), or for self-aggrandizing ("they can't move without their cellular telephone," M5: 53), a criticism exacerbated by the fact that the MP in question was a religious-party representative and, therefore, could be expected to be less interested in worldly possessions and technological innovations. Volunteers to help homeless immigrants, still living in caravans, were praised: "It's a good thing that there are people like that in this country" (F6: 5). Satisfaction was also expressed at the unity of 'our' political camp: "It's nice that everybody in *Meretz* [a coalition party to the left of Labor] agrees with one another" (F6: 7).

Specially involving were characters who played a part in ongoing news stories, which run intermittently on the news in much the same way as subplots in soap operas. When such a potential victim or villain appeared, family members would engage in detecting signs that give away guilt, innocence, or scheming, and thus make the character fit into one of several possible, competing narratives (Murdoch 1974). One such character was Arieh Derei,

Minister of the Interior at the time, who underwent a lengthy police investigation for corruption. Seeing Derei on the screen evoked a 'mini-forum' in the home of the Ilan family. Husband Yiftach commented, "I always notice that Derei is under pressure" (M3: 23), to which his wife Irit offered an interpretation – "suffering." Yiftach, not quite satisfied with this empathetic framing, was searching for the right definition, "not suffering but . . . ," to which Irit offered the less benevolent framing – "twisting and turning." This exchange conveys a much debated public confusion about Derei, a star in Israeli politics, who founded an ethnic religious party that could secure the power of a government of either the right or the left. Did he dig his own grave by breaking the rules, or was he just less experienced than other politicians, and therefore got caught?

The credibility of TV news

How do Israeli viewers evaluate the credibility of television as a source for learning about reality? Statements indicating an awareness that what one is viewing is indeed constructed, as well as attempts to point to the biases of this mediation, were voiced throughout the interviews. Such statements further divided into two types, namely, the more commonly expressed awareness of ideological construction, and the less commonly expressed, aesthetic awareness of the constraints of the medium, its form and production (Liebes and Katz 1993). Newspapers were on the whole considered less credible by these respondents because they were thought to express the partisan positions of their journalists. This may be due to the different forms of mediation in print and television news. TV seems more transparent.

Ideological criticism argues that television serves either the interests of the press owners or the journalists' own ambitions, or it may be seen to serve the interests of the political establishment. Each of these options has implications for the way in which the relationship between reality and its representation is conceived. Thus, if 'they' (for example, politicians) 'are trying to manipulate us,' everything that is being shown may be interpreted as its opposite.

We found that the most common critique of media construction was that television, or, rather, its producers and journalists, are hostile to 'us,' and work to destroy our morale. Otherwise, why would they show only bad news – failures, corruption, and defeat – ignoring any indications of success or progress? As a rule, this type of ideological criticism refuses to accept the principle according to which the press in a democracy is supposed to play an oppositional role in order to carry out its 'watchdog' function. Viewers noted time and again how television would show 'our' soldiers shooting rubber bullets at Palestinians, but would fail to show when the soldiers themselves were hurt: "They make a noise in the news when any Arab is injured by a stone or by a settler, but they never make it public when the opposite occurs [when a soldier is injured]" (M3: 27). In the same vein, "It is really annoying that our soldiers in the [Occupied] Territories are shown to hit, and slap, and curse" (F7: 22). Clearly, this type of criticism expects TV news, in case of conflict, to be supportive of 'our' side, often because it is concerned about the effect on 'third persons' of coverage which focuses on 'our' faults (Davison 1983). Thus, for Israeli viewers concerned with the effects of the medium on ignorant audiences, public broadcasting may not be hegemonic enough, at least inasmuch as the Arab–Israeli conflict is concerned. Parenthetically, it is worth noting how rare was the opposite type of ideological criticism, that is, that TV operates as a government agent, promoting its point of view.

In certain cases, belief in strong media effects on others would bring viewers to wish there was some kind of censorship. One anxious mother, for example, thought the kidnapping of kindergarten children in Paris should not have been shown because it may cause others to imitate the act: "The situation in the world is deteriorating," she claimed, "because all sorts of crazies learn all sorts of tricks from television. The Arabs too" (F2: 35).

Aesthetic criticism of a cool and distant mode – relating, as it were, to the forms and formats of the stories, to the interaction between verbal and visual aspects, and to the interaction between medium, form, and content – was much less common than ideological criticism. We did find an awareness among viewers that TV news stories are about "all sorts of action," "mostly violent," "good stories," "with visual items." Sometimes an explicit concern was expressed over "ways [used by the media] to keep us from turning off." But, in spite of its seeming sophistication, aesthetic criticism is often indistinguishable from moral outrage. For instance, complaints about bad taste, vulgarity, and melodrama may be ways of expressing concern about too much violence. To exemplify, is a comment such as, "Yuk, I cannot watch all this blood" (Gb1: 22), a protest against bad taste, or does it express a reluctance arising from the moral unease of confronting 'our' soldiers in Gaza who are involved in brutality?

The social uses of news

The social uses of television news, according to the Israeli interviews, take two forms. First, the daily management of family life through the displacement of internal tensions, and the surveillance of threats to the family. Second, the framing of social and political issues through negotiation with the screen and with other family members.

Management of everyday life

Displacement and surveillance – the two ways in which TV news is incorporated into the family's management of everyday life – are different but intertwined. While displacement of family tensions is more concerned with the medium, and with taking a 'time out' (Jensen 1995) from the daily routine, surveillance is focused on the content of news.

Displacement, then, relates not so much to the content of news (indeed, it may relate to any content), but rather to the ritual aspect of viewing. In this respect, the news becomes a focus for diffusing or setting aside interpersonal tensions within the family by displacing personal problems onto the realm of societal problems. The shared experience is used for diverting the energy invested in strained family relations into another sphere.

While any television program may be used for this purpose, the news is particularly suitable as it represents common, legitimate concerns and anxieties. In this sense, news (not fiction) is an escape from the immediate 'real' and personal issues over which there is family controversy, to issues that involve the family through its membership in community or society. These are issues which family members may worry about and unite around while, at the same time, being freed from the responsibility of decision making. In this way, news – by virtue of its dependability, its status, and its assurance of offering bigger problems around which to rally – provides a refuge from the petty slings and arrows of family relations.

Thus, unlike the newspaper which may be used, at times of family fights, for raising a (physical and symbolic) wall between the reader and the rest of the room (Noelle-Neumann 1973), television news suggests a different tactic for the diffusing of tension. News viewing serves as a means of turning away from intimate and emotional disputes, to unite around not just 'a good story,' but a story which is relevant to all family members and, therefore, may allow for the gradual melting of the ice into smiles, or tears, and a resurrection of family unity.

Tactics of diffusing tension by displacement were used, for example, by Yael, a wife (F6: 7) whose husband, acting out some protest, busied himself in the kitchen throughout the first part of the newscast rather than joining the rest of the family who were viewing. After listening to the constant rattling of dishes in the kitchen, Yael took the initiative and cajoled her husband, Yossef, to rejoin the fold. (This interpretation is based not only on the interview dialogue, but also on general comments by the observer who noted a tension between the father and the rest of the family.) She pointed to various "good stories" which he "should not miss." The first attempt at appeasement was evoked by a fire in a toy factory in Thailand, as commented on in several countries. This distant tragedy gave Yael the opportunity to call Yossef to "come and see" a good human melodrama, adding that "there were four thousand people in the factory [while it was being burnt]!" Yael's efforts at uniting her family are apparent in her adding color of her own to the story by making up the number of victims which was missing in the actual news report. The failure of this first attempt did not discourage Yael from trying again, this time calling Yossef to join the rest of the family in shrieking admiration of a motorcyclist jumping over the Great Wall of China. The partial success of this attempt – Yossef rejoined, but was still sulking – encouraged her to involve him directly in 'his' area during sports, when she would make a point of being interested in Israel's football team: "It lost badly, our team, didn't it?"

Unlike displacement, surveillance – obviously a more active form of personal management – does relate to the content of news which, by definition, serves as a warning light, signaling potential risks, threats, and dangers in various realms of life. The threat may be to physical survival, to economic well-being, or to moral norms of self, family, community, or the polity. In some cases, the threat is at least partially alleviated when the broadcast itself points to possible ways of control or containment. In other cases, seeing a threat in the news only contributes to making the danger more real.

The more relevant the risk is to the viewing family, the more 'functional' it is in terms of reinforcing solidarity, but also the more 'dysfunctional' in terms of alleviating anxiety. When mother Gila exclaimed, "seeing the soldiers [in a Palestinian village] searching for arms inside the houses is scary" (F6: 25), she was referring to the potential danger to the Israeli soldiers in the *intifada* from Palestinian terrorists. To make sure that we as visiting researchers understood, her husband explained that "Gila has a son in the army, this is why she is worried." The husband used the explanation also to distance himself from her worry; Gila reinforced his remark by adding that "soon Hagai [the younger son] will also be a soldier." Parenthetically, it is interesting to note that although it is also the husband's son, both parents seem to imply that it is socially accepted for mothers to have the prerogative of worrying explicitly, and not for fathers.

Surveillance, of course, also has to do with less dramatic risks to life, such as illness. Reactions to a nurses' strike in May 1993 followed a pattern similar to the reactions to terrorism. Again, its importance was judged by estimates of how close the danger was to oneself and to one's family. In the following examples, the risk seems distant enough and the anxiety is, accordingly, speculative: "It [the nurses' strike] creates tension (...) If one of us will have to be hospitalized ... " (M6: 10), or "we are not affected because we have no connection [with it]. If we had a relative who needed treatment, God forbid, we would be much more interested. But, as it is, we are far from it, and the further away you are, the less interesting it is" (M2: 27).

The framing of social and political issues

We distinguish between two types of frames used by viewers for decoding and incorporating news items: First, meta-frames, which make sense of TV by mapping the social and ideological elements of news in terms of 'our' camp and the camps of various enemies, and by drawing analogies between news items and 'real-life' incidents. Second, substantive categories of super-themes according to which news stories are sorted out.

Mapping

The purpose of mapping, or charting, the structure of relationships among various social or political groups as portrayed in news stories is to pinpoint 'where I belong' on the map. Mapping was the most common, but also the most implicit, meta-frame that was used in order to make sense of the news. This form of mental organization was often done non-verbally by parents pointing to or nodding or smiling at 'our' politician, and by discarding and sometimes booing a politician from the opposite camp. Such mapping is not quite spontaneous as it also serves parents in ideologically socializing their children. The accumulation of these signals, through evenings of viewing, will train children to a reality of warring camps in which they know where they stand and who stands with them, and in which they find out whether they are in the majority or in the minority, and, in the latter case mainly, perceive what 'they' are doing to 'us.'

Analogies

A more complex form of framing news items is accomplished by feeding the stories into the evolving and changing ways in which we interpret the world and define our own identities. In this manner, news stories serve to illuminate, to expand on, or to contrast with, experience gained in life. In parallel, knowledge and understanding gained from other sources in life serve to enrich one's insight into news stories.

Analogies between stories in life and on the news are often drawn by 'trying on' a news story in order to examine how it might fit with a personally experienced event. Such analogies are considered relevant because they point to shared elements which may either prove or disprove the credibility of a news item. The process also works the other way around – by examining personally experienced stories in the light of a news story. Specifically, this commuting involves an activation of roles – cultural, professional, or ideological – whereby the implications of general social issues for particular roles and situations can be considered, weighed, and reevaluated with illumination from various sources of knowledge and experience.

An analogy from life to story was applied, for example, in the interpretation of an item about Shulamit Aloni, the Minister of Education who refused to resign her post when Shas, a religious ethnic party, made her resignation a condition for joining a coalition government. "Aloni," said Enat, a teenage daughter, "reminds me of a class friend who rather than play a secondary part in the school play preferred not to take any part at all" (Ga4: 34). Enat interpreted the Aloni item by drawing on the analogy from her own life, which framed Aloni in terms of a spoiled, egocentric, and unreasonable girl, who ruins everybody's game because she feels insulted. This example shows the way in which meta-frames operate to highlight one aspect of a story, in this case the need to sacrifice one's position for a higher goal (the preservation of the coalition government). The frame has to ignore other aspects of the story, such as the question of giving in to political blackmail, and of compromising ideological principles. In the case of Aloni, giving in would imply admitting that a liberal ideology constitutes a bad influence on the children in Israel.

The meta-frames, inherent in the organization of news characters in terms of 'our camp, their camp,' and in the analogies between stories from the news and from life, are not expressed explicitly. Such meta-frames identify what viewers do by raising an eyebrow when an extreme right-wing politician appears on the TV screen, or by associating between a news story and what happened on the way home from work. There are, however, other ways of framing news stories which give meaning to items by providing them with an explicit label. The rest of this chapter focuses on the organization of particular stories in generic groups according to such semantic super-themes.

Super-themes

Four semantic super-themes ran through the conversations. One connects the individual family and Israeli society, the others address society with 'us' (the family) being a part of it. We named the four super-themes 'our family's small problems/our state's big problems,' 'gridlock,' 'we are at the center of the world,' and 'they are outwitting us.'

Our family's small problems/our state's big problems

Beyond the shared experience of news, which, as shown, at times provides an opportunity for family reconciliation, relevant news stories often serve to set right the proportions between one's – and one's family's – personal aggravations and the really big problems of the polity. Israel's generic social and ideological controversies not only create a comfortable focus for discussion, but can be weighed opposite the everyday problems of the family. For example, one mother summarized an *intifada* story, and another a story of terrorist attacks on Israeli soldiers on the Lebanese border, by pointing out that their own family's problems shrink to insignificance in light of the problems that society is facing (F6: 7, F3: 10): "If only the intifada would end," said one mother, "we promise to manage our own problems" (F5: 2).

Gridlock

This super-theme, according to which 'we' (Israeli society) are stuck in insoluble dilemmas, trapped whichever road we choose, links up directly with the previous theme that makes little of 'our' family's problems in comparison to those of 'our' state. In the following argument, for instance, one viewer (F5: 3) made an observation about the closing of the border between the Gaza Strip and Israel, a measure taken following terrorist acts: "When we open the border between the Occupied Territories and Israel we subject ourselves to the dangers of terrorism. When we close it we condemn the Palestinians to unemployment and idleness, which breeds violence against the occupying soldiers." The underlying notion is that of a double bind.

In another family, the wife, mentioned above, who made a conscious effort to involve an uncooperative husband in the family conversation, addressed an item featuring Israeli soldiers in a Palestinian refugee camp. She asked, "What are they [the soldiers] there for?" – and answers herself that, "Now that they [the Palestinians] are locked in [a reference to the temporary closing of the border between Israel and the Occupied Territories], they [have nothing better to do other than] fight with the soldiers" (F6: 10). "But," she added, "if the soldiers would leave, we might endanger our own security." This fatalistically stated remark, pointing to the futility and hopelessness of the Israeli soldiers' presence in the Occupied Territories, also echoes the super-theme of gridlock. One adolescent (B5: 8), relating to the same issue, concluded that "we are damned if we do and we are damned if we don't."

The nurses' strike was also brought up within the super-theme of gridlock, demonstrating the double bind of doing justice and, at the same time, creating a dangerous precedent. There was a broad agreement that "the nurses work really hard and they absolutely deserve a raise, but if the government gives in to their demands the teachers will follow suit . . . " (M1: 22).

They are outwitting us

Although 'we' are stronger, this super-theme argues, 'they' manage to gain the upper hand. 'They' are often the Palestinian or Arab enemies, but may also be competing ideological groups within Israeli society, such as extreme leftists ('PLO lovers'), or extreme rightists (often nationalist-religious groups). Two reasons were mentioned for 'them outwitting us.' One reason is that 'they' (violent minorities) exploit the fact that 'we' act according to the rules, and so our hands are tied, while 'they' are not stopped by such constraints. The second reason is that 'they' learn our methods, and therefore, in time, 'we' lose our relative advantage.

Of course, 'they are outwitting us' arises out of a pinpointing of 'our position,' and of gauging whether 'my' political camp is winning or losing. The power relation between foes and allies is charted within the framework of the major controversies in Israeli society – the conflicts between the secular and the religious, between oriental second-generation immigrants and the second-generation establishment of European origin, and between hawkish and dovish positions vis-à-vis the Arab–Israeli conflict.

Recounting news stories often means charting an aspect of these three conflicts. One example in our interviews, repeated in a number of versions, was the retelling of the government crisis mentioned above in which Shas, a new ethnic religious party, exploited the fact that the government rested on an extremely narrow majority to blackmail the government with increasingly larger partisan demands. Hence, although Shas is a small party (with six Knesset members in 1993, which rose to nine in 1996), it can be 'outwitting us.' The party boss is Rabbi Ovadia Yossef, who at the time of the study was frequently visited by the then Labor party Prime Minister Rabin, and by his ministers (and no less frequently by current Prime Minister Netanyahu).

Guy, a teenage boy, told that story in the following way: "There is one person who sits and decides what is going to happen with the government and the opposition, who is going to be Prime Minister, and who is going to be a minister. Rabbi Ovadia Yossef actually decides what will happen. He gives instructions to everybody — he instructs Shas, and Shas has the power to topple the government. And it's a pity that something like that happens" (Ba7: 24). A similar map of the structure of power was drawn by another viewer while watching another Shas Member of Parliament on the screen: "Look who is running our state. Derei [the head of Shas, then Minister of the Interior] has to get used to one thing — prison" (Ba9: 33). This map, drawn with reference to the coalition crisis, consists of the corrupt, manipulative, unjustifiably strong 'him' (Rabbi Yossef, Minister Derei) or 'them' (the Shas party) *vis-à-vis* 'us,' in this case the Labor majority, who should have the power to rule, but do not, or the whole country, which deserves better. And a comparable chart was drawn in the re-telling of news items about Israeli soldiers and Palestinians in Gaza, in which 'us,' who are strong but bound by the rules, cannot exercise 'our' power and consequently end up allowing 'them,' who are much weaker but do not abide by the rules, to win against us. The powerful, in the framework of this super-theme, are emaciated and power does not lie where it should.

'They' – the opposition, the government, the party of Shas, Rabbi Yossef – may reside *within* society; 'they' may also constitute an enemy from *without* – the Palestinians, Syria, Iraq, or the rest of the world. This distinction connects with a further sub-theme, according to which even when we seem strong, we are very vulnerable, as the Jews always were. Enat, a teenage daughter, described it in the following words:

(Ga4: 42) The Arabs find methods to get away with it. He [a Palestinian who threw stones at a soldier in Gaza] did it when there were lots of people around and the soldiers could not shoot at him. Then he ran into the alleys, and when the soldiers wanted to shoot he escaped. People started to come, and they could not shoot him because they would be killing people for no reason.

Enat's mapping of the Palestinian–Israeli conflict repeats the pattern according to which 'they' are weak, but use our self-imposed limitations to gain the upper hand.

The two super-themes of 'gridlock' and of 'they are outwitting us,' may provide alternative framings of the same news items. For example, on 13 May (for logistical reasons, some of the interviews had to be conducted in the days following Newsday, 11 May, see Appendix B), two stories of terrorist attacks, one reporting the injuring of an Israeli soldier by a hand grenade in Nablus, the second reporting the stabbing of two soldiers in the Gaza Strip, were, not surprisingly, chosen by several of our interviewees as the most important items. But, while, for a father, the attacks on the soldiers were proof of a double bind, for daughter Enat these items not only pointed to imminent dangers to their lives, but also indicated a remedy. "As long as we are letting them," said Enat, "they are outwitting us," offering as proof that "as long as there was a blockade [on the West Bank and Gaza] nobody was injured, and when they opened it up — soldiers started to be injured again." The lesson for her was obvious: "We are letting them gain the upper hand by not re-sealing the border between Israel and the Occupied Territories" (Ga4: 11).

A more pessimistic view was offered by Ruthy, another daughter in the same family, who, while also choosing the stabbing incident as the most important item, believed that it offered no such solace, but instead entailed the risk of things just getting worse. "For me the most important [item] was when the two terrorists attacked the two soldiers and stuck knives in them, because the Arabs are starting to learn our methods, and this is scary" (Gb4:12). Whereas the two sisters shared the super-theme of 'them outwitting us,' Enat believed that Israelis could reestablish their superiority by doing the right thing, while Ruthy had no such hope.

Accordingly, the viewer's choice of framing depends not only on television's framing of the story, nor entirely on the family's culture and ideology, but also on individual cognitive and other psychological dispositions. In contradiction of Wright's scheme (1960), which distinguished between various types of news items as either functional or dysfunctional, these examples suggest that, to a great extent, it is the recipient who will determine whether the message conveys a sense of control (as expressed by Enat's formulation of the super-theme) or of anxiety (expressed in Ruthy's more pessimistic variant).

We are at the center of the world

The opening statement in the following exchange demonstrates a last substantive super-theme. Unlike, for example, Danish viewers, who may feel that they are marginal to events ('nothing ever happens in our little corner of the world'), this theme implies that 'we are at the center of the world.' The idea that almost anything, originating anywhere, has a bearing upon 'us,' is exemplified here by the collapse of the Soviet Union, which shook the world ("all this mess") – but which also led to the mass immigration of Russian Jews to Israel. The conversation was carried on in the Brandt family at the sight of a group of new Jewish immigrants from Birobidjan. Ayelet and Yosh are in their forties and have four children, two of whom are present. He is an insurance agent, she a housewife (M1, F1: 33–34):

F1: Isn't it surprising that they have [actually] immigrated to Israel as the result of all this mess?

M1: What is important in this story is that they have come from a place in which our state should have been established. [M1 refers to an idea of offering a zone of self-rule to Soviet Jews in the 1930s.] That's the most interesting.

F1: Why? How come?

G1: Is that what *you* believe?

M1: No! They offered it.

F1: OK, I didn't know this.

M1: It was an offer which, with a little bit of pressure, they could have accepted.

F1: I don't know if it wouldn't be better than it is here.

Beyond finding 'ourselves' at the center of things, there is an ideological lesson to be learned from the irony that Jews living in a place which, at a certain point in history, was thought of as a possible refuge from anti-Semitism, are now seeking refuge in Israel. This lesson, in turn, allows for a questioning of Zionist ideology, raising the larger question of the success of Zionism itself – was it all worth it?

Later in the same conversation, in a move from life to text, Ayelet nostalgically framed these Russian immigrants as "pioneers," "who are already looking for work, they would like to work" (F1: 35), thus making them the bearers of major, but long lost, values in Israeli society. The label 'pioneers' in Israel refers to the first Zionist immigrants who came to enact the ideology according to which Jews, who had had to live on parasitical occupations in exile, should resume a healthy existence based on productive work in their own state.

Conclusion

Several points emerge from the analysis of news viewing in Israel in 1993. First, viewing was both active and interactive, although, evidently, there is no way of proving conclusively that this was what viewers would do when the researchers were not there. A great deal of other evidence supports the conclusion that families will view together, making use of the news not only as a gallery of characters to gossip and joke about, but also as a forum for discussing the central issues with which society is struggling and, in the process, socializing their children ideologically. (However, it should be noted that, as mentioned earlier, the role of television in Israel as a focus for family viewing and discussion was drastically affected by the introduction of a multiplicity of TV channels and by the addition of several TV sets to family homes.)

Second, interacting about the news is encouraged by the characteristics of the medium. Unlike the case of reading a newspaper, the explicitly social situation of viewing, and the assumption that others are viewing elsewhere, promotes interaction and negotiation. Third, in relating to the news, viewers draw on preexisting schemata for understanding reality, into which items can be fitted. The three cognitive mechanisms emerging from the family conversations are: the management of personal relationships, as translated into news through displacement and surveillance; the interpretation or framing of reality that is accomplished by commuting between life and program, and by mapping structures of power so as to identify 'my' position (winner or loser); and, less often, the monitoring of medium and genre in order to discover ideological and aesthetic biases.

Finally, importantly, the substantive super-themes seem to be drawn on by viewers in all of these three modes of interacting with news. In Israel, four super-themes could be identified: 'We are at the center of the world' – whatever happens has a bearing on us; 'we as individual families have small problems, compared to our state's big problems'; 'they are outwitting us' – whether 'they' be the opposition, the government coalition, religious groups within society, or an external enemy; and 'gridlock' – we remain stuck in insoluble dilemmas, between the devil and the deep blue sea.

6

ITALY

Paolo Mancini, Elena Alemagni Pimpinelli,
*and Stefania Di Michele**

Italian television and society in transition

Around the time of this study in May 1993, the Italian television system was undergoing a rapid evolution, partly in response to changes in the wider political system, a process which has continued in the second half of the 1990s (see Mazzoleni 1992, 1995; Statham 1996). The television system was, and is, dominated by two main organizations: the RAI, which is a state-regulated, public-service broadcaster, and the privately owned Fininvest. Both organizations own three television channels and broadcast throughout the national territory. While there is RAI 1, RAI 2, and RAI 3, Fininvest owns Canale 5, Rete 4 and Italia 1. Another single channel, Telemontecarlo, is also broadcast throughout the country. In addition, there are about 750 local stations broadcasting within limited local areas.

RAI has always been dependent on the party-political system, which has exercised control over the broadcaster through the *Commissione Parlamentare di Vigilanza* (Parliamentary Vigilance Committee). As recently as 1993, the committee still nominated the RAI Board of Directors. This dependence is perfectly in keeping with the strong tradition of political partisanship in Italian journalism. In television, this resulted in the *lottizzazione* (lotting system) whereby each of the three RAI channels was controlled by one of the principal political parties. At the time of this research, RAI 1, the main channel, was controlled by the Christian Democratic Party, RAI 2 by the Socialist Party, and RAI 3 by the Communist Party. Problems with the lotting system often emerged in the household interviews.

In 1993, all three RAI stations presented news programs, whereas Fininvest offered only two. One of the Fininvest programs, *Studio Aperto* shown on Rete 4, had low audience figures, and the other program, shown on Canale 5, had

*   The Italian part of the *News of the World* project has been funded, in part, by VPT-RAI and RTI-Fininvest. For the interviews with Italian households, only the longer quotations are identified by respondent number and page in the transcripts.

just begun broadcasting. Today, all three Fininvest stations have daily news programs with an appreciable audience, particularly the one on Canale 5. In comparison, TG1, the news program shown on RAI 1, is, and has always been, the prime-time news program with the largest audience. TG1 is broadcast at 8 pm, the traditional supper time in Italy. Accordingly, this RAI 1 newscast was the program chosen for discussion and observation in our research.

After the 1994 elections, the Italian political landscape and, hence, the television system which has always been an integral part of national politics, has undergone dramatic changes. Two of the main government parties, the Christian Democratic Party (DC) and the Socialist Party (PSI) have disappeared, while the owner of Fininvest (now Mediaset), Silvio Berlusconi, has established his own party, *Forza Italia*, which gained a relative majority of the votes in the 1994 elections. The fact that Berlusconi became prime minister, has created a much-discussed overlap between the institutions of political power and the main private media conglomerate in Italy. Even if, after one year, Berlusconi was forced to resign as prime minister, he is still active as a political figure, and the overlap between politics and television has not yet been resolved.

The structure of Italian television has always been an important issue in public debate, since television has a very large audience compared to a low level of press readership, and the changes which have taken place following the 1994 elections, have not entailed the end of the political affiliation of the Italian media. Since 1994, the media system has formed new alliances with both the government and the opposition parties.

Television consumption between public and private spheres

Several authors have considered television to be an instrument through which the outside world enters the family during one of the few moments when it comes together as a unit (e.g. Ellis 1982; Gamson 1992; Livingstone and Lunt 1994). In Italy, as in several other countries (Lull 1988b), the time of the evening news broadcast corresponds to the time at which family members gather for dinner. Having supper together while watching the news has become a sort of modern tradition.

Such a use of television informs particular procedures of interpreting news: this is the time when the private family sphere – with its hierarchy, its more or less established roles and identities, as well as internal communication processes – measures itself against the public sphere as represented on television. At this time, and in this context, a division is created between an interior and an exterior family, between a domestic and an external space (Ellis 1982), with significant consequences. Our findings suggest that this division may produce "a sense of isolation from the events shown and consequently a sense that they invade the viewer's domestic space" (ibid. 166). This sense can be reinforced by the perception that the world 'out there' is a world of conflict, contention, tragedies, accidents, and murders, all very far from the tranquillity or, at least, familiar routines of everyday life. Every evening, the news covers such topics to a family group that becomes an interpretive micro-community (e.g. Lindlof 1987; Jensen 1990b).

We conclude that a distinctive perception of 'risk' arises from this meeting between the public and private spheres. Risk, as the English sociologist Anthony Giddens has underlined, is characteristic of the very idea of modernity. He argues that a condition of 'disembedding,' that is, of "lifting social relationships out of a context of local interaction and restructuring them across indefinite spans of time-space" (Giddens 1990: 21), invariably accompanies modern humans. The historical shift from an agrarian society constituted by small groups to an industrial society made up of large units has resulted in a loss of temporal and spatial context, as well as of a common identity. Having been deprived of the certainty of an interactive relationship with a community that is defined both spatially and symbolically, one finds oneself, at least in a phenomenological sense, exposed to an experience that is often antithetical to the world of everyday life. Instead, individuals experience a continuing global-ization of their relationship with the community. The 'distanciation' from everyday experience, typical of the modern condition, thus generates a continuous sense of risk and, in turn, a search for a micro-community within which one may feel secure and defend oneself against the inherent risk of 'de-localization' (ibid. 1990). The family can be said to represent a first elementary level of such a self-defensive community, as hypothesized also by Meyrowitz (1985) in his analysis of how television engenders 'decontextualization.'

An interpretive process of this sort may be particularly in evidence in contexts such as Italy where family identity remains strong and plays an impor-tant role in the organization of society. The following sections trace the several levels of interpretation in the interviews, as applied by the households to selected news items. Some 'continuing stories' (Tuchman 1978) dominated the Newsday of the project in Italy: new stories about political corruption, new developments in the war in Bosnia, and the ongoing political fight between the Italian government and its opposition. Great importance was also given, however, to a fire in a doll factory in Thailand which killed many women workers.

Multi-level interpretation

Four interconnected levels

Within the complex process of communication, we identify a multi-level interpretation, a self-regulating mechanism with levels that are distinct one from the other, but interconnected through established procedures of decoding. Viewers incorporate information into the rest of their daily activities and appro-priate the surrounding reality by giving significance to what they see and hear.

In progressively taking possession of external reality, they interpret the news at different levels: the event, the story, the self, and the medium. While these levels represent distinct and specific moments in a sequential, vertical development, the progression is also continuous and circular: the event and the story are enriched through the experience of self, just as the self is influenced and enriched by the news story. The news, thus processed, enters into super-themes (Jensen 1988) or schemata (Graber 1984) – that is, macro-aggregates of meaning and values which allow the viewer to give sense and significance to the news shown on the screen.

Next, we attempt to trace the course of the news through the process of 'decodification,' including, in our terminology, the actual reception of visual and auditory stimuli from the screen, the use of language and other communicative competences in recognizing the codes, and the cognitive interpretation and insertion of information into an organized set of meanings (see Cheli 1988, who also refers to memorization of the message received). The interpretive course of the news begins with 'the event itself,' defined as the first level in the working of super-themes, the level at which single fragments of a story are simply highlighted before they are inserted into a more complete framework of meaning. The event is here perceived as a series of facts, places, and people. But in order for it to assume a unified meaning, even in the personalized interpretation of each viewer, the event must be given a narrative structure through the complex set of rules by which language and other signs produce significance, and thanks to which viewers come to form their 'own images of the world' (Hall 1975).

Passing, at this point, to the more articulated level where the event is transformed into a 'story,' the viewer relies on various sources which are not necessarily contained in the news text. They include a rich package of ideas offered by different media, as well as by the context of family consumption, in which an exchange of ideas equally takes place. Added to these ideas are a number of other experiences from the viewer's own reality. From this overall informative context – the context which becomes text through interpretation – the viewer is able to accomplish a first stage of contextualization, giving a certain finality to the events represented. The event-as-story becomes a resource, activating an interpretive process in which a theme, sub-theme, or issue, as mediated and filtered by the self, grows more complex and articulated and is further enriched by other elements and details until it is inserted and transformed, as we shall see, within a super-theme. It is, then, the category of super-themes, closely tied to the viewer's self, which can be seen, time after time, to bring the viewer closer to certain events/stories. And it is through an analysis of the discursive construction through which the viewer recognizes the profound ties between event and self that one may attempt to comprehend the social interaction that arises between them.

The 'self,' accordingly, has been introduced as an entity comprising many components such as personal life, everyday experiences, professional activity,

106

general knowledge, emotions, etc. Importantly, the self emerges already during viewing in the households when only family members with a personal interest in a particular topic will expressly invite attention to it, but it manifests itself more clearly during household discussions when each family member will define his or her specific identity in relation to such interests as well as the intended uses of the news. The self will decide the choice of one event over another; it will inform decodification; and it helps to explain selective memorization of different news items. Having gathered information from several sources, the self will ascribe relevance and informative value to those events it most readily remembers. By way of introduction, it should be emphasized that the information deriving from the immediate context of viewing appears to affect both the processing of and, probably, the memory for news, sometimes gaining the upper hand to such a degree that it may inadvertently influence how sense is made of the news and, hence, the reconstruction of the real world. As the findings indicate, occasionally the urgency of speaking about facts that are particularly dear and close to an individual's own reality causes a distancing of the self from news items along entirely individual, independent tracks, even to the point of misremembering them, so that nothing substantial remains of the original piece of news that engendered the family discussion. Personal life may thus prevail over the public news item as viewers refer an entire story to the personal dimension of their individual past, needs, and interests, or to their family acting as an interpretive community.

The last level of interpreting television news is that of the 'medium.' Competences which viewers have developed previously, primarily through the mass media themselves, but also through personal experience, allow them to interact with the medium, interpreting and judging both the quality of the information and the television angle as opposed to the angle taken by other media. This makes it possible to compare the editorial slant respectively in the private and public television systems as well as the possible machinations of political reference groups affecting the way the news is presented; to discuss the manner in which news readers communicate the news; to comment on the excessive attention paid to political events in Italy, coupled with too little attention paid to foreign news; to underline omissions and recurrences; and to criticize the repetitiveness of the news and its disinterest in listening, to the point of expressing a generally negative opinion of the journalistic profession as such.

Whereas the event, the story, the self, and media criticism all constitute possible levels of interpretation, the super-theme is, so to speak, the final product of extracting a certain sense which is an intermediary between the viewers' exposure to the medium and their everyday life. While the story remains tied to the television journalist's narrative, the super-theme may depart completely from it, taking a hint in the story as a suggestion for going in other directions and arriving at an entirely different meaning of news. This multi-level interpretation of news may be specified with empirical examples of each of the four stages leading up to the super-themes.

The event

During the phase of observing the Italian households watching television news on Newsday, it became clear that, to them, much of the information remained simply a series of events, facts, places, and people, not connected by a narrative plot. At this stage, the news items seemed to have no relevance to viewers other than as a source of information to be conferred with their memory of real events from personal experience or with information obtained through another medium. Some news items went by without arousing much interest and did not become a subject of discussion because they were not anchored in personal life.

It is the emotional and cognitive 'heritage' of people, their context in a broad sense, which determines their response to the message. At the same time, the way in which, in the flux of information, attention is given only to specific events would suggest fairly automatic procedures that are simple and immediate. These may be expressed in the following forms:

Exclamations or simple statements which express a judgement:

- "Mostar! [a Bosnian city central to hostilities in 1993] It was so beautiful!"
- "Great!"
- "Shameful!"

Half sentences which express a comment as a sort of immediate, instinctive action:

- "Lo-o-ok at that!"
- "Unbelievable!"
- "My God!"
- "Where? In Thailand?"

Fragmented observations in a logical sequence, but without a unifying theme:

- "But they're killing all the communists." [with reference to Bosnia]
- "Show it better so people will get emotional." [with reference to the fire in Thailand]

Disconnected phrases, not inserted into a narrative plot, were particularly evident during viewing. Facts such as a location or the names of people were picked out of the event, and comments were brief, ironic, amused, critical, sympathetic, or could express the satisfaction of being confirmed in one's own position. For the most part, however, the news topics did not acquire any fully developed meaning during viewing.

The story

Just as only some specific events arouse the curiosity of viewers, only some were important enough to be remembered when viewers were asked to recall the most important items. The 'stimulus' event may be transformed into a story only if it possesses the right characteristics from the point of view of the viewer's personal interests, thus activating the further process in which social meaning is produced. Viewers elaborated on events through a narrative construction only when a news item activated their previous knowledge or experiences, their inclinations, or their work. The findings show that the criteria which are applied in determining relevance are strongly related to the viewer's 'self,' increasingly so as the process of meaning production progresses.

A woman who, during viewing, had already expressed some consternation at the news of renewed bombings of the city of Mostar, intervened again during the household discussion. She had been struck by the news of the destruction of Mostar, a city she had had occasion to visit and therefore had direct knowledge of. This may explain her shift from an exclamation about the event, to a more elaborate story with historical background as well as personal evaluations:

- Event: "Mostar! It was so beautiful!"
- Story: "What a shame, it was so beautiful! Have they destroyed the Turkish quarter? They are crazy! Now they are fighting among themselves. There was a civilization in which Turks, Muslims, and Bosnians lived together . . . "

The self

Although departing initially from the interviewer's questions, the respondents would proceed in an autonomous fashion once they arrived at more sophisticated levels of interpretation. Moving away from the news item and articulating their answers, not with reference to a shared topic but on the basis of everyday interests and repeated or even occasional events in their own lives, viewers' observations might become free associations, tied to their mood. Such specific interests emerged as the focal point of the process in which the self interprets the news.

As already noted, the process of interpretation has both a sequential and a circular dimension. One example is found in the comments about the war in Bosnia, offered by the household that had had direct experience with the city involved in the conflict, Mostar. The mother, when viewing the broadcast, suggested that to her the news of the war in Bosnia resulted in consternation rather than a desire to get more information on the conflict as such. The reason, as indicated, was that she had personally visited and had direct knowledge of the city being destroyed. At the first level of interpretation, then, the event was reduced to a location, Mostar:

- Event: "Mostar! It was so beautiful!"

At the next level, the story opened up the simple theme of the destruction of beauty:

- Story: "What a shame, it was so beautiful! Have they destroyed the Turkish quarter? They are crazy! Now they are fighting among themselves (. . .)."

However, the actual news item almost disappeared from this respondent's discourse as Mostar along with the last few items on the news gave way to her vision of the conflict. The political issues were soon transformed into a human issue: "In a civil war, one member of a family can be against another, that is the tragedy of civil war, you saw them. Now that they are going to bomb Mostar, who will they kill? Who is right and who is wrong? You tell me!"

The stepwise interpretive process contributed to a position from which this woman could make sense of the news – her self:

- Self: 'The war is in Mostar, which is a beautiful city.'

To sum up this third stage of interpretation, 'war' came to be seen as something that necessarily wiped away a city, its objects, and its people, but, perhaps most important, also the memories of a place where this woman had had a pleasant experience in the past. Her involvement seems to be strong precisely because the event not only gave rise to a story, but destroyed a part of her self. In the process, the sequential stages of interpretation have been complemented by a circular movement involving her direct experience of the city in the past as well as her mediated experience of similar instances of 'war' as reported daily in the news.

The medium

The different communication strategies that are signaled by journalistic headings, for example, did not go unobserved and were not always accepted uncritically. Also within the context of the family, the medium itself became an object of discussion, evaluation, and criticism. In Italy, the debate concerning the value of the information, of what the information should be, may in fact be growing stronger and more critical in conjunction with the great space which, probably more here than in other countries, newspapers dedicate to television and its programs, discussion and criticism – even to the point of newspapers becoming dependent on television. As noted earlier, television audiences in Italy are substantially larger than the readership for the printed press.

Discussion of the media not only occupies a growing space in Italian newspapers, but a central position on the public agenda of people and politicians. Accordingly, it is also an issue that Italian families wish to discuss. However, the present responses suggest two rather different, partly opposed, attitudes toward television. The extreme attention given by the media to the matter of corruption was said to produce a kind of addiction to such news which paradoxically, in the longer term, may result in inattention:

> M4: 38: The bribes scandal cannot surprise me, I have it up to here. Today they arrested this, that, or the other person, indictments . . . it's very confusing. And then these discussions of the new course, the new image. Such good people, those who have harassed us for forty years and have reduced us to this state. If a new face comes along and says, "OK, it happened, but let's roll up our sleeves anyway."

On the one hand, then, news is to be consumed every night. Waiting for the evening news broadcast was conceived almost as a ritual sacrifice to which Italian citizens must subject themselves. On the other hand, television was said to produce boredom because of the repetitiveness of the – again, paradoxically – predictable events following from the corruption which has overrun Italy: "Really, this going on and on about the bribes . . .," or "Yes, no, but we are tired of bribes." Television further provokes indignation, disdain, and profound irritation: "Bribes and more bribes, it's shameful." And television comes to be perceived as a threat to the family because – whether they like it or not – viewers are reminded of the lack of dignity and the progressive loss of credibility of the political class which has governed the country for years: "It is a painful thing for us Italians to see the news, we who are a free people, and we who have seen that not seeing the news is good for the liver, the heart, and the brain, important parts of the body." Nevertheless, television can be said to "grip with pincers" the viewer with a need for information. Viewers want to attend to the news, and find it difficult to distance themselves, because the next day it will be necessary for them to be informed, in the workplace, among friends and other people. Thus, the requirements of the public sphere govern media consumption in the private sphere.

The interpretive capacity of viewers has also been made evident by other research. Livingstone and Lunt (1994), dedicating an entire chapter to 'the critical viewer,' have underlined how "listening to the audience also reveals that people are aware that programmes are constructed: they comment on biases introduced by production processes, on the constraints of programme form or scheduling, and on the uses and effects of programmes" (p. 71). Our research supplies many confirmations of this capacity for intervention *vis-à-vis* the medium, although, obviously, the high critical capacity demonstrated by these households must be correlated with their social and cultural characteristics and cannot be assumed as a universal among Italian households.

In particular, items on the news which viewers have been waiting for, and which involve information that cannot but affect public opinion, may provoke a reaction in this respect. Criticism can serve as the viewer's means of censoring and keeping at a distance news that is not considered credible but rather manipulated, full of risks and threats, itself a fruit of the corruption of which the programs often speak:

> M8: 101: (. . .) all the news programs, all journalists . . . all three news programs are different in the sense that the Italian television is allotted by the politicians. Therefore we know the Channel 1 news is Christian Democrat, the Channel 2 news is of the Socialist party, and the Channel 3 news is of the Social Democrats or of the ex-Communists. Then perhaps an event recounted on TG1 will probably . . . comment on the event in a different way than other channels. They are therefore three different news programs because sponsored by three different political parties.

Another respondent found that "the TG1 conceals because there are the priests etc. . . . things to do with priests and Christian Democrats" (M8: 102).

Strong criticisms were directed by respondents at the medium, its editorial slants, and various political colorations. In any event, the partiality of the news was considered evident:

> F4: 41: The news? Items are distorted. I think that as far as objectivity, TG3 is the best, the journalists are the most objective, see? Because they say things in a more straightforward way, a more realistic way . . . whereas TG1 distorts a bit . . . also because the television news is manipulated. I have sometimes watched all three channels, and they are all completely different. TG3 is sometimes aggressive, often catastrophic. TG2 is so so . . . TG1 smoothes everything over and changes the news.

Media criticism often unfolded as part of the interactional use of televised information. Everyone would use television news to strengthen their own position and, within the families, every member of the household would try to interpret television so as to convince others of their own point of view. Moreover, in doing so, parents may perform their duties as educators, in certain cases in opposition to television as an unreliable teacher:

> F4: 45: TG1 does not give the impression that it is reporting. It comes off like a lesson about something which has happened, not a report. It suggests how one should behave, like a teacher. It does not tell you a story about a question, it's always like a lesson. Yes, this has happened, but there is always a solution for everything, everything is fine, even when everything is a mess.

Traveling among super-themes

Political corruption

The super-themes, being the preliminary end products of multi-level inter-pretation, begin to suggest the relevance and potential uses of news in the everyday life of viewers. Previous research in the Italian context (Mancini 1991) had found a generalized super-theme of 'politics,' an all-encompassing and vague catch-all, which, by association, incorporated many news items that had little to do with politics in a traditional sense. With the breaking of the bribes scandal in Italy from 1992 – the dominating events and discussions regarding corrupted politicians and officials, summed up under the term *tangentopoli* (city of bribes) – the super-theme of politics, while remaining general, stereotyped, and negative, seems to have acquired better defined, sharper outlines, as well as a clearer connotation of 'political corruption.' The viewer's thoughts about the meaning of things political may be directed by this perspective from the outset, implying a judgment which soon prevails and overwhelms other possible perspectives. The general super-theme, however, can be divided into several more particular thematizations, which we now examine in order to clarify their contents and connotations.

Political information, especially when it pertains to kickbacks or public debt, tended to be linked immediately by viewers to their own daily lives. On a scale of commonly accepted values and sentiments such as justice, trust, and honesty, political information was thematized in negative terms and associated with 'bad government and corruption': "The Italian political system operated for years with dishonest and thieving politicians who robbed and victimized honest citizens." Discussions concerning this subject in the households were very heated and lively. Here, everyday life experiences and shared opinions were confirmed and voiced openly with reference to the bribes scandal. The identification of respondents with their everyday lives was strong enough to overcome their identification with individual political factions, "They are all thieves, none excluded":

Oa6 (Grandmother): 67: They are all thieves, even one who steals only a little is a thief.
M6: Of course, but the Christian Democrats, or the governing parties bear a greater share of responsibility, as they were administering and governing.
F6. It's hard to say, there are a hundred thieves within the party, they are all thieves.
M6: . . . The problem is that the parties within the system made a system of it. The other parties certainly also benefited . . . as well as local agencies. We saw them, here too, they all got something out of it . . .
F6: People still see them as thieves.

The constant conflicts among parties and between politicians and judges, the quarrelsome climate seen daily in political news – all presents a picture of politics as being out of control, confused, and defined negatively by a search for political advantage and a struggle for power. The victim of this confusion is always the citizen, harassed by taxes and "everything": "(. . .) lately everything has been compounded by the blow to families . . . from health to taxes, everything." The dishonesty of politicians, as well as the incompetence of such thieving governments, were under accusation because they touch everyday life in a very tangible way. Bad government and corruption affect, and will increasingly affect, everyday life through growing social burdens for each family and growing taxes for each television viewer to pay. The politicians' dishonesty was seen in juxtaposition to the family's labor and savings. Politicians, and politics in general, were thus viewed as a tangible threat to the family's pocket and whole economy, and the family, used to watching television together, feels this threat very strongly, a general feeling to which every member may add something.

In the group discussions, we found that concrete items of information from television news were rarely mentioned by viewers, who instead appeared greatly affected by the general climate of political warfare. For example, the words of politicians seemed secondary, even irrelevant, and were often omitted by respondents from their narrative of the news. The very appearance on the screen of a political figure representing any movement within the old political system could be sufficient to unleash heated discussions among viewers concerning the old corrupt system, together with verbal outbursts of contention and intolerance which, more often than not, had nothing to do with the news item itself. The super-theme, then, has 'taken flight,' gone beyond the level of the story, and has, in its form and contents, assumed a more general pattern of associations and evaluations which serve to define and interpret events recounted on the news while ignoring the original item. The value judgment may become more important than its object in the news: "Why don't they just bomb the Parliament!"

In the super-theme of political corruption, families seemed to be brought together by their readings. In this respect, the interviews discovered no divergent opinions in the interpretive community:

> F6: 65: I would just kick out all these people who are being investigated! Right away! At the regional level and at the national level! Some of the people in jail are still president of this or that, council here, council there . . . where is it written . . . if I steal a thousand lira they fire me and never give me back my job. Why should these people have this kind of privilege, where is it written, these guys already have a lot, wanna see that the race to go there comes to an end . . . because they are all counseled, protected and do as they d . . . , no, I can't swear . . . whatever the hell they want with our money /
> M6: / and they give them a large pension on top of it /

F6: / after five years they get ten million, those parliamentarians, the regional councilors get five, and they have asked for a raise, I guess they want seven!

A second thematization – apart from the consequences of political corruption for individuals and families – can be traced within this super-theme: namely, the 'hopelessness of the old system.' This implies a severe criticism of the entire Italian political system, excluding no one. Above and beyond party lines or political ideology, 'everything' is corrupt and hopeless. What emerged was a complete distrust of the political class in general, which was seen as hopelessly corrupt. A certain feeling of distance as well as disaffection had broken out among these viewers, who had been "cheated and taken for a ride." Now, feelings were also directed towards the medium of political information itself, so that the super-theme related to the level of media criticism. All of this viewer's critical capacity was expressed (see further, pp. 110–12), organized around a specific super-theme:

F4: 41: (. . .) television news is manipulated. I have sometimes watched all three channels, and they are all completely different. TG3 is sometimes aggressive, often catastrophic. TG2 is so so . . . TG1 smoothes everything over and changes the news.

Again, the very medium of television and the news itself are kept at a distance because they are seen as untrustworthy, the result of the corruption of which they speak. The accusation leveled at the medium is that it is entrenched in the political game, reminding viewers daily of the sad reality of a political system that does not seem to change.

War

The super-theme of 'war' appeared frequently in the interviews and presents itself as logical yet complex. The principal object of this thematization is the conflict in the former Yugoslavia, which has a special dual characteristic. On the one hand, it is a 'far away' conflict – difficult, unclear, and not felt to be close to home, because it is a religious–ethnic–cultural–civil conflict, distant from the viewers' culture. This was expressed strongly in statements such as: "Let them kill each other off! They have no right to involve everyone . . . let's hope they'll drop an atomic bomb." On the other hand, it is a 'very close' conflict, (a) because of the short geographical distance and the territorial threat it represents, (b) because of the memory of World War I and comparable events, and (c) because of the common human involvement with people who are suffering and actually living the dramatic situations we see daily on television.

Local and global elements intertwine in the super-theme of war, showing how viewers are able to follow several perhaps opposing courses of interpretation. In speaking about war, respondents clearly considered it to be of worldwide importance, something that could not fail to involve everyone, both from the emotional point of view of its impact on humans and from a historical and economic point of view. The emotional involvement with people who are suffering and with the drama that has befallen them, together with viewers sharing the preoccupation with the potential worldwide economic consequences of conflicts, shifts the perception of the event onto a general plane and into a global setting. War is a universal issue involving a very wide transnational public sphere.

World news, such as the Bosnian war, thus assumes universal importance because of the degree of viewer involvement and, more specifically, the emotional reactions toward a sister people at the moment of its annihilation. The process of globalization, the knocking down of spatio-temporal barriers by new technologies, may be transforming national identity, as formerly associated with small nations, into a collective identity where the traditional confines between nations, and between night and day, are demolished (Silverstone 1994). Whether the outcome is a real community seems to remain an open issue. Still, electronic media have reduced the globe to not much more than a 'village,' intensifying human interaction in an extraordinary way and involving quite different social groups in our lives, as we are in theirs:

> F1: 8: When we were in Nocera I met a couple, he was Muslim and she was an Italian Catholic. I felt ashamed and embittered when he spoke of the attitude in the West toward Muslims during the Gulf War: "I'd like to see, if those women that were raped in Bosnia had not been Muslim, how everyone would have reacted." As a Westerner I felt like . . . burying my head, I assure you.

This globalization process, as mentioned in the opening paragraphs, is countered by an opposite reaction, that of seeing international events in personal, domestic, or national terms – the private side of public events. With this reaction, the transnational identity of citizens of the world comes to be overshadowed by their economic concerns as well as by their physical and emotional safety. As the public sphere threatens the private, viewers may create a defensive barrier and may no longer acknowledge as theirs the problems of a humanity to which they in fact belong. When an interpretive community originating in the nation (macro-level) or the family (micro-level) takes the upper hand, the event will be brought back to a domestic, private sphere where the historical and global threat becomes geographic and domestic. In this local setting, daily preoccupations serve to redefine borders, recreating the dimensions of the war while simultaneously reinforcing a sense of belonging. In the super-theme of war, the double process of globalization and localization, the passage from the universal to the particular, is particularly evident.

The consequences of war, in becoming localized, are brought back onto a national scale. Whereas the events are made universal in the sense that they are understood with reference to a global setting, such international events are reintegrated at the national level. As such, they are tied to notions of threat and risk:

> Oa9 (Nephew): 108: We can take aim at Yugoslavia with our missiles.
> Ob9 (Nephew): They've already gotten out the Patriot . . .
> B9: In Cesenatico [Italian city on the Adriatic sea, facing Yugoslavia] there are Patriots.
> (. . .)
> M9: 109: Our coastline cannot become an American outpost.
> B9: Yes, it can! Four of them left the other time too . . . one fell right away.
> Ob9 (Nephew): But that's not to say it will be Italians leaving . . .
> M9: In any case the Americans won't go fighting on the ground like in Vietnam.
> Oa9 (Nephew): They're not going to fall for it again, they bomb from the sky and as usual it's the innocent that get it.
> F9: They aim at military targets.

The notion of a 'threat' is key to the super-theme of war. War is a physical threat to the respondents, who feared eventual involvement in the Bosnian conflict on the part of Italy, which borders on that country. The proximity to a country at war, geographically "a step away from home, 200 kilometers from here, here in front," engendered preoccupation and fear. And, anxiety appeared to grow as an American intervention became more likely. Yet the American intervention was evaluated positively by some viewers as a solution to the conflict, a necessary move, whereas others saw it as a sign of the imminent involvement of Italian soldiers and of the Adriatic coast and, hence, a loss of both local and national tourism. The physical threat had become an economic threat:

> M8: 79: By the way! There's something you don't hear anymore: all the arms they put on the Adriatic coast, no one knows anything anymore.
> Ga8: They are there, but how can they talk about it? The tourist season is just beginning. If people were to know there are ground-to-air missiles, they'll all go to Tuscany by the sea.

In several interviews, the viewers' historical memory associated to the idea of a civil war in Yugoslavia being a potential catalyst for a World War III. The war would then become a global threat. Further, those viewers with some knowledge of history and cultural background saw Sarajevo as a distinctive symbol of World War I:

Ba4: 42: The fact is this: Serbia wants a great Serbia because of the Serbs. But this is not right, because in '38 Hitler wanted Czechoslovakia because it was his, and when he invaded Poland, the French, the English, and the Americans kept out, but when he invaded Belgium they woke up.

Certain interview passages almost seem to offer a historical justification of the war as a necessary logical consequence of previous events in history. The repeated parallels and comparisons, not only with World War I, but also with the Vietnam, Korean, and Gulf wars, may be not so much an attempt to ask oneself what a possible solution might be – a concern voiced only by male respondents – as much as a way to criticize American interventionism, the collapse of Communism, and other historical events preceding the conflict. The parallels can be a way of removing oneself from any responsibility and possible involvement in the conflict:

F4: 46: Machiavelli's principle has always worked.
Ba4: For those who told about it, not those who are six feet under.
Bb4: In Vietnam too they got there first.
M4: Too late.
Ba4: Clinton like Kennedy.
F4: Bush should have already intervened.
Bb4: You know when Kennedy sent the first marines? In 1964, during the Cold War, a first difference that no longer exists. The second thing is that Vietnam is a step away from Communist China. Here we're talking about Serbia, which is a step away from nothing, because there is Bulgaria which has nothing but problems.
M4: Now Clinton has this hot potato. When they elected him it was already a mess.
Ba4: But there is another reason: Yeltsin who has the Slavs in parliament and had to have a referendum to get out, if they didn't let him go he would have had to appease the Serbs. When they gave him the go ahead, Yeltsin said, "Now you Serbs behave." So then America was off.

War is human suffering and violence, but it also involves indifference and therefore a threat to conscience. One way for the respondents to try to distance themselves from it, to defend themselves, was to direct specific accusations at the television medium, which could be guilty of not making the situation clear, preferring to show just the spectacular, most threatening, side made up of violent images, "Blood, show more blood":

F8: 78: Now they probably have extermination camps too.
Ga8: They probably do . . . but no one knows anything.

While the conflict shown daily on television may be too violent and too unclear, it can force viewers to identify themselves with it, to suffer, to feel pity and shame. Not only is personal conscience threatened, but the images on the screen may cause indignation and consternation, threatening family tranquility as well, as suggested by a son in one family:

> Ba4: 42: They can't show these things! The wounded I've seen are upsetting, without arms, legs, it's incredible. All these states that lived peacefully together and that are now killing each other. I heard of a married couple, he is Serb and she a Croat, and they attacked them, and the poor things are married . . .

Social violence and/or defense of the family

The following super-theme departs from various thematizations dealing with the 'victims' of the events spoken of on the news. It shows that one of the main interpretive categories of the modern world is, in Giddens' term, 'risk'; so much so that it generates a super-theme in itself. Among the events shown on the news is not just the war in the former Yugoslavia, but also things of local concern such as public health, accidents, and unemployment. And the victims are not just those televised, but the ordinary citizen and viewer, the families who are forced to pay higher taxes in order for the national debt to be repaid, and all those who live in insecurity and everyday 'social violence.'

References to this particular super-theme revealed an emotional sympathy for others, but was rooted in a preoccupation with self and family. It is primarily the possible social impact that may create involvement, participation, and collective identification among these viewers, who extended the information to refer to their own daily existence. The respondents felt themselves to be victims in effect, just like the victims shown on the screen. This electronic empathy which viewers established with other social actors, both in front of and behind the screen, is encouraged by the opportunity for direct involvement in the event through human interest which allows for participation in someone else's experience, especially when the human categories relate to socially close entities – family, colleagues, and social group.

Such 'social' participation, however, also creates anxiety and, in order to defend themselves, viewers may thematize the victims with a certain distance – 'It could never happen to me!' – or otherwise see an event entirely in their own terms. The Italian respondents discussed topics, once again, with constant reference to themselves and their own lives, ignoring other social aspects of the facts presented. In the following passage, for example, the news of an increase in automobile insurance rates is decodified not so much as social violence on harassed citizens in general, as much as a threat to the family economy. The pocket of the head of the family is touched in a concrete way and this is what is of interest:

M9: 107: Again? N-o-o, are you sure, it's increasing again! This is unnerving!
Oa9 (Nephew): You'll see if for the Saturday night crowd...
[a reference to the large number of car accidents on Saturday nights]
M9: But not us, not us.
Oa9: Why us?
Ob9 (Nephew): They don't do anything, anything.

In their thematizations of the news, then, respondents did not discuss the specific information of the program or its social value, but how, and how much, a particular piece of news would affect them personally, how to defend themselves and their family from these threats, whether they were in fact concrete threats or not. The most important thing remains preserving the integrity of the family and the tranquil world of everyday life from social threats – a defensive mechanism is engendered from within the family. In this respect, the self becomes a familial self that is key to the understanding of television news.

The threat that news items bring into the home creates preoccupation, anxiety, and fear, which must be controlled and managed. In doing so, viewers may put certain interactional strategies of 'family management' into action, in the sense that news items can be used by the mother or father to suggest acceptable behaviors to other members of the family. Events in the outside world can imply, either implicitly or explicitly, models of behavior, as well as underlining what is not just and offering an occasion to condemn it. This was the case with the major fire in a toy factory in Thailand:

G2: 19: Mother of God! Poor things!
F2: What a disaster, oh, what a tragedy!
M2: Do you realize where they made their daughters work?
G2: They explained it to us in school, that they pick children up on the street and put them to work for a few pennies.
B2: At least they do something and don't hang around the streets.
G2: Yes, but they also work with toxic substances.
F2: Like here, those who work in illegal factories in the south that make fireworks... things like that... so many die...

In several of the quotations above, it becomes clear that distant events such as the fire in Thailand and the war in the former Yugoslavia, as seen through horrifying images of violence, could be perceived as close threats to everyday life – the victims of the story directly involve viewers. The thematizations offered by the mother and father, endowed with pity and pietism toward the weak, women, and children, suggest that they see a need to teach their children with reference to the news. On the other hand, the defensive mechanism of the family can also produce a rejection of the images seen. In the following quotations, a veritable warning is expressed, not only as a rejection of the images as such, but also in the form of a direct, determined criticism of news coverage in general which not only involves but threatens the viewer. While the reactions may seem rather superficial, criticism of media as well as of self inform the process of interpretation.

About Bosnia:

> Ba1: 7: They can't show these things, they make you lose your appetite.

> Oc9 (Daughter in law): 100: What about the people running away from Bosnia . . . those poor children and the old soldiers . . . their children.

About the risk of the Bosnian conflict spreading to other countries with US involvement:

> Oc9 (Daughter-in-law): 99: It makes you feel like crying.
> Oa9 (Nephew): Cry about what?
> Oc9 (Daughter-in-law): Look at those images.
> M9: My goodness.
> Oa9 (Nephew): They make them disappear!
> B9: They have to clean out.
> Oa9 (Nephew): You'll see, you'll see.
> M9: Look at the children, how can you watch them this way!

About the fire in Thailand:

> F4: 42: The images of the fire are too crude.
> M4: I'm really furious. (. . .) Terrible images.

About the bribes scandal:

> M4: 39: It is a painful thing for us Italians to see the news, we who are a free people, and we who have seen that not seeing the news is good for the liver, the heart, and the brain, important parts of the body.

The Church

The sustaining element of this last super-theme is the Pope. Thematizations revolved around individuals in the Church, particularly Pope John Paul II. This super-theme did not, however, emerge as often as found in other research (Mancini 1991), and the thematizations had other, unusual connotations. Added to the image of the Pope as a pilgrim and traveler, as seen on television during his travels (Guizzardi 1986), was the image of someone highly politically aware who has turned more and more to social concerns outside the Church. Thanks to the Pope, the Church was said to have had an important role in the collapse of the Communist regimes in Eastern Europe and as a spiritual guide in the social, political, and moral rebirth of Italy after the bribes scandal:

B9: 100: A Pope that will go down in history for many new ideas which he has spread with his travels, in any case an important person . . . for many reasons he will go down in history.

F9: Probably if it hadn't been for this Pope, there would still be the Berlin Wall. It would have fallen in the end, but clearly the Pope's action speeded up the process. In any case he is a great political figure, even within the Church, beyond the spirituality of the Church.

M6: 66: The Pope came home, I think the speech he gave in Sicily has no precedent.

Oa6 (Grandmother): Ah! you see . . . youth?

Ob6 (Grandmother): No, no, if they didn't want to hear, they wouldn't have gone to listen . . . the Mafia and of course . . . they may be afraid they will kill them too . . . so the Pope goes around like he was on an outing, but for him it's a sacrifice if he runs into a madman that shoots him . . . what perseverance to go everywhere in the world this way.

Oa6 (Grandmother): And he brings with him the New Testament, and these are no lies. The Pope does his duty, he went to Sicily and did his duty.

This political enterprising on the part of the Pope was tied by respondents to his institutional role, which was evident on his trip to Sicily 'against the Mafia,' Sicily being a special stronghold of the Mafia. First of all, it should be emphasized that although there was no explicit reference in the news program on Newsday, respondents singled out the Pope's intervention as the most important event of that week. Second, the political image of the Pope came out in two separate recurring thematizations which were tied to his trip to Sicily: the meetings, or confrontations, of the Church and the Mafia, and of the Church and the state. On the one hand, there is the Pope, who takes a personal risk, travels, gets angry, makes a move. On the other hand, there is the state, which is not very manifest and, moreover, involved with the Mafia:

G1: 6: The Pope is angry.

F1: He got angry. Usually he is the good pastor, this time he seemed particular, uh, . . . an angry person. We always saw him as a priest. A priest does not yell and does not get involved in politics. Whereas the Pope has now behaved like a real head of state, someone who expresses his opinion, although he is a priest . . . the Pope.

The political action of the Church was thus alive in the viewers' thematizations, emerging clearly in the household discussions. The Pope's trip to Sicily took on political importance as his presence there was connected to recent occurrences such as the assassination of the two judges Giovanni Falcone and Paolo Borsellino (a few months before the present study), men who symbolized the fight against the Mafia. All these factors served to place the Pope at the center of events and to reinforce his figure as a brave man, one who is angered and determined, just as he is very direct in relating to young people and therefore a symbol of the moral rebirth of Italians.

The Pope's political image becomes even clearer when juxtaposed, as happened in many thematizations, to a church which for years was connected to a corrupt political regime, made up of corrupt mafia priests:

> F9: 113: The priests who were in Sicily did nothing against the Mafia, in fact they agreed with the Mafia! During Paul VI there was the Aldo Moro affair.
> Oc9 (Daughter-in-law): And Andreotti.
> F9: Call that man a saint . . . Saint Julius the Hunchback. No, I never liked that Pope. The Russians were hitting and he said nothing, he said whatever he pleased.

By contrast, the present Pope, who goes around doing his duty, turns out to be the only real politician, just as the public investigator Antonio Di Pietro stood out under the super-theme of 'political corruption' as the only serious person around:

> F1: 9: The Pope in Sicily is the most important news . . . not so much the trip, but the position he has taken with regard to the Mafia, what he said, the message he sent. I would say that the connection of the Pope and the Mafia is something that makes you think. It is a direct accusation, he has taken his position on the battlefield . . . he is a serious politician.

The super-theme of the Church, above all, serves to reemphasize how difficult the political situation in Italy was and is. It is for two figures from outside the political system to act as agents of purification, the Pope and Di Pietro, representing the viewer's hope for justice. Moreover, it should be noted that the super-theme was constructed by associating bits and pieces of information, perception, and knowledge, all of which have come from different sources and at very different times. While being related to facts and examples that are rather distant in both geographical and historical terms, the super-theme of the Church is also colored by evaluations which normally pertain to other spheres of social conduct. As such, it suggests how viewers may travel, not just between several levels of interpretation, but also between several thematic perspectives on social reality.

Conclusion

While television news creates a global universe of images, values, myths, and knowledge, it simultaneously accentuates the separation of the context of reception from that universe: each family is alone in front of the screen. Since dinner time in Italy, as in some other countries, coincides with the time of the main newscast, the family is the primary context of television news consumption – though not of all TV programming. This serves to highlight the distinction between 'us' and 'others,' between private and public spheres, generating, as we have seen, a widespread perception of the risks associated with what is shown on the screen, be it political, economic, foreign, or war news. Moreover, the perception of risk would appear to be related with the specific role of the family in the given social, national context. In Italy, the family is still the main cell of community life and, as such, can be seen to enter into conflict with the extraneous events on the screen (Casetti 1995). This suggests an increasingly complex interpretive route of news into the wider social context, mediated not only by the individual self but also by a familial self.

Responding to the opposition between external and internal factors, which may thus reinforce the identity of the family as a community in the face of the vast problematic world represented in the mass media, the family appears progressively to close in on itself and to erect barriers around itself. Furthermore, the peculiarities of each family group as an interpretive entity may prevail over all the problems and mishaps – the constant sense of danger which arises from the news as disseminated by television as well as other mass media. It is likely that larger communities develop from this first nucleus of consumption if still rooted in the experiences and personal relations of the family, its common cultural and symbolic perceptions, and tied to traditions which are shared and consolidated. Such groups, no longer built only around shared information and direct interaction, presumably exist in a relationship of opposition to the images of the world transmitted by the mass media.

We conclude that this is the key mechanism of how modern societies are redefining the relations between the universal and the particular, the global and the local. The idea of a global village is created not at the level of community identity, but as an accumulation of information and images, emotions and perceptions, which, though significant in producing affinities of attitude and behavior above and beyond national borders, cannot build a single symbolic identity (Tomlinson 1994). From the moment of television consumption, in an ever-widening circle of interactional situations, a contrast is created between the outside world, as represented on the television screen, and the viewing group as linked by ties of common interests, everyday relations, and personal experiences – real-life conditions which are clearly defined in terms of time (the moment of news consumption) and space (the shared dining room). Consequently, the world represented seems to become progressively something else, even if one may more or less negotiate it and share attitudes and behaviors. The global information one receives remains essentially something outside the viewer. And, it is this world which is perceived to be full of danger and threats to the very community which is busy consuming images of itself. Even the least dramatic news items can be seen as potentially dangerous. Unless communities retain, or find a new spatial and temporal identity as it confronts the world as represented, they risk living in isolation, frustration, and a loss of their sense of themselves. The dynamics between the global and the local are complex rather than linear, but may identify one of the common processes of interpreting the news in different countries, and thus may contribute to comparing and explaining the interpretation of events such as the conflicts in Bosnia and Israel or the fire in the Thai doll factory.

If news is indeed a cause of fear, why watch television? A virtual experience of the public sphere through television news remains essential if one is to be somehow active in it. Otherwise, one would not have the necessary information, nor be a part of that common universe of emotions which characterizes the daily activities of the members of today's vast global society, a universe established primarily through information from television and other media. The point of interconnection between the public and private spheres in this historical context of globalization may be a perception of the risks that the outside world can bring to the community of the family. The globalizing processes of mass communication (Sreberny-Mohammadi 1991) also contribute to the micro-communities of reception and interpretation which produce divergent views on the news and the world.

7

MEXICO

*Guillermo Orozco**

Mexican mediations

In Mexico of today, both the reception of television news and the making of news by the media, are fields of study with growing social importance. This is because of the popularity of TV news as a means for audiences to stay informed, and because of the mediation which both television companies and political institutions exercise in the dissemination of information and the construction of news (Alianza Cívica 1994; Molina 1989; Sánchez 1994). But, above all, television owes its current importance to the fact that the very process of viewing has been recognized by political parties, non-governmental organizations, as well as by researchers, as a battlefield in and of itself – an arena in which the television system, politicians, and members of the audience, all in different ways, contribute to the mediation, negotiation, and appropriation of messages. Along with other political and economic events that have put Mexico on the front pages of the international press (Orozco 1994c), the Chiapas conflict (see below pp. 128–9), which exploded on 1 January 1994, just a few months after the present study, has widened the interest of Mexicans in the media, especially given the controversial role played by TV news programs in covering this event.

The viewing process may be conceptualized as a dialectic in which viewers construct their particular strategies of reception within specific socio-cultural conditions and contexts and with reference to the concrete information televised (Orozco 1994a, 1995a). The dialectical characteristic of television viewing makes it all the more significant to explore comparatively the multiple interactions

* The author expresses his special thanks to his colleagues Salvador Martìnez, Sergio Inestrosa, and Luis Menéndez for their collaboration at different stages of the research process. For the interviews with Mexican households, the quotations are identified by respondent number only, not by page, because of the format of the transcripts. In addition, while fifteen interviews were conducted, three of these had to be left out of the analysis for practical reasons. The original sequence numbers were kept in the analysis of the other twelve interviews, which explains why the chapter refers also to Households 13–15.

involved, with the aim of arriving at a better understanding of the role which televised news plays in the daily life of different segments of the audience. Prior research in several countries (Ang 1985; Jensen 1986; Lull 1988b; Morley 1986), including Mexico (Cornejo 1994; Orozco 1988; Renero 1992), has amply demonstrated the fundamental role of the family as a mediating institution and interpretive community in between its members and the televised message. Further Mexican research has explored the role that individual viewers, especially mothers, have in defining other family members' viewing (Orozco 1995b).

This chapter shows how individual and family viewing have common characteristics, without necessarily being identical, because of factors such as the gender, age, interests, or super-themes of each family member. Super-themes generate interaction with the news by serving as catalysts and concentrating the audience's dominant interests. The specific super-themes explored in this study show themselves as categories with an important potential for explaining the way in which Mexican viewers take an interest in, prefer, discriminate, relate to, and appropriate particular items of news broadcast on television.

The main unit of analysis in the project was the household: for the Mexican study twelve households were examined. Besides the group interviews with families, additional individual interviews with family members were conducted. The households were selected according to criteria of 'comparative sufficiency.' Given the qualitative nature of the methodology, no attempt was made to produce statistically representative data. Rather, the object was to explore different habits of TV news reception in households that were differentiated according to criteria of socio-economic strata, educational levels, place of residence, and predominant cultural orientation. The families selected ranged from lower-middle to upper-middle class. Every family had at least two children, half of them more than two, up to six children. Of the twelve households, half resided in Mexico City, the other half in three Mexican states: Queretaro, Michoacan, and the State of Mexico. Family interviews were conducted on 11, 12, and 13 May 1993, and the individual interviews between 6 and 14 May 1993. The analysis below of the interviews stresses common aspects, with the aim of identifying a shared discourse regarding the reception of television news across different families, while differences between them, as well as variations among individual viewers, are pointed out when appropriate.

Violent peace and perennial resistance: Mexico before 1 January 1994

Mexican society has become increasingly stratified. Of the more than eighty million Mexicans, forty million are classified as poor, and 60 percent of the gross domestic product is in the hands of only 10 percent of the population. Following the last economic crisis of 22 December 1994, which abruptly devaluated the Mexican peso by more than 30 percent, more than two million workers lost their jobs. By the middle of 1997, figures showed up to ten million jobless around the country.

Together with the deterioration of the job market, Mexicans have experienced a political crisis too, as manifested in a deterioration of traditional institutions, particularly of the ruling party, PRI (the Institutional Revolutionary Party), an authoritarian and centralized corporativist structure in power without interruption for seventy years. Corruption and drug trafficking are two of the most acute problems in public life. Violence has manifested itself in the form of several political assassinations since 1994, peasant massacres, and, in general, a political unrest prevailing since then throughout the country. Mexicans may be witnessing the beginning of a collapse of the country's political structure, especially after July 1997 when, for the first time in history, the PRI lost its majority in Congress.

In this scenario marked by economic and political crisis, traditional Mexican culture is also in a process of transformation. At the time of this study, the effects of a neo-liberal model were being felt to the full, pushing to the fore values of individualism, competitiveness, and distrust of others. These values contrast with traditional ones of solidarity, love, enjoyment of life, and hospitality.

Historically, Mexico has not been a participatory society. As a result of its 'authoritarian' regime, the label commonly placed on the Mexican government, citizen participation was controlled and redirected by various government agencies, such as the National Workers Union (CTM). In political elections, the absenteeism of voters ran to 70 percent, and public debates about democracy were conducted mainly around elections, and then only by political parties.

The past administration of President Salinas (1988–94) propagated the belief that Mexico was entering the First World. The NAFTA trade agreement and various macro-economic figures helped the government to spread the image of a prosperous country, a partner of the USA and Canada. These ideas of prosperity circulated during the time of this study. However, the Chiapas conflict of January 1994 made evident the ancestral differences among Mexicans themselves, the structured lack of justice in the country, and the poverty and exploitation suffered by the majority of the population in spite of the macro-level financial indicators. In a nominally peaceful country, accepted as a member of the OECD at the end of 1994, the guerrilla war in the Chiapas province, a confrontation between the original 'Indian' inhabitants and the government over land and other rights, reminded Mexicans of the true conditions underneath the wishful future for the development of the country. The seriousness and profound implications of Chiapas for the self-image of Mexicans also opened up a new role for media, particularly for the press and for journalists. Many independent reporters risked their own lives by going to Chiapas to cover what was going on in that corner of the country. Chiapas thus became a turning point in press coverage, traditionally under the control of the Ministry of the Interior. In order to give a sense of what this change means in the Mexican context, the *Mexican Journal of Communication* (No. 2, 1995) published a report on censorship, violations, attacks, and assassinations of journalists during the Salinas six-year presidency. According to this report, forty-two journalists were killed.

A 'dictatorship' of four decades: Mexican TV

In order to understand the nature of television news reception in Mexico, one must situate it in the context of the national television system (see further Sánchez 1983; Sinclair 1986). In contrast to other Latin American countries such as Chile or Argentina, where several models have coexisted simultaneously, in Mexico the audience has been subjected to a 'dictatorship' of the Televisa consortium, an oligopoly which controls the majority of programming and has grown under the aegis of the Mexican state itself. Since the first TV transmissions in 1950, then, Televisa has been the main model of programming available to the Mexicans. This means that, today, the Mexican television audience can be said to have been molded as viewers *à la Televisa*.

In all these years of commercial broadcasting, different governments have attempted to compete with Televisa. During the 1970s and 1980s, the government was able to develop Imevision, a parallel television system, to ensure a more 'faithful,' positive construction of its public image and, particularly, a more appropriate focus for its newscasts (Bohmann 1989). However, the second system followed the same pattern and style as Televisa – light entertainment. With very few exceptions, Mexicans had no opportunity to watch other types of programming than that introduced, developed, and now growing under the model of commercial television and its networks (Orozco 1994b).

The model adopted and developed by Televisa is, to a great extent, similar to that of television in the US, but with one enormous difference: the only competitor – a highly relative term at that – has been the government itself. Unlike in the American context, there have been no competing commercial networks to stimulate Televisa and improve the quality of its programming, or to broaden the options available to the viewing audience (Sinclair 1990). This situation might change, however, as a consequence of the privatization of media which was initiated by the government during the second half of 1993, only a few weeks after this study was carried out. As a result of this policy, TV-Azteca, a second private enterprise, entered the Mexican TV scenario, and might alter it in the near future.

The history of Mexican television programming can be summed up as the simulated competition of alternatives. The crucial element has been not an innovative differentiation, but a reassurance of the government that its preferred self-image will be presented to the viewing audience, while the owners of Televisa have been assured of the maximum possible profits. While, during certain periods, there has been a noticeable tension between the programming criteria respectively of Televisa and Imevision, at other times there has been no difference whatsoever. Mexicans even joke that Televisa's anchorman – who is also the company's news director – is the true Minister of Communications in Mexico.

In 1993, as part of the Mexican government's policy of privatizing its cultural companies, it put its TV channels up for sale. However, again in contrast with deregulation in other Latin American countries, in Mexico the state did not lose control over the national television system. This has been thanks to top level agreements between current government officials and the owners of the old private companies (Televisa) as well as with the more recent (TV-Azteca). These agreements have also been made possible by the very accumulation of power by the ruling party (PRI) throughout its seven decades of uninterrupted government, and by the growing number of sweet deals offered first to the Televisa group and, more recently, to the emerging TV-Azteca group that bought the stations sold by the government at the beginning of 1994.

The fact of continued government control over commercial television was first made clear when, during the presidential elections on 21 August 1994, the signals of CNN and CBS were jammed so that during the preliminary vote count on election day itself they could not broadcast viewpoints other than those already agreed upon. Second, transmission of the same signals was prohibited during the Congressional elections of 6 July 1997. This violation of the rights of audiences in general, and of the pay-television audience in particular, demonstrated simultaneously both government control over private television – itself a proof of the abuse of power that is characteristic of dictatorships – and a lack of respect for the audience, a day-to-day trait of Mexican TV.

Other international television systems are not a major challenge to the model established by Televisa. Cable television equally belongs to this consortium, and only the coded Multivision is the property of another group (Crovi 1995). CNN is part of this other group's programming. Pay television, however, only reaches a small part of the audience, the upper-middle classes in the big cities, who can afford it. For instance, at the end of 1994, the number of subscribers to Multivision and Cablevision (the cable company of Televisa) was only around one million, which accounts for six million potential viewers in cabled households in a country of more than eighty million inhabitants.

Lots of news, little information

At the time of this research, a total of 182 hours of news a week were aired on Mexican channels with nationwide broadcasts. The two most important programs, and the ones watched by the households interviewed – Televisa's *24 Horas* (24 Hours) and Imevision's *Desde Mexico* (From Mexico) – broadcast 22 hours a week in total.

Admittedly, 182 hours of television constitutes a huge amount of news, offered to the Mexican audience. On the other hand, there will necessarily be a lot of repetition in the information televised, as verified by content analyses (Orozco and Viveros 1996). Several of the programs air more than once a day.

For example, *24 Horas* is broadcast at lunchtime and at night. Other news programs on the same Televisa network are broadcast up to five times during its 24 hours of continuous programming. The night-time newscasts are perhaps where the freshest news is found. After midnight and in the early morning, a combination of new and old news items can be seen. Paradoxically, there are no news programs during weekends, except on cable and pay television. Furthermore, several programs on different channels carry a number of stories which are presented as news, but which are more like features, stories that the networks use to fill all those hours of newscasts. It should be added that news commentaries are almost non-existent on Mexican television. The only two such programs are aired very late at night, one being sponsored by the National Polytechnic Institute, and with a signal that reaches only central Mexico around the capital.

A well-known study (Sánchez 1994) showed that the Mexican public prefers to stay informed through television. Fifty-six percent said that they preferred news on TV, compared to 25 percent who favored radio, and 16 percent who chose newspapers. Such figures, however, must as always be treated with caution. Although 56 percent prefer television as their source of news, they do not necessarily consider it the best medium of information. Rather, they may consider it the easiest way to have rapid and cheap access to information, as suggested by the analysis of household interviews below.

From medium to mediation

The two news programs which were included in the content analysis for the present study (Appendix A), and which served as points of departure for the household interviews – *24 Horas* and *Desde Mexico* – are long-standing broadcasts on their respective channels. They are produced in Mexico City, and give priority to national news over both local and international news. The name of one, "From Mexico," is indicative of an informational centralism in Mexico, consistent with the centralism prevalent in its political, economic, as well as cultural systems.

Whereas, for practical reasons, households interviews had to be conducted over several days, a summary of the night-time *24 Horas* on 11 May (Newsday) suggests the nature and focus of Mexican television news at the time. Somewhat unusually, the newscast included eleven foreign and only nine domestic news items. The time allotted to foreign news was 17 minutes, 51 seconds, with two items about the war in Bosnia accounting for a total of 5 minutes, 46 seconds, while domestic news summed to 15 minutes, 12 seconds. In this newscast, three thematic focuses could be identified for foreign news, as suggested by two items about each theme: Bosnia, the hunting of whales, and NAFTA.

The foreign news items were presented in the following order:

"The tragedy of the former Yugoslavia seems to have no end"

"An assassination in Sarajevo in 1914 was the motive that started World War I"

"Drug dealing and drug use in Russia"

"The Prime Minister of Israel maintained his government intact after the resignation of the Minister of the Interior"

"In Lebanon, deported Palestinians rejected a plan for repatriation"

"In Tokyo, the future of whales is being discussed"

"For more than a century, humans have been engaged in the destruction of whales"

"In Washington, the Democratic Majority leader said that NAFTA is good for the three countries"

"Washington Post editorial: Time to rescue NAFTA"

"Elections in Spain will take place on 6 June"

"In Caracas, the Supreme Court made no decision regarding Carlos Andres Perez."

Such television news may, on the one hand, foster civic participation. On the other hand, the family serves to mediate each member's reception of that news. The findings of this study suggest that there are at least five aspects of mediation enacted in the household, which may inform the individual family member's processing of the news with a view to some eventual civic activity:

- The preconceived notions of what a news item is, and what its uses may be;
- The motivation for the individual to seek out news;
- The knowledge or understanding which the viewer supposes may arise from the news;
- The personal or collective power considered to be a prerequisite for action;
- The nature of the action which could be undertaken to change the aspect of reality that has been made known through the news item.

We watch the news, not what's behind it

First of all, it is important to note that, strictly speaking, news is a television genre that is seldom watched as a household in Mexico. According to one respondent, "It's rare that we watch the news together. Each one of us watches it, but for us to watch it together is unusual" (Ba13). Respondents also freely stated that other genres such as sports or soap operas, tended to attract the whole family more easily than the news: "We do tend to watch soccer games or the soaps together" (F5).

The respondents gave little weight to family discussions as a reason for changing their individual opinions, at least about the news. After a family discussion of the news, one housewife said, "I still think the same thing I said at the beginning [of the discussion]" (F9). Yet, several respondents emphasized that news is basically useful for stimulating discussions, even if they stressed that this occurs mainly outside the home, with other people: "I watch the news because when you go out and people start to talk about something, well, you have to know what they're talking about, don't you?" (M3).

Only occasionally was the news referred to as something capable of fostering action or activity. For example, regarding an item about the killing of whales, one respondent commented, "I think that's why they ran it, so we would protest and those killings would stop . . . " (F9). Using the news as an aid for action was not a widespread notion. With reference to a news item which explained the existence of a seismic alarm in Mexico City, another viewer commented that it "is useful at least to temper or lessen a tragedy of incalculable proportions. That's why I think it's a good thing" (M8).

With regard to the function of news, several respondents conceived it basically as entertainment or amusement. The news may not only be broadcast as entertainment, but may also be received as such, as part of a flow with which viewers interact with pleasure:

> M1: Well, yes, [the news] is entertaining. At least it makes you forget your routine or your problems a while when you see national or international problems that are a little more real.

In other households, the very opposite view was expressed, that TV news is a means to situate oneself socially so as to not to be surprised by events:

> F6: I think it's a good idea to be up on the news. Otherwise what happened to the Germans could happen to us. They were caught up in a way that they never knew what was happening.

Still other respondents find that information is "mainly [a question of] general cultural level" (Bb2).

In terms of the defining characteristic of a news item, the spectrum of opinions was very broad. For some respondents, news is what is new, as in the case of a head of household who said with reference to an item on the decentralization of Pemex (Mexico's state oil monopoly): "I don't think that's news because we've been hearing that for a long time" (M5). For others, news is what is important, understood almost in tautological terms: "It's simply something that is happening and if it's happening it must be important" (F2). News "shows history in the making" (M10). Still others thought of news as looking at big events – for example, a housewife who said, "We all know that Pemex is one of the biggest and most basic industries in Mexico, so everything to do with it is noteworthy one way or another" (F5). Respondents also paid special attention to 'non-news' that might not deserve air time: "Why should I be interested in whether the President jogs or not in the morning, or whether he jogs at night . . . " (M15).

Both the respondents' comments and various observations by the interviewers suggest that very few families will watch a whole news program. One head of household said, "We don't pay attention to 100 percent of the news. Some very particular items that we are interested in do hold our interest" (M5). It also comes out that many family members may only listen, but not watch the news:

> M15: For example, I listen to half the morning news and I watch the other half. You see? That way you don't lose touch and, since the news is presented by formulas...that way you don't waste your time watching the set.

In summary, the preconceived notions of what a news item is, and what its uses may be, include neither interaction or mediation in the family, nor mobilization of the viewers as citizens.

Between pleasure and duty

The families interviewed moved between two motivational poles *vis-à-vis* the news: watching for enjoyment or as a duty. The following commentaries exemplify these attitudes:

> F8: I tell her [the speaker's daughter], don't get mad. I don't know if it's the environment or the general state of things, but they're not interested in anything that's not right under their noses. If they don't read, at least they can listen to find out what's going on around them.

> M11: To be truthful, the news I like is the sports. That's when I say, "Now I'm going to hear something enjoyable."

> F1: I saw that thing about the whales and the wars and, it's not that I'm a sensationalist or anything, but it really had a big impact on me. And I remember it, and then, like I told you, I can't really do anything about it. So, I'd rather not watch.

This tension is even more clearly articulated between the younger members of the families and the adults. The young said that they either do not watch the news, or watch only the stories they like, while the adults, to a certain extent, appeared to feel duty-bound to watch it. A young man commented, "I hardly ever watch the news." He added, referring to his friends, "The truth is that not many watch the news. Most just listen to records and things like that" (Ba1). Conversely, an adult, head of the household, said about watching the news, "Yes, it's a professional interest...sometimes, I don't have time to read the papers and so I watch the news. I have to see the news, see it or read it" (M10). And the mother in the household, concerned about the question, commented:

> F10: There's an enormous vacuum among young people: nothing

surprises them anymore . . .it's the same to them if Mexico wins a game
or the bishop is murdered. It's all so ordinary and normal that there's
no discrimination [between news items], no selection, no surprise.

Another source of tension is gender differences: adult women did not refer
to or justify a need to keep informed. A housewife said, "To tell you the truth,
very few news items get talked about among women. They're not interested in
hearing them, unless they're really sensationalist" (F2). On the other hand,
there were those who would watch the news because it is easier than reading
the newspaper, or because they do not have the time to read a paper. "It's easier
to find out what's going on through a news program than by having to read the
paper," said another housewife (F15).

Some respondents watch the news to be aware of what is happening to their
relatives. A young woman whose brother lives in California (USA), said:

> Ga9: 'Cause, like I say, what if one of my relatives takes a trip . . . I pay
> more attention [to the news] because what if the situation stays bad or
> if it settles down [in reference to the recent Los Angeles earthquake]?

Others stated that they do not watch the news because there is more bad news
than good news. A young women, completely sure of herself, said that she
hardly watched television at all, because of "all the news they show, 90 percent
is bad news and only 1 percent good news." And, she added, it should not be
like that: "They should at least make it 50–50" (Ga4).

An entirely different line of reasoning was taken by those who may decide to
watch a particular news program because their television set gets better reception
of that channel. This was the case with a woman who said, "We watch Channels 2
and 5 . . . we prefer 13, but the thing is, we don't know if we have a problem with
how the antenna is aimed or what, but we don't get Channel 13" (F10).

In summary, the interviews documented a clear generational difference, a
moderate gender difference, and almost no difference relating to socio-economic
status, in these viewers' formulation of motives for keeping informed. Other
contributing motives for watching the news were easily understandable images,
the type of information broadcast, and the expectation that particular news items
would be reported. In this respect, the mediation enacted in the family appears to
be related to the generational difference: older family members felt that they
should urge younger members to watch and discuss the news.

I see it, but I don't believe it, or I don't understand it

Viewers envision two main obstacles to achieving the knowledge that might be
needed to take action. The first arises from understanding fully what is going
on, and not merely knowing what happened. Two brothers had the following
exchange about the war in the Balkans:

Bb6: Because I don't really know what they're fighting about, because until now, I don't know what the fight is about.

Bc6: Yes, because sometimes they're reading the news and they say such-and-such a country intervened, but they don't say why.

The second obstacle to potential uses of news is that viewers may not really believe what is being reported. Expressions of skepticism were numerous:

M11: In this country the news is filtered first and then they pretend they're not pretending.

M13: They just report what the government wants and what other countries want them to.

F1: All the information nationwide is paid for by the government.

M8: The communications media follow the politicians' game and play up to them.

Besides the ideological manipulation which was perceived clearly by viewers, there was a certain perception that the form of experience promoted by the news is vicarious and that, therefore, something more is needed to really know what is happening. This situation of broadly distrusting the news seems to be a major obstacle to viewers' taking any kind of outward action. One head of household emphatically stated:

M3: For you to be able to form a political judgment, you need to live through the moment and perhaps be close to where the event is taking place . . . that's what you see [on the news], as opposed to what you might actually be able to experience yourself.

And a young girl said:

Gb6: It would be good if it were repetitive and with each news item they repeated why the problem arose.

Taken together, the statements in families of lower socio-economic status suggest a slightly more accentuated criticism of the media for their dearth of information and for the lack of other comments that may be needed to understand the news. In accordance with this criticism, members of these families would also accept more easily the help of other members in understanding what is happening. Correspondingly, members of families with a higher status could be seen to emphasize slightly their disbelief of what they see on the news. Apart from making the denunciation, however, they did not mention what they or the family would have to do to overcome this condition.

Everyone else is so large, and we are so small

Faced with news items that might call for action, the families interviewed expressed a general feeling that nothing could be done. One respondent emphatically said, "You can't solve anything . . . I think the information is only there [for you] to stay informed" (M1).

This feeling of impotence is apparently due to the fact that others are perceived as stronger. The man just quoted also said:

> M1: The powerful countries lead the pack. If you look at them side-ways, they look back and say, "What about it?," because you look very small to them.

Two agents appear to stand out as the strongest of the strong. One is the United States:

> M1: Countries with low[-level] economies and technology, well, unfortunately, they really can't do anything. We face that here. Like, if Clinton yells loud at [Mexican President] Salinas, Salinas quiets down.

The other agent that was perceived as strong was the Mexican government. In this respect, a girl remarked with certainty that "Everything is politics" (Ga2). In the same vein, her mother said, "I think to myself that it's all totally controlled. They don't give you any alternative . . . " (F2).

Given these conditions, the only possible sphere of action is the domestic sphere of everyday life, basically its economic aspect:

> F5: [We] very seldom [do anything about a news item], but I think I remember one that talked about a devaluation [of the Mexican peso] and, to tell you the truth, we did do what they call panic buying.

An analysis across all the interviews showed that, on this point, there were no differences between families. The feeling of a collective helplessness seems to be overwhelming. Perhaps for this reason, no mention was made of family efforts to change the situation.

Action should be taken, but I'm not the one to take it

Once having recognized that the above mentioned obstacles to engaging the news (understanding and confidence) could be overcome, and having accepted at least the possibility of action, nevertheless respondents would immediately elude personal action. One girl said, "Mexicans look for lots of pretexts . . . [We'll] say, 'Well, you see, I can't because I'm working,' or something like that" (Gc6). For this reason, the responsibility for acting is deposited with 'others':

F11: We have that problem [traffic] in Mexico City. As long as nobody calms those people down [public transport drivers], we're going to continue to have traffic problems.

For this aspect of reception, as for some others, no significant differences could be noted between the households analyzed, nor did any of them make reference to a mediation within the family of this sort of concrete news use.

Having detailed the elements of possible family mediation (p. 132), we now turn to some of the related super-themes. These themes could be seen to orient not only news reception; they also give more substance to the suggestion emerging from the respondents that they are not the ones to take action after watching international news on television.

Super-themes

War there, peace here

The international item which evidently caught the viewers attention was the war in the Balkans. The feeling expressed about it, was one of great relief because the war was happening somewhere else, far away, and because Mexico is a country at peace. With such relief, one man noted that "It's a good thing I'm in Mexico, where there's no war" (M1). And a housewife said, "We are a country which fortunately has never, or at least in the last few generations, has not gone through a war like that" (F5).

Perhaps the fact that Mexico – until the period of this study – had not suffered a war in its territory since the Mexican revolution of 1910, makes war seem far off, even unreal for the respondents. It could even be said that, in Mexico up until 1994, when the Zapatista movement manifested itself in the Chiapas conflict, war was seen as something which only happened on TV. That is why the following comment by a young girl is not so odd:

Gb6: I have my doubts about whether it was a war or they were rehearsing. But rehearsing what? Since you could see that the boy was launching them [the grenades].

The respondents certainly recognized the cruelty, violence, and madness unleashed by war, but they preferred not to talk about it. That is why comments such as, "It really is terrible to see how they kill people" (M5), could coexist with other comments like, "If you have a family gathering, well, you don't really want to ruin it talking about wars" (Gc6). In the final analysis, the respondents did not perceive the war as their business, but as someone else's. "Here we almost don't notice that [war], because we're busy with our affairs" (M5). In other words, the popular sentiment may have been that war does not directly involve Mexicans. This sentiment, however, may likely have changed following the Chiapas conflict, even if it remains an open question whether the attitude to (not) taking action has been modified or not.

Our policy is non-intervention

As a principle of the international policy of the Mexican state since the last century, non-interventionism has permeated deeply into national consciousness. The condemnation of intervention may be understood almost as an obligation for practically every Mexican. One man assured us that the United States pries into all other countries because it is the most powerful country in the world, and because "it's got interests to defend there that it can't afford to lose" (M1). Along the same line, a girl found that the United States "has always been a busybody butting into everyone else's business" (Ga9).

However, some of those interviewed did doubt whether this national 'principle' was really a principle, or if it might be more a matter of convenience:

> Ga2: The thing is that Mexico doesn't intervene . . . with the policy of non-intervention. But it doesn't intervene when it's not in its interests. It does intervene when as a Third World country someone insults it or tries to belittle it. But in a situation in which it could have an opinion [the war in Bosnia], it doesn't express one because supposedly it has a non-interventionist policy.

Thus, the principle of non-intervention can be seen to operate more as a smoke screen which capitalizes on international problems by translating them in such a way as to politically suit the Mexican government. The principle may, then, come to imply that the government always does the right thing.

How bad and cruel others are

Besides Bosnia, the remainder of the international news items which captured the attention of respondents had a common denominator that could be summed up as cruelty, or unjustified evil-doing. Items about the killing of whales, the death penalty carried out on a Mexican in the United States, and the kidnapping of some children in France were all the cause of disapproving comments. Identification with the victim was the natural main reaction:

> F9: Well, you know, those killings [of the whales] aren't right . . . And by the Japanese, who are so smart!

> Ga2: What I noticed was the kidnapper who got into a kindergarten. That seems awfully cruel, don't you think? With such little kids.

Only one person wondered whether we, the viewers, are not as cruel as them, the characters in the news: "Look at the thing about the [great sea] tortoises. It's banned [killing them in Mexico] too, but people go and . . . " (M9). Further, the identification of Mexicans with 'victims' may resonate with a deeper feeling that they harbor of being victims themselves – for example, *vis-à-vis* their northern neighbors, the citizens of the United States (Paz 1974).

Hope and Utopia

Some optimistic thoughts also were triggered by television news and expressed by the respondents. The great national hope seems to be the North American Free Trade Agreement (NAFTA); the Mexican government has gambled the country's future development on this instrument of economic policy. That news item was, indeed, one of the first to catch the eye of the respondents. As one man said confidently, "A fair treaty could fill us with hope" (M11).

The other main hope expressed in the interviews was an end to corruption and drug trafficking. This is another heartfelt desire of Mexicans, since the two ills are widely considered to be firmly entrenched in the country. One woman, discouraged, said that seeing the enormous corruption in the unions and their complicity with the authorities made her horrified (F1). Another woman, slightly hopeful, stated, "They caught some trucks [full of drugs] and they say that now they are finally going to put an end to all this drug business" (F9). Similarly hopeful, a man pointed out that it was good news to know that an honest man had been appointed as Attorney General (M11).

One additional hope expressed by the Mexican respondents was that the ills besetting the capital be eliminated. The news about the extraordinary trials and tribulations of inhabitants of Mexico City – traffic congestion, itinerant sales-people, and pollution – was widely commented upon:

> Gb6: I think the decentralization of Pemex [Mexico's state oil monopoly] is important because of pollution.

> Ga3: I was pleased that the pollution levels were low.

> M11: They've given them [itinerant sales people] a plaza for themselves, fortunately, because in a city this size, regardless of unemployment, they're a problem.

It should be noted, on the other hand, that there is also a feeling among viewers that, because of the predominant centralism, the Federal District, Mexico's capital, gets priority on the national news. A person who lives outside Mexico City indignantly said, "It seems like nothing happens outside the Federal District, unless there's a flood or a murder" (F10). Another respondent, more measured, commented that, "There is news that, like on *24 Horas*, is centered on what happens in the Federal District" (M3).

There's no place like Mexico

Without a doubt, Mexicans vacillate between chauvinism and *malinchismo* (an expression referring to a fondness for everything foreign, and a corresponding disdain for everything Mexican), but when they describe the situation in the country, a feeling of 'there's no place like Mexico' prevails. Even if it was to criticize vulgar patriotism or Mexico's supposed perfection, the respondents agreed on the uniqueness of their part of the world:

> F3: I've seen other news that really has a big impact, like seeing how people live in those countries, you know, and you say, "I've got it great!" I mean, you tend to compare your country with the others and you realize that we are really a free country and that makes you happy.

> M3: Mexican politicians are always shouting that we're the best country, the best city . . . the way they talk, we're practically the world's perfect country . . . and the media seem to play their game.

> M1: Well, the truth is that we thank God we have a country like ours, despite the problems we have, the problems we confront every day, because the truth is we have it good. Like they say, "There's no place like Mexico."

Conclusion

The analysis has suggested a model of the world in which Mexican viewers see themselves as small, ill-informed, far away from events broadcast by television news, and impotent to take action on these events. Although recognizing that action should be taken, the Mexican respondents expressed a feeling that they are not the ones to do so, ridding themselves of any responsibility by arguing that, as Mexicans, they follow the national policy of non-intervention, as traditionally invoked by Mexican governments. When looking at a particular event, for example, the war in the Balkans, they saw it as something happening in a different part of the world and, therefore, those whose interests are at risk in that war are the ones to intervene. This line of reasoning, however, may also entail a feeling of being the victim of those other bad agents – whoever they may be – even if, not least, NAFTA represents a hopeful future, and even though there is no place like this small remote country known as Mexico. (The model of the world, according to the Mexican respondents, is summed up in Chapter 9.)

Moreover, a synthesis of each family's strategies of reception allows us to discern differences between families according to their social status. Families of a higher social standing tended to give priority to international news, and to note its seriousness. Families of a lower social status, in contrast, said that they pay less attention to international news and, when they do give it attention, will give priority to its human side or sensationalism. Further, the families of higher social status were clearly and harshly critical of national news, whereas the families of a lower status, while critical, were more accepting – there were even those who confessed that they were only interested in the national type of newscast. This can be taken as an indication that among the lower-middle classes, the news may be appropriated in more emotional categories than among the upper-middle and upper classes. That is partially explained by the fact that these latter families have a higher educational level as well as a broader cultural background, which allows them to relate to news items in more logical, rational terms. Regarding gender, it was interesting to find a case of a family in which the father was 'in charge' of keeping up with international news, and the mother with national news.

Some respondents mentioned that, for local news, they resort to other media, and that they would not expect a nationwide program to broadcast news from every local area. One of the news programs which was not considered in this study does have a section about what is happening outside Mexico City in which it attempts to present at least one item about each region, thereby covering the demands of local audiences. Another important consideration was articulated with regard to the ongoing debate about excess information about the capital city. While this may seem natural to those who live there, since it is the center of the country, those who live outside the capital found that the national news should dedicate more air time to the rest of the country.

In addition to the interrelated set of super-themes, certain other themes were found to organize the reception of television news by the Mexican respondents. First, when viewers felt that their country might have the possibility of winning a contest – the world soccer cup or the Miss Universe contest – their interest in following these particular items seemed to increase. One young man said, "If Miss Mexico wins [the Miss Universe crown], then it's important to watch [the pageant]" (Ba6). Second, the religious feelings of Mexicans were hinted at in expressions such as, "The news about the Pope going to Spain is the only positive one they had on the whole program, wasn't it?" (F4).

The fear stemming from each change of presidential administration was also expressed clearly among these viewers. Even though a change of administration was not yet on the political agenda during the period studied, what is in Mexico called 'futurism' – speculation about who the presidential candidate for the ruling party will be – had already begun. As one of the interviewees said, "Each administration has its own style" (M11). Indeed, each administration differentiates itself by the specific measures taken within its six-year term. The former administration (1988–94) put special emphasis on prosecuting tax evaders, and their arrests were widely publicized in all media. In that context, one woman said, "Then there's the business with Lupita D'Alessio [a popular singing star] who didn't pay her taxes. They arrested her and she paid up. She got out with the help of Julio Alemán [the leader of the writers' union]" (F9).

Probably, if the period studied had been longer, evidence to strengthen these and other themes as actual super-themes might have been found. It is also likely that, following the Chiapas conflict, some viewers' perceptions of news coverage both on television and in other media, and of the viewers' link to news items, will have changed.

What certainly has changed since 1994 is a general feeling in Mexican society about participation in public life. This has manifested itself in the increase of non-governmental organizations in the country; the emergence of democratic citizens' institutions; the development of other, both local and national movements around the country; the increasing debate in the media about what is troubling Mexico; and citizens' active participation in elections, referenda, and opinion polls about specific social issues. Mexican society has been shaken up by the political events since January 1994. The hope of many Mexicans is that the many changes may prefigure a better country – and better television.

8

THE UNITED STATES

David L. Swanson, Ann N. Crigler, Michael Gurevitch,
*and W. Russell Neuman** *

American political culture

American political culture is not known for its internationalist bent. Perhaps in part because of their relative geographic isolation, Americans tend to pay less attention to international news, know less about international affairs, and express more reluctance to support international aid and peacekeeping efforts than the mass publics of most other industrialized countries (Kohut and Toth 1994; Schlesinger 1995). Nevertheless, it would be incorrect to label Americans as isolationist: they see their country as playing a leadership role in international politics and pay close attention to issues of international trade (Times Mirror Center 1994).

The remarkable and increasing diversity of American society makes efforts to describe a single 'American political culture' doubtful. Still, traditional American political values emphasizing self-reliance, individualism, active participation in civic life, and equal opportunity continue to figure prominently in much elite and popular political discourse (Almond and Verba 1963). Correspondingly, American institutions and traditions tend to rely more on the private than the public sector, and the myths and legends of the public sphere tend to celebrate the values of capitalism and private enterprise (McClosky and Zaller 1984). Electoral politics, dominated by a centrist, two-party system, tends to be stable, moderate, and less ideologically polarized than most multi-party democracies.

* The authors wish to express their gratitude to graduate students and colleagues at the University of Southern California, the University of Maryland, Tufts University, the University of Illinois at Urbana-Champaign, Purdue University, and Indiana University at South Bend who conducted individual and household interviews for this project. In addition, Nicole A. Fink of the University of Southern California and Anandam P. Kavoori of the University of Georgia provided important assistance in some aspects of data analysis and the project's theoretical conceptualization, respectively. Portions of this chapter are based on papers presented by the authors at the annual meeting of the American Political Science Association, 1–4 September 1994, New York City.

144

Although at the time of this study there was an evident public mood of cynicism and political conservatism in the US as in a number of other countries, this mood is probably most accurately characterized as a cyclical swing in public opinion rather than a sea change in the American ethos (Stimson 1991). Many of these elements become evident from the super-themes which emerged from the analysis of public discourse on Newsday.

The *News of the World* project, in attempting to understand the role of television news as a political resource for information and awareness, a potential vehicle to support citizens' participation in political culture and the public sphere, focused specifically on the process by which viewers understand and interpret television news stories. Thus, the nature of our research leads us away from classic themes in US political communication research such as media dependence, agenda-setting, powerful communications effects, and, more recently, hegemony. By focusing on the tensions between the reportorial discourse of the television journalist and the rich, diverse, and personally-grounded interpretations of the news audience, we are drawn to a constructionist perspective which emphasizes an active, interpretive, dynamic interchange between public opinion and the world of television news. We find that although television journalists commonly adopt a formalized and routinized political-conflict news frame emphasizing what might be termed a 'policy horserace' between the American President and Congress, most viewers virtually ignore that frame and interpret news in more personally relevant terms.

After reviewing the form and organization of national television newscasts in the US and describing the methods by which our data were collected, we analyze the news texts which our respondents saw and their context of viewing. With the structural, textual, and contextual elements of our subject thus defined, we move to the focus of our interest – the way in which viewers actively construct meaning in their interpretation of the political world around them. In the analysis that follows, we concentrate on how super-themes are employed in the interpretive process, how they relate to manifest content and themes in news stories, and how they arise from the world of everyday experience.

National television news in the United States

The broad contours of the US television system are fairly well known and cannot be explained in detail here (see Head, Sterling, and Schofield 1994; Webster and Phalen 1997). Briefly, there are about 1,200 television broadcasting stations in the US. The majority of these stations are affiliated with the major commercial broadcasting networks (principally, ABC, CBS, NBC; to a lesser extent, Fox and newly evolving networks associated with the Time Warner and Viacom media empires). There are also over 300 non-commercial, publicly supported stations affiliated with PBS, the Public Broadcasting System (Nielsen Media Research 1993). Each station broadcasts to its local area a mixture of programs which it receives from its network, programs which it produces independently such as, for the commercial stations, local news programs, and typically some programs purchased from syndication services. Local news (usually several hours of programming broadcast around the dinner hour and a late-evening half-hour) constitutes the great majority of the locally produced programming on most of these stations, and it is a source of significant revenue for them.

The penetration of television in US households is virtually universal, and a wide array of programming services is available nearly everywhere. As of 1991, US households received twelve television broadcast stations on average. In addition, roughly 60 percent of US households subscribe to a cable television service from which they are able to receive an average of thirty-five different channels, including usually specialized news channels such as CNN and public affairs programming such as C-SPAN (Nielsen Media Research 1992).

The major networks' (ABC, CBS, NBC) national newscasts are thirty-minute programs broadcast at 6:00 or 7:00 pm, and viewed in about 28 percent of US homes on an average week night (*Electronic Media* 1995b). The three newscasts are quite similar, with studio-based anchors and correspondent story packages. The programs consist of about twenty minutes of news divided into an average of ten different stories (Straubhaar et al. 1992). The remaining time is distributed between a minute or so of anchor lead-ins and previews of upcoming stories, and six to seven minutes of advertisements presented during three to four commercial breaks throughout the program.

In addition to the half-hour early evening news programs offered by the major commercial networks, hour-long evening national news programs are offered by CNN (*Prime News*), which is available through cable services nationwide, and by the Public Broadcasting System (at the time of this study, *The MacNeil-Lehrer Report*). However, the size of the audiences for these longer programs is very small when compared to the audiences for the major networks' national newscasts. For example, CNN's 1994 average rating during prime time, when its main newscast is offered, was 1 percent of households (*Electronic Media* 1995a). Network television news is big business, with the three largest networks (ABC, CBS, NBC) together budgeting about a billion dollars a year to maintain their news staffs and infrastructures including news bureaus in major capitals around the world. In recent years, however, financial and competitive pressures have been forcing even these largest networks to close some domestic and overseas bureaus and reduce staff (Bogart 1995).

Americans continue to read newspapers and news magazines regularly, but increasingly large pluralities, especially among younger Americans, say they rely primarily on television as their main source of news. Nonetheless, the percentage of people who will read a newspaper on an average day is about twice the number watching a network newscast. There continues to be some methodological controversy over the accuracy of studies of reliance on television versus print news. This debate is perhaps an unfortunate distraction, because most Americans have considerable and regular exposure to both media (Bogart 1989).

Methodology

In the United States, researchers' interest in television news as a provider of political information dates back more than three decades to the ascendancy of television as Americans' self-reported main source, and most trusted source, of news (Griffin 1992: 122; Nimmo and Combs 1990: 25). The dominant approach to studying the subject has endeavored to chart the flow of information about political actors and events through newscasts to viewers. Attention has focused on the quality of the information offered to viewers – that is, whether the truncated formats and entertainment values of television, especially in comparison to print journalism, serve democracy's need for well-informed citizens – and also on the extent to which viewers understand and remember the information offered in newscasts. Generally, this line of work has led to pessimistic assessments of citizens' political knowledge, often linked at least in part to attributes of television news (e.g. Bennett 1988, 1992; DeWerth-Pallmeyer 1997; Neuman 1986; Patterson and McClure 1976; Robinson and Levy 1986).

Somewhat more recently, numbers of researchers turned their attention to the social and psychological processes that come into play in viewers' reception of news. Cognitive psychology has offered one important way of understanding these processes. From early agenda-setting studies of newspapers and television news to more recent research on cognitive schemata in political perception, cognitively oriented studies of news viewers' information processing have produced generally more optimistic judgments of how much information audiences may find in news, and have shown that such learning reflects both the abilities and motivations viewers bring to the news and particular attributes of news stories themselves (e.g. Graber 1984; Iyengar 1991; Iyengar and Kinder 1987; Kraus and Perloff 1986; Popkin 1991; Shaw and McCombs 1977).

Most recently, reception analysis, as reviewed in Chapter 1, has been used to explore more deeply and on its own terms the way in which the meaning of news stories is constructed in situated transactions between audience members and news texts. This view of meaning is compatible with cognitive approaches to studying news audiences, but offers also something of the more textured conception of interpretation found in critical media work. We attempt to capitalize as well on the ability of reception studies to bring media texts into the analysis, which continues to be a difficulty for cognitively oriented studies of information processing, and to do so in a way that recognizes the polysemic or multivocal qualities of news stories that typically are ignored or are acknowledged only with difficulty in the information-focused studies of learning from news. Thus, our conceptual perspective attempts to integrate views from several different approaches to studying news and its audiences.

Reception analysis, then, focuses on the relationship between discourses in particular media texts and discourses audience members produce describing their interpretations and experience of those texts. One preferred method for eliciting audience discourse is the intensive, loosely structured interview, as employed in this study on Newsday, 11 May 1993. Prior to this day, interviewers recruited a selection of households where members were willing to be interviewed. We sought a diverse selection of households along such dimensions as age, socio-economic status, race and ethnicity, and geographic location. The number of households to be interviewed was set at sixteen, which was judged to be a manageable set of interviews to be conducted simultaneously given available resources, yet large enough to represent a range of interpretive strategies and decoding practices. (The small number of households clearly does not permit us to make claims about how the interpretive practices we found are distributed through the population of network news viewers.) Six interviews were conducted in the midwest, three in the Los Angeles area, three in the Boston area, and four interviews were conducted in Maryland communities near to Washington DC. With the exception of a woman who was separated from her husband and living with her daughters, all interviews were conducted with traditional households consisting of a married couple, most of whom had children. Both husband and wife took part in most interviews; older children were present and took part in some interviews; a family friend took part in one interview. Ages of those interviewed ranged from fourteen to seventy-three. A variety of blue-collar and white-collar occupations were represented. Persons taking part included African-Americans, Mexican-Americans, other Latin Americans, and native Americans, as well as white Americans.

Of the sixteen interviews that were conducted, three were dropped from the analysis that follows. Two interviews were dropped because they were conducted on 12 May due to logistical problems on the 11th, so the newscasts to which they refer are not included in the corpus of texts from the 11th. For convenience, the one household that chose to watch *CNN Prime News* was dropped from the analysis. The remaining thirteen households chose to view either the *CBS Evening News* or *NBC Nightly News*. However, to gauge the television news context that immediately preceded 11 May, the national news programs of Newsweek that were recorded, transcribed, and analyzed (Appendix A) were *ABC World News Tonight*, *CBS Evening News*, *CNN Prime News*, as well as *NBC Nightly News*.

The news texts

The news agenda

The television news agenda for the week preceding 11 May is shown in Table 8.1, which lists the lead and second stories on each network's newscasts for the period 5–10 May. With NBC airing no newscast on Sunday, 9 May, there were seventeen network newscasts during this period. Events in Bosnia were the lead story on fourteen newscasts; two lead stories focused on proposals offered by President Clinton concerning the economy and new regulations to govern the raising and spending of private money in electoral campaigns, respectively; the final lead story concerned the controversy about whether to lift the ban on gays serving in the military. On a daily basis, Bosnia was the lead story on all three networks on two days and the lead story on two of the networks for the other four days. Bosnia thus dominated the news agenda immediately prior to 11 May. The remainder of the news agenda was fragmented across multiple topics with none receiving repeated emphasis to distinguish it as more important than others.

The network news agenda on 11 May, the day our household interviews were conducted, is shown in Table 8.2. Only three stories were covered by all three networks on the 11th: Bosnia; the policy issue of gays serving in the US military; and reform of the health care system. The latter two stories were featured in the first segment of all three newscasts (that is, the stories appeared in the initial six- to eight-minute portion of the newscast that preceded the first commercial break). Bosnia was the lead story on one newscast (ABC) and was given special emphasis on the other two newscasts. CBS devoted a three-minute story to Bosnia comprising all of the newscast's third segment; NBC made Bosnia the longest hard news story of the day and gave it all but twenty seconds of the newscast's second segment. Given the strong emphasis in both story position and amount of time allotted to story that all the networks gave the three stories, it was determined that the content analysis would concentrate on

Table 8.1 Network news lead stories, 5–10 May 1993

Day	Story	ABC	CBS	NBC
Wednesday, 5 May	1	Bosnia	Bosnia	Bosnia
	2	Health care	Hate crimes	Colon cancer discovery
Thursday, 6 May	1	Bosnia	Bosnia	Bosnia
	2	Radiation overdoses	Post Office shootings	Health care
Friday, 7 May	1	Bosnia	Clinton reforms, popularity	Bosnia
	2	Technology & unemployment	Bosnia	Post Office shootings
Saturday, 8 May	1	Bosnia	Bosnia	Clinton's problems
	2	Bush assassination plot	Bush assassination plot	Bosnia
Sunday, 9 May	1	Bosnia	Bosnia	No newscast
	2	Clinton's economic plan	Storms in Texas, Oklahoma	No newscast
Monday, 10 May	1	Bosnia	Bosnia	Gays in the military
	2	Bush assassination plot	Clinton's economic plan	Clinton's economic plan

these stories and that analysis of audience discourses would focus primarily on what viewers had to say about them.

Table 8.2 Network news story line-up, 11 May 1993

	ABC World News Tonight			CBS Evening News			NBC Nightly News	
Pos.	*Story*	*Time*	*Pos.*	*Story*	*Time*	*Pos.*	*Story*	*Time*
1	Bosnia	5:50	1	Gays in the military	3:10	1	Gays in the military	2:50
	Commercials	1:00	2	Health care reform	2:10	2	Health care reform	2:00
2	Gays in the military	2:40	3	Role of Perot after election	2:50	3	Hospitals cost-shifting	2:10
3	Health care reform	1:50		Commercials	1:00		Commercials	1:00
4	Smoking and AIDS study	0:20	4	Autopsy on David Koresh	0:20	4	Bosnia	4:30
5	Fire at Bangkok toy factory	0:20	5	LA riot liquor stores	2:20		Commercials	1:30
6	Yeltsin fires senior officials	0:20		Commercials	1:40	5	Lead in drinking water	0:20
	Commercials	1:30	6	Bosnia	3:00	6	FDA approves female condom	1:40
7	Trade Center investigation	0:20		Commercials	1:40	7	Consent issue, Texas rape trial	0:30
8	Clinton to lift PATCO ban	1:40	7	Japan whaling controversy	2:10		Commercials	2:10
9	Senate passes 'motor voter'	0:20	8	Cyclist leaps Great Wall	0:30	8	Chattanooga cops not indicted	0:10
10	Stock market report	0:10		Commercials	2:00	9	Home schooling examined	3:30
11	ATM fraud in Hartford	0:20	9	Flight attendant weight	4:20	10	Chancellor commentary on Perot	1:40
	Commercials	2:00				11	Senate passes 'motor voter'	0:10
12	German health care system	4:20				12	Stock market report	0:10
	Commercials	1:40					Commercials	2:10
13	Drug trial held in KC school	2:10				13	Cyclist leaps Great Wall	1:00
	Total news story time	20:40		Total news story time	20:50		Total news story time	20:40
	Intro, previews, upcoming	0:50		Intro, previews, upcoming	1:10		Intro, previews, upcoming	0:30
	Total commercials time	6:10		Total commercials time	6:20		Total commercials time	6:50
	Total time of newscast	27:40		Total time of newscast	28:20		Total time of newscast	28:00

Textual themes and frames

The following analysis identifies the major themes and overall frame offered in each network's treatment of the three stories of interest on 11 May. In concentrating on themes and frames, we follow the lead of numerous previous studies that have demonstrated the importance of these story elements to the narrative content and coherence of news stories and as resources for interpretation by news viewers (e.g. Cohen and Wolfsfeld 1993; Gamson 1989, 1992).

Gays in the military

The three networks offered similar treatments invoking a President-versus-Congress conflict frame to report that day's testimony in the Senate Armed Services Committee's hearings on President Clinton's proposal to lift the ban on gays serving openly in the armed forces. The highlight was the testimony of retired US Army general and Desert Storm commander H. Norman Schwarzkopf. Each network's story included sound bites from: Schwarzkopf's testimony that lifting the ban would reduce combat effectiveness; Fred Peck, a Marine colonel who gained visibility as chief spokesperson for the allied forces in Somalia and had learned only two days earlier that one of his sons is homosexual, telling the committee he would fear for his son's safety in the military; Peck's son noting the contrast between many gays who are shunned by their families and his father expressing pride in him before the Senate Committee; present or former gay service members testifying about their family difficulties and pain; and, on ABC, a service member opposing the view that gay service should be regarded as a civil rights issue.

ABC framed the story as an episode of political conflict between President Clinton and Senate opponents of lifting the gay ban, led by Chairman Sam Nunn of the Senate Committee. Anchor Peter Jennings introduced the story as "resistance" to Clinton's view, and reporter Bill Greenwood concluded that the outcome of the testimony was that "it didn't change any minds. Most members still believe admitted homosexuals don't belong in the military." NBC also highlighted the political conflict, with Schwarzkopf dropping "the political equivalent of a smart bomb," "the President's plan already in big trouble," and a widening rift between the President and Senator Nunn. However, correspondent Lisa Myers judged that the Senate Committee is "headed toward allowing gays to serve in the military, but only if they stay in the closet." CBS broadened the frame, casting the story both as a political conflict in which Schwarzkopf's speaking out weakened Clinton's position and, in the words of reporter Bob Schieffer, as "a gut-wrenching illustration of America's deep division over a painful and complex social issue."

151

Bosnia

On all three networks, 'the Bosnia story' was, in fact, two stories packaged together. The first story revealed that President Clinton was considering sending US troops to Macedonia. The second story consisted of reports from the scene in the former Yugoslavia. Each network cast 'the Bosnia story' in a conflict frame, noting the possibility of an upcoming clash between the Executive and Legislative branches of the US government over whether US troops should be sent to the region.

Structurally, the possibility of US military involvement was used as the 'news peg' for the Bosnia story by all three networks. Each network framed the Bosnia story first as an intractable problem for the President with the possibility of deployment of US troops and second as a difficult-to-understand ethnic and religious civil war involving, on CBS, "genocide." ABC and NBC featured political difficulties and opposition to the President's announcement. NBC's Lisa Myers noted that questions about sending troops to Bosnia frustrated Clinton's effort to sell his economic plan during a trip to Illinois, and her package included a sound bite from Senator Joseph Biden expressing bitter opposition to deploying troops and anger at the Europeans' desire that the US do so. ABC offered more detailed coverage of the objectives of the proposed deployment and sound bites from both Biden and Senator Richard Lugar offering criticism. Reporters on both networks concluded that the Bosnian conflict continued to create problems for Clinton's leadership domestically and in Europe. The domestic political conflict attracted less notice on CBS, however, where anchor Dan Rather introduced the on-scene package from Bosnia by noting that Clinton "was still trying to decide what, if anything, to do" and was considering sending troops "for the purpose of keeping the war from spreading." A sound bite from Biden criticizing the Europeans was included in the package from Bosnia.

The three on-the-ground reports from Bosnia, however, were quite different. CBS offered the briefest report as Bob Simon described the Croat offensive against the Muslims, with Mostar already under siege and an assault on Travnik expected soon. Simon also narrated video of the Serbs' continuing siege of Sarajevo. ABC and NBC offered longer soft news stories from Bosnia. ABC's Hilary Brown provided a feature on the plight of orphaned refugees in Tuzla while, on NBC, Martin Fletcher's package described the plight of Muslims, Serbs, and Croats living amicably together in one Sarajevo neighborhood where they all suffered under Serb shelling and did not understand what the war is about.

Health care reform

The third story covered by all three networks on 11 May concerned health care reform. Here, too, the policy-conflict frame dominated the structure of these television news stories. It would later turn out that the partisan gridlock over health care reform and the numbing complexity of the proposals and counter-proposals would doom Clinton's high profile attempt to both raise and resolve a nagging policy conundrum. In May 1993, news attention to the still-developing Clinton proposals was increasing with the approach of the Clinton administration's self-imposed June deadline for revealing details of the plan.

This evening the networks emphasized somewhat different aspects of the health care reform story. Prompted by a *New York Times* report that the administration might be considering discontinuing Medicare, ABC focused on a meeting between health policy adviser Ira Magaziner and representatives of senior citizens groups. With sound bites from both sides, reporter George Strait framed the story as political manipulation, with the administration giving seniors assurances for now because it would be "political suicide" to admit the truth that Medicare will have to be phased out eventually. On NBC, Robert Hager's package focused on political conflict. His story described administration plans for a campaign to win public support for its proposal and stressed strong opposition from senior citizens worried about Medicare, from employers worried about higher payroll taxes, and from two men interviewed in a bar in Queens, New York, who opposed new taxes on beer and wine. The reporter concluded that "the administration expects a long, hot summer, and a long, loud debate." CBS framed the health care story also as conflict between the administration and the plan's opponents. Here, attention focused first on the "political minefield" of including abortions in the benefits package, where Clinton was depicted as caught between his pledges to abortion rights groups that have long been his supporters and the powerful opposition of abortion opponents. The worries of senior citizens about Medicare were noted as another political difficulty but received less attention than on the other networks. Despite differences in their stories, then, all three networks constructed the topic of health care reform as a site of intense opposition and political conflict with no winner or solution in sight.

Before leaving the subject of story frames, it is perhaps worthwhile to note some similarities in these three stories across all the networks. All three stories began by focusing on events in Washington, as is typical for US network news. This was true even for the Bosnia story, where the possibility of deployment of US troops set the stage for reports from the scene. All three stories focused first on actions and statements of officials, which defined the context in which the views of representatives of other groups and the views of ordinary citizens later were placed. And, all three stories focused primarily on political conflict between the administration and its opponents, emphasizing especially the intractable problems facing the President in each of the three domains.

The viewing context and uses of the news texts

Despite the proliferation of alternative information sources through specialized cable channels and other media (Neuman 1991), the three major commercial networks continue to dominate national television news in the US. Although most viewers continue to watch the network newscasts with some regularity, public confidence in television news declined sharply from a 55 percent confidence rating in 1988 to only 25 percent in 1993 (Merritt 1995: xv). According to Briller's (1990: 108) analysis of long-term trends, this declining confidence in television news reflects the increase of 'tabloid journalism' on television and growing suspicion that US journalists generally are "often influenced by powerful people and organizations" (a suspicion held by 62 percent of respondents in a 1990 poll).

Accompanying declining confidence in network news is widespread suspicion that the news is biased or slanted to favor one side of an issue and sensationalized, driven more by the need to attract an audience than by the desire to inform viewers in detail. As one of our respondents observed, "I think television news (...) has a very strong liberal slant. And if you aren't aware of it, they really do kinda brainwash it" (F5). "They always give a slant to the issue," agreed another respondent (M7). Another respondent explained, "The national news a lot of times will not necessarily give a very great explanation of the overall problem. (...) they put everything down on such a really fundamental and very simple focus that the whole picture is hard to understand at times" (F4). Added this respondent's spouse, "I think the major networks just go so much for the mass appeal that it just kind of turns me off" (M4).

While most Americans select television when asked to single out their most important source of news, the persons we interviewed indicated that television most commonly is only one among a number of different sources from which they learn about the topics and events they regard as most important. These combinations of sources through which our respondents become informed about particular stories almost always include interpersonal as well as mass media sources.

In assessing the role of interpersonal voices in the various combinations of information sources from which people commonly learn about events, it is important to recognize that television viewing continues to be largely a social activity which is closely intertwined with family life in the US as elsewhere (e.g. Lull 1988b; Morley 1986, 1988). In twelve of the thirteen households that our interviewers visited, the television set on which the news was viewed was located in the social center of the home (living room, family room or 'den,' kitchen/dining room). In the same number of households, the news typically is viewed in a social setting by multiple family members who commonly discuss the stories and other matters during the newscasts. Our respondents echoed the findings of numerous other studies (e.g. Levy and Windahl 1984; McDonald 1990; Rubin and Perse 1987) which suggest that the motives which underlie decisions to watch television news are as much social as informational and that viewing commonly occurs within a stream of ongoing activity that includes leaving the room and returning frequently during the newscast, engaging in other activities such as preparing and eating the evening meal, and talking with others about topics not connected to the news.

The picture of news viewing that emerges from our interviews sketches a portrait of television news as occasionally the subject of focused attention, but equally often as background to social and other activities. In the flow of activity during a newscast, viewers may 'tune in' to a story that catches their attention, then 'tune out' less interesting stories. In learning about a story or event of interest to them, viewers typically acquire information from a mixture of sources, including other people as well as television and other mass media. Thus, the voice of television news is heard in a swirl of ongoing activity and social interaction in the home, and often it is supplemented, elaborated, and perhaps even contradicted by other voices that provide information about the same topics.

Television news is rarely used directly as a resource for political action, according to our respondents. Instead, viewing the news serves social purposes, both in the immediate context of viewing and in later conversations with acquaintances, and also provides viewers with some of their information about 'what is going on,' even if television's reports are thought by many viewers to be slanted, sensationalized, and not very helpful in understanding the full context of complicated events. Of course, the sense of 'what is going on' is a critical element in a complicated, variable, and context-dependent process that ultimately may lead to political action.

Audience decodings of the news texts

The more than 600 pages of transcripts from the household interviews provide a detailed and complex picture of how television news viewers individually and collaboratively construct the meaning of news reports from their own vantage points in particular contexts. In order to describe the more important elements of that complexity in an economical way, we trace an analytic thread that begins with discontinuities between the interpretive frames inscribed in the news texts versus the frames invoked by viewers, and winds its way ultimately to the central role of super-themes as overarching frameworks for situated, local interpretation.

Polysemy

Although a new wave of experimental and survey-based research has reminded us once again of the media's subtle power to frame and cue our thinking and influence our 'agenda' of political significance (Ansolabehere and Iyengar 1995; Iyengar 1991; Iyengar and Kinder 1987), the analysis of our viewers' constructions of the news stories demonstrates the overwhelmingly active interpretation, dramatic diversity, and individuality of viewers' decodings. In case after case, viewers structured and framed stories and story elements in ways that made particular sense to their own interests and experiences. For example, when asked to identify the main point of the story about gays, viewers gave such differing answers as: "freedom of choice" (F1: 9); "most of the military is against [lifting the ban]" (M3: 5); "they're afraid gays only go there to check 'em out instead of fighting for their country" (Ga8: 6); "whether we are willing to accept homosexuals as equal" (M4: 4); discrimination and fairness to gays; a strong military; whether gays would be safe in the military; politics; and, "the minority against the overwhelming majority" (M6: 14). Similarly, viewers' perceptions of the main point of the story about health care included: "we're going to be paying for this" (M7: 27); "it's gonna make it easier for people to [get abortions]" (F3: 10); "not all the people have medical attention, and this is very important" (F8: 24); "why we have to pay for people who don't have insurance" (G10: 40); and, "people who are in power who are now making these decisions" (F15: 35).

Despite the fact that, in one way or another, all three of the stories of interest were framed by reporters as episodes of political conflict, the interpretive constructions of the stories offered by our respondents in most cases ignored the political aspects of the stories. Instead, viewers' constructions focused on the underlying events or merits of the proposals that were the subject of political controversy (see Asard and Bennett 1997). So, for example, viewers' representations of the health care story centered on whether health care reform was needed, would be effective, would be fair to them, and similar matters. Constructions of the ban on gays serving in the armed forces tended to ignore the conflict between President Clinton and Senator Nunn and to look instead to whether viewers thought the ban was a good idea.

An interesting case in this regard is the story about Bosnia, which actually consisted of two stories. The first story reported the political difficulties the President faced and the possibility of sending US troops into Macedonia. The second story came from the war zone; on CBS, the story described the continuing conflict at several sites, while NBC offered the story of Muslim, Croat, and Serbian neighbors living together harmoniously in one Sarajevo neighborhood and unable to understand why the war was being fought. Most viewers' representations of 'the Bosnia story' concentrated on the second story and failed to acknowledge or incorporate the first story about the President's search for an effective and feasible US policy. Viewers' constructions of the Bosnia story tended especially to draw links between the victims of the war and ordinary people like themselves, and the viewers reacted accordingly as the four examples below illustrate.

> F13: 11: The Bosnians and Serbs and Muslims all live together, they are able to live in harmony.

> M15: 15–16: It was interesting to hear the Croatian, Serbian, Bosnian, Moslem all living in the same household saying that they don't know what the war's about. People that want to have these wars are not the

typical person, they're the fanatics (...) and the focus of the media that elevates them to important status.

F3: 8: I thought it was [about] anyone, children getting killed, innocent people getting killed.

M3: 16: [The story is about] the destruction of the common people in that country.

For many viewers, as the following excerpts exemplify, 'politics' entered their constructions as a synonym for a desire to control even when the result of such control is tragic, senseless destruction:

F11: 15: The whole thing is politics. They show regular people in their houses all getting along. It's basically the same everywhere. People can get along if there isn't so much, people trying to be in control.

F9: 6: People was just sitting and a bomb went in their house and hurt somebody there. People are fighting and their own people don't know why they're fighting. It's just a politic war.

F7: 18–19: I feel bad for the people, there's a mixture of everybody in a family, Serbs and Moslems, and it's power, it's political, innocent people are standing there waiting to get killed.

The relatively few respondents who focused on the political and practical difficulties for US policy tended to be the more highly educated viewers among our households. A graduate student pointed out:

M6: 8: It's not just the Serbs, also the Bosnians and the Croatians. If we march in, all the factions will gang up against us like happened to the Russians in Afghanistan.

A law student described the story as, "It's just a big mess, no easy way out for Clinton" (M4: 6). A research scientist offered a similar construction of the story as about "what Clinton's going to do" (M14: 11). The main point of the story, as he saw it, is that "it's a lose, lose, and a lose situation. This guy's in a terrible spot" (M14: 13). It is perhaps ironic to note that the overarching political frame offered by the networks in all three stories of interest was perhaps the least relevant and useful interpretive dimension for the viewers in our households.

Each of the viewers' interpretations described above is more or less warranted by the news story in that the interpretation is founded on one or more elements within the news text. But many of these interpretations differ sharply from the frames inscribed in the broadcast texts. Thus, despite the stories' reliance on convergent and familiar journalistic frames, it would be misleading to characterize those frames as somehow determining how viewers perceive the issues.

Where do viewers' constructions come from, if not the news texts? They come from many places, of course, including the various sources in addition to television news from which people learn about events. However, audience members' individual and family biographies and everyday life experiences seem to play especially important roles, as we discuss next.

The fundamental role of personal experience

A striking, but not surprising phenomenon in the household interview data was evidence of the power of personal and family experience to filter interpretations of news texts. In the interpretations of the Bosnia story described above, there are repeated instances of viewers constructing the main point of the story in an opposition between 'politics' or 'fanatics' and 'the typical person,' 'the common people,' 'regular people,' and 'family.' In doing so, the viewers turned to their own life experience in order to translate a story about horrific events in an exotic locale into terms that are personally relevant and meaningful.

The same move to everyday experience for interpretive guidance was displayed again and again with reference to all three of the news stories. A 52-year-old midwestern appliance service technician, for example, saw most of the news stories as demonstrating how powerful people and institutions "force something on people that they don't want" (M3: 15), leading him to take a skeptical stance toward government and corporate actions and proposals. But he embraced the idea of a government health care plan because:

> M3: 11–12: I have a son in (...) [Name] Hospital that's on public aid, and that could affect his health care. (...) He hasn't been able to work for two years, and has no insurance. (...) You've gotta have some form of health care when you've got major problems like he's got. (...) I think there's a lot of importance to that, because (...) there are a lotta people that don't have health coverage.

Similarly, a 42-year-old west-coast white-collar worker explained that he regarded an NBC story on home schooling which came ninth in the story line-up as 'most important' because:

> M10: 6–7: it hit home. (...) I see from time to time whether or not we are getting a quality education for our children. And if the teachers are letting us down, or are they burned out (...) I have my daughter involved (...) in a class (...) that she's not doing very well in, and when a third of the class is not passing, it makes me wonder, "Well, why aren't they passing?" And I've made four or five attempts to talk to the teacher and still haven't been able to sit her down and, you know, specifically say, "What is the problem?"

The salience of everyday experience sometimes led respondents to draw links between distant events in a news story and local community concerns. In some cases, the result was a personal interpretation that could barely be recognized from the text of the news story. For example, a 33-year-old midwestern postgraduate student regarded the story on gays in the military as "most important":

> M6: 4–5: because it's just not in the military. And we've seen it in the schools already where [a teacher] (. . .) was fired a couple of months back for that very reason, (. . .) he was teaching the homosexual curricula. And he basically brought suit against the school (. . .) claiming that they were [discriminating] against him. (. . .) And if we continue the same line with the, uh, homosexual line as we would any other civil rights legislation, we would say we'd have to have quota laws and homosexuals (. . .) where it's a teacher, whether it be anyplace in the business, and you'd have to hire a homosexual in preference over anybody else.

The critical role of super-themes

The interpretive structure by which viewers are able to translate the exotic events of news stories into terms that are readily understandable and personally meaningful is the super-theme. The excerpts from viewers' discourse that we have quoted to this point offer various examples of these broad interpretive structures. Some of the super-themes that appeared most often in the discourse of our respondents are described below. The richness and dynamism of the super-themes reinforces a sense of 'conversation' between the audience and the media rather than a one-way effect.

Controlling powerful interests versus the common people

The super-theme invoked most frequently by our respondents was an opposition between ordinary people, understood as people like themselves, and diffuse powerful interests, typically described in vague but threatening terms as persons, groups, or institutions that seek to advance their own interests by controlling ordinary people through economic or political means and are heedless of the consequences of their actions for the lives of the common people. This venerable super-theme was serviceable for our respondents not only in constructing meanings for individual news stories, but also in providing an overarching interpretive orientation to multiple news stories.

In the case of an east-coast couple in their late fifties, for example, several stories were seen as instances of political and corporate interests pursuing profits and power at the expense of ordinary people like themselves. A story in sixth position on NBC's line-up about the Food and Drug Administration's approving the sale of female condoms was described by the husband as important in part because:

> M7: 10: certain stations seem to be throwin' all this stuff at you, (. . .) all you see on TV is condoms, pro-choice, (. . .) the gay issue (. . .) I think it's a big, ah, thing to sell condoms. (. . .) Who pays their check? (. . .) the advertisers. (. . .) that's why they're trying to get 'em in the restaurants, (. . .) I mean, who profits by all this?

Deploying the same super-theme, the wife described health care reform as the most important domestic story because:

> F7: 27: I have a relative (. . .) and, I hear (. . .) [welfare] patients (. . .) gold chains, leather (. . .) We're payin' for this, you know, and (. . .) our insurance is goin' up and up. And, and it's just not fair to the middle man, we're carryin' everbody!

Added her husband, "This is Hillary Clinton's, uh, baby, and she wants it. And she don't care what it's gonna cost" (M7: 26).

In the same way, concern for the plight of common people like themselves facing the powerful interests arrayed against them allowed a middle-aged, blue-collar midwestern couple to draw parallels between stories about gays serving openly in the military ("the power to force something on people that they don't want" [M3: 15]), Bosnia ("the destruction of the common people in that country" [M3: 16]), and the conflict between an airline and its flight attendants over mandatory weight restrictions ("this is happening in many businesses [. . .] they will only hire part-time employees [. . .] trim budgets and avoid paying benefits [. . .] and the older people are being left out" [M3: 14]).

Fairness and personal freedom

A second super-theme that emerged frequently in our respondents' discourse about the news texts concerned the values of fairness and personal freedom. A middle-aged professional couple living in the midwest invoked this super-theme to connect stories about gays in the military (the story is about "sexual rights and freedoms" and "supposedly America is based on freedom of choice" [F1: 7–8, 9]) and about the flight attendants (who are victimized by unfair images). The same connection was drawn by a Mexican-American mother and her teenaged daughters living on the west coast who saw the military's ban on gays serving openly as "unfair" because "it's not their fault they're gay" (Gb8: 10) and the story of the airline flight attendants as proving "there is discrimination going on for a woman" (F8: 38).

The fairness super-theme was echoed in interpretations of these stories offered by a diverse group of other respondents, although these respondents did not use the super-theme to connect the two stories. Concerning the weight requirements for flight attendants, a 71-year-old woman who is married to an attorney mused, "I don't know the standards for how many pounds over-weight, but I just can't see how it's being fair to someone who has nine extra pounds and looks good [. . .] and apparently it isn't affecting her health" (F5: 7–8). A midwestern married student couple described the story about gays serving in the military in similar terms: "amplifies some of the intolerance people have for one another" (F4: 4), "about whether we are willing to accept homosexuals as equal to us" (M4: 4). A middle-aged Mexican-American woman who works in a manufacturing plant explained that the same story made her feel sad because "a lot of gays have been in there for a long time and now, just because they're gay, they're not allowed; I think it's so unfair" (F10: 10). An African-American woman living on the east coast invoked the super-theme of fairness to connect the story about gays in the military ("banning gays is discrimination; you should never judge a person by, you know, what they prefer or anything like that" [F13: 7]) to the story about events in Bosnia (the main point is about "acceptance of difference" [F13: 25]).

The fairness super-theme as used in these examples mediates between news events and the viewers' own lives because, almost universally, fairness is seen as a necessary condition for the viewers' happiness and success. As an older woman explained concerning the health care story, "You see what's happening to your-self and you're struggling, and then you see somebody getting something for nothing and you're paying for it!" (F7: 26). A west-coast woman said about the same story, "When we moved here and didn't have insurance and our daughter was sick, they wouldn't take her; we had to go to the bank and prove to them we had cash" (F10: 40–41). Her son added, "I don't understand why we have to pay for people who don't have insurance" (B10: 40).

Human potential

A third super-theme employed by many of our respondents celebrated the potential of ordinary people, working alone or collectively, to accomplish great deeds. Concerning the Bosnia story, an African-American teenager invoked this super-theme to construct the story as explaining how "that little small group of them live together and try to help each other, (. . .) how they're trying to survive and come out with their lives" (Gb13: 21–22). In a story about parents who are educating their children at home rather than sending them to school, the 40-year-old male maintenance supervisor of an apartment complex found the theme of "people who are dealing with problems that they have in creative ways" (M15: 34). In the same story, a 33-year-old Honduran woman who is an east-coast homemaker and student saw that "instead of being a problem, [youngsters who drop out of school] are doing something else, even though at home, something that's good, that will help them in the future" (F9: 9). The home schooling story showed "that people accomplish their goals and dreams if they are really interested in doing it, and they don't necessarily need guidance" (M10: 55), according to a 42-year-old man who works for an insurance company on the west coast.

A noteworthy feature of the three common super-themes described above is the way in which they can be seen to cohere in a consistent and familiar orientation to life experience. At base, this orientation focuses on the individual and the family, and it suggests that the actions of powerful interests ultimately are to be judged by their consequences for individuals and families. With the fair treatment from government and powerful interests that is hoped for, but not expected, individuals and families can shape their lives to attain their goals. News stories that seem to relate to this general orientation are likely to be noticed and regarded as important. Viewers' individually and socially constructed understandings of such stories are likely to find within the stories enactments of this general interpretive orientation. The orientation itself serves individuals holding quite disparate views equally well. For example, viewers who oppose lifting the ban on homosexuals serving openly in the US military may see in this issue validation for the belief that powerful interests often seek to impose their will without regard to the wishes of the majority of ordinary people. Viewers who support lifting the ban may find in the same issue validation for the importance of fair treatment as a pre-condition to achieving happiness. Similarly, President Clinton's health care proposals were seen by some viewers as an arrogant exercise of power and by others as an attempt to help those in need, yet viewers of both opinions were able to find in coverage of the health care debate further support for their shared general interpretive orientation.

Of course, many super-themes emerged in our respondents' discourse in addition to the three most common ones described above. For instance, a 43-year-old Mexican-American mother of two who is employed as a babysitter and housekeeper listed "stories about children" as the most important current issue and saw violence and harm to children, families, and innocent people as the theme that linked together stories about health care (as she explained, "This problem take too many lives, too much life for babies" [F8: 25]), about Bosnia (the US should "stop the killing of innocent people" [F8: 12]), and about the controversy over rebuilding largely Korean-owned liquor stores that were destroyed in the Los Angeles riots ("Families is very affected for this" [F8: 8]). Moreover, not every news story was readily interpreted by our respondents in terms of a super-theme. Respondents seemed to have particular difficulty with news stories that they regarded as 'not very important' and could not easily relate to their own life experience or to the general interpretive orientation described above. Often, the respondents' discourse about these stories merely glossed one or two elements in the texts of the stories and did not offer an integrative thematic interpretation.

Conclusion

We have concentrated on the dynamic relationship between the evening news broadcast and the viewing household. Our families demonstrate a stubborn and perhaps practiced capacity to virtually ignore the dominant journalistic reporting frame of partisan political conflict. They draw instead on the importance of personal experience as the grounding of interpretation, the ability of super-themes to link multiple stories about disparate subjects, and a shared interpretive orientation to the news, a public sphere that makes sense to them, not one that was dictated to them.

Reception analysis, by its nature, draws the analyst to a thick description of the process and product of viewers' active and creative construction of the news. These dynamics are less evident when our research methods focus on the learning of discrete facts or before-and-after shifts in attitude or issue salience. Reception analysis, however, is not well suited to precise assessments of the distributions of interpretive practices across large populations. Perhaps we need to heed Hovland's sage advice and find new tools for the integration of insights from diverse methodological traditions in the study of human communication (Hovland 1959).

Some of the most interesting questions raised by our findings are comparative questions. Readers who are familiar with similar studies of news discourses and audience members' constructions of news events will have noticed often close parallels to some of the themes and super-themes we discovered. In interviews with American and Danish respondents about a variety of political issues, for example, Crigler and Jensen (1991) noted that respondents frequently conceptualized political issues in terms of such themes as 'powerful others' who control individuals through governmental and other means, and "human impact [...] marked by feelings of caring, worry, compassion, or disregard for others" (pp. 181–2, 184–5). Similarly, in a study of how 'the bomb' and the Cold War were represented in various US news texts, Gamson and Stuart (1992) found that ordinary citizens most often were depicted in the roles of passive victims or observers of the actions of powerful political actors. Moreover, the three super-themes we observed can, if taken to a higher level of abstraction, be seen as all concerned with the individual versus the collectivity, especially as the collectivity is controlled by powerful interests and institutions. In each super-theme, viewers reflected upon their relationship to society and the ways in which society impinges upon them or upon people like them. Thus, our findings lead inevitably to comparative questions concerning whether there may be, across countries, a common stock of super-themes that viewers use to decode news stories.

9

CONCLUSION

Klaus Bruhn Jensen

Comparative studies lend themselves to, among other things, theory development about the place of media in the everyday lives of their audiences. The distinctive features of a particular aspect of media use can be identified more clearly when compared and contrasted across different cultural or historical contexts. In this respect, cross-cultural research may be a special case of social and human science generally. Beniger (1992), for one, has argued that all social-scientific research is essentially comparative and, further, that some of its main theoretical advances have been due to comparisons of seemingly disparate matters:

> After we designate researchers who compare across time (historians) and across space (geographers), researchers who compare communications content (content analysts), organizations (organizational sociologists), institutions (macrosociologists), countries (international relations specialists), cultures (ethnologists), and languages (linguists), and researchers who compare individuals in terms of gender, race, social class, age, education, and religion, what remains? (p. 35)

Whereas an extended definition of 'comparison' can contribute to a broader theory of science for the communications field (see below), specific comparative projects such as the present one may offer a particular opportunity for theory development because such research, relying on a qualitative methodology, is designed to focus on 'difference,' seeking to develop, refine, and substantiate its systematics with continuous cross-reference to particular cultural and historical contexts. Accordingly, this concluding chapter discusses the contributions to theory development of the empirical findings on television news reception in different cultural settings. Apart from summarizing the main similarities and differences between the seven countries, this chapter presents a model of how reality may be conceived by viewers, depending on their contexts of socialization and acculturation. In addition, some policy issues in international communication are reconsidered in the light of the present findings; a comparison of these radically different countries may also serve to highlight a range of political choices and

164

possible interventions. Finally, the chapter discusses the implications of the *News of the World* project for further research, with particular reference to the different nature of 'comparison' within qualitative and quantitative methodologies, and, hence, the complementarity of each of these approaches for understanding how world cultures make sense of reality through the modern mass media.

A model of 'the world in the head'

From super-themes to interpretive dimensions

One of the chief characteristics of qualitative communication research is that its findings emerge from the detailed examination of selected constituents of communication in context, as part of what is commonly known as a 'grounded' research strategy (Glaser and Strauss 1967). Whereas the super-themes occurring in each of the seven countries are documented and discussed in the relevant chapters, the purpose of a second-order analysis of the super-themes is to detect structuring principles which might unite or divide the groups of national respondents along similar analytical dimensions. This section first traces a set of interpretive dimensions underlying the super-themes, and proposes a configuration of the dimensions in the form of a model. Next, the section situates the findings from each country according to the dimensions of the model, further noting substantive similarities and differences between countries in this respect. With reference to previous theoretical and empirical research on social aspects of cognition and action, the last part of the section discusses the explanatory value of the model and its contribution to a more comprehensive, cross-cultural theory of communication and reception.

A preliminary analysis of the diverse super-themes suggested that, for example, beyond cases of a near-overlap of the references in several national samples to war and other forms of conflict in the viewers' distant, and sometimes not so distant, surroundings, a number of seemingly rather distinct categories could be understood as interrelated along more abstract conceptual dimensions. A total of four such dimensions were established, which in different ways address aspects of the social organization of time, space, and interpersonal as well as institutional relations.

First, a dimension of space, from 'here' to 'there,' not surprisingly, helped to explain the occurrence of several super-themes in the different countries. News anticipates events, near and far, which may affect the audience's basic sense of 'ontological security' (Giddens 1984): 'Am I safe, is my family safe, is the nation or culture to which I belong safe?' Further, super-themes along the space dimension suggest the respondents' perceived distance from the center of events and thus their sense of place in the world. In the present samples, distinctive examples come from Israel and Denmark. On the one hand, Israeli respondents recognized a preoccupation with themselves as 'the center of the world' (Chapter 5), while, on the other hand, Danish respondents assigned themselves to the periphery of world events – 'our little corner of the world' (Chapter 3). It should be stressed that this dimension refers to what is simultaneously a mental and a social space, bounded not by absolute, geographical distance, but by experienced distance from events. In the respondents' own concepts, events can be placed on an axis from the highly familiar and culturally bound to the entirely unknown, alien, and, perhaps, threatening aspects of news.

Second, a dimension of power, indicating relations of the 'individual' to 'authority,' captures a variety of agents, be they national or foreign, religious or secular, which affect the living conditions of individuals. Certainly, the interviews draw attention to variations in terms of how respondents placed themselves on this dimension, depending on where they are situated in a social hierarchy and on an 'international news map' of the world, as expressed also in news contents (Appendix A). Nevertheless, the relations between social institutions and individual viewers come across as a key to the latter's interpretation of many different types of news items, regardless of their social or national background. The conceptions of what may remain the most immediate source of power, namely, the nation-state, also range from a classic, monolithic state in the case of India, attempting to appease and reconcile its religiously and ethnically diverse citizens (Chapter 4), to the case of the United States, where authority may be understood in more diffuse terms as the powers that be, restricting and perhaps infringing on the enterprising of ordinary people (Chapter 8). Across the different cultures, however, many respondents express a sense of powerlessness in the face of either identifiable powers, such as the state or particular enemies, or more abstract forces, such as fate or a generalized threat to the individual.

Third, a dimension of time, stretching far back into history as well as into the future, is introduced in various degrees by respondents as a means of orientation in relation to the day-to-day events reported in the news. The clearest examples come from Belarus, a new nation following the break-up of the former Soviet Union in 1991. For the Belarusian respondents, the notion of 'the country we want to live in' (Chapter 2) even served as a common denominator for the other super-themes, signaling their hopes for a future that is still far from realized. However, also less radical changes and hopes for the future may guide the interpretation of the day's news, as when, in Mexico, the present is evaluated in terms of what the new trade agreement, NAFTA, might bring (Chapter 7). While the news media are frequently criticized in research as well as public debate for supplying only snippets of information without historical background – often with good reason, despite the incidental nature of the news genre (Park 1940; Schudson 1982) – audiences may thus, to a degree, compensate for this feature in the interest of coherence and relevance.

Fourth, a dimension of identity is introduced to account for super-themes which broadly concern the social and cultural identity of viewers in relation to a variety of 'others.' Along this dimension, one encounters especially potential enemies and allies of the respondents, either at an individual or at a national level, and sometimes more abstract references to forces of various kinds, whether economic, religious, or social-systemic in nature. Among the potential destabilizing elements in Belarus, the respondents identified other regional nationalities in the area. Among the possible healing forces in a society increasingly torn apart by corruption and violence, Italian respondents mentioned the Pope, who was described as an active social leader as well as being a spiritual leader. Whereas the agents along this dimension may not always be seen to participate actively or immediately in the everyday life or political processes affecting respondents directly, they remain important points of reference for the respondents' understanding of themselves, since humans derive their identity – socially, culturally, ethnically – and, hence, their justification for participation and action in society, from their interaction with others and the perspective of these others on them. The agents along the dimension of identity represent, in Mead's (1934) term, the respondents' 'significant others.'

It should be added that the super-themes along this last dimension of identity were sometimes interrelated by respondents with the space dimension and/or with the power dimension. This is understandable, since we become 'ourselves' in relation both to the rest of our embedding social structure (power dimension) and to the rest of the world (space dimension). Nevertheless, in many cases these 'others' were articulated in the interview discourses as distinct entities – for example, the several ethnic and religious factions which constitute Indian society, but which do not come together precisely in a unified state along the power dimension, or the Pope who, while being a powerful authority in Italian society, has set himself apart from the corrupt powers of the state and thus represents a hope for moral rebirth. Also in more stable contexts such as Denmark and Mexico, the various 'others,' comprising international powers and victims, were often not identical with either the immediate political authorities or with the participants in distant wars. Thus, the identity dimension appears to have independent explanatory value for an understanding of the respondents' construction of social reality as it serves to identify the allies, values, and goals for action which enable the very process of becoming a social agent in relation to the other dimensions of power, space, and time. As the following reexamination of super-themes from the seven countries suggests, also the nature and distribution of super-themes along the identity dimension differ in important ways between the countries.

The full model, displayed in Figure 9.1, constitutes an interpretive matrix, with the individual respondent at the symbol in the bottom left corner. It is an instantiation of his or her orientation at a given time in relation to particular events, rather than being a social field in which the respondents might locate themselves, for example, either relatively high up or low down on the dimension of power. In the context of news reception, the model may help to explain the nature and interrelations of the super-themes as they were applied by the respondents to specific news items. The section later returns to a discussion of the relationship between the super-themes and the conceptual dimensions. In itself, the proposed model constitutes a heuristic device, a theoretical prototype, derived from a small set of empirical data whose possible manifestations in the interpretive practices of individuals, social groups, or even national audiences should be examined in further studies.

Before proceeding to a discussion of the status and implications of the model, this section next reconsiders the findings about super-themes from the seven countries. For each country, the analysis relates the super-themes, as identified in previous chapters, to the four dimensions and to the model as a whole, notes the relative salience of each dimension for viewers in that particular cultural setting, and discusses the implications of the national versions of the model.

Local empiricism

Belarus

The interviews from Belarus (Chapter 2) reflect a continued preoccupation with the momentous transition to being a sovereign state following the dissolution of the Soviet Union in 1991, which made the respondents citizens of a different order. Probably more so than in any of the other countries studied, the historical or time dimension tracing the development from Belarus being a part of the USSR 'then' to being a sovereign state 'now' shines through in the interpretations of many, if not most, news items. To this extent, a feeling for 'the country we want to live in' amounts to a common denominator of the other super-

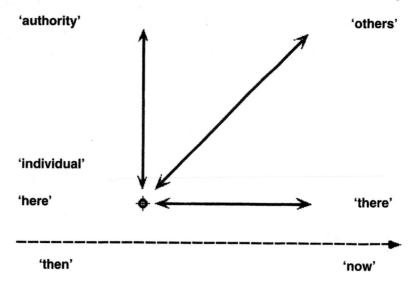

Figure 9.1 A model of 'the world in the head'

themes, offering the most salient interpretive principle. As a result, the individual super-themes may be less distinguishable here than in some of the other countries, and the scale of change even leads some respondents to refer to notions of 'fate' as an explanation of events.

Sovereignty has brought overwhelming challenges, not least in the economic field. At the individual level, the respondents noted that Belarusians had found it difficult to adapt to the new form of market economy. At the national level, oil as well as a strong independent army were noted among the requirements of sovereignty that have been difficult to procure. Thus, the super-theme of 'economic crisis' serves to characterize not only the historical period following sovereignty, but also the present state of domestic affairs, which might most appropriately be summarized as a 'status quo,' regardless of the hopes for the future. Nevertheless, on the space dimension, this status quo is relatively distant from, and certainly preferable to, a state of 'war,' as has affected some of the other newly independent nations in the region.

On the power dimension, the sense of status quo was reasserted as ordinary people were described as 'victims' of various 'threats,' including those of different state bodies representing the 'system' serving its own interests. State violence or abuses of power apparently were conceived of as a threat to the safety and prosperity of citizens which is on a par with terrorism, accidents, and crime. Although the interviews contain appeals to the state as an instrument of law and order, in addition to other services being provided to citizens, the state or government as such was not depicted as an authority at the top of the model, as was the case in several other countries. Instead, the state comes across as one of several vaguely defined but severe problems for ordinary citizens.

Along the identity dimension (see Figure 9.2), the Belarusian respondents identified, and evaluated negatively, foreigners from other nations in the region, who were seen as being among the perpetrators of physical violence and other crime. It is worth noting at this point that a recurring feature of interviews from the countries which, like Belarus, are going through a crisis is a single negative 'other.' Such an entity may provide an explanation for current problems as well as an identifiable target for criticism and opposition.

Denmark

In several respects, Denmark constitutes a diametrical opposite to Belarus. Its stable, entrenched, and affluent social system, coupled with a long and predominantly peaceful history, can be seen to inform the Danish respondents' decodings of news (Chapter 3). The dimension with the greatest salience, as suggested not only by the degree of concern expressed, but also by the amount of detail provided by respondents, appears to be that of space. The interview discourses repeatedly situated Danes in 'our little corner of the world.' At the other end of this continuum is the 'war,' which was still conceived as being

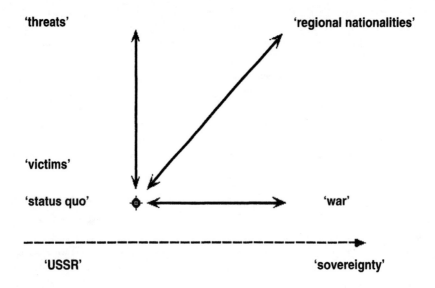

Figure 9.2 Belarusian model

quite far away, even if it had recently moved somewhat closer in the shape of the conflicts in the former Yugoslavia (see Figure 9.3).

This is not to imply that the power dimension was ignored by Danish respondents. 'Those who take the rap' at the bottom of the social hierarchy include various innocent third parties, ordinary people, in addition to the victims of war and hunger as well as of street violence. In the most inclusive sense, this third party equals those citizens and tax-payers who, for instance, have to live with decisions regarding economic policy that have been made at the top of the hierarchy, and who will ultimately have to foot the bill. Yet, their relationship with 'those in charge' was not given the shape of a sinister conflict, but rather that of minor skirmishes which, in any event, may follow from the complex nature of modern political organizations and state bureaucracies. Also in the case of foreign news stories, including those of the European Union, the Danish respondents noted that there is a gap between those with concentrated power and those with hardly any say. However, even though power was said to corrupt, the sense of urgency found in interviews from other countries was virtually absent from the Danish interviews, presumably because comparatively little is at stake here. Instead, there were general references to the small people and nations that have to make do, and to defer to the realities of big-power politics.

This accommodating attitude may help to explain the way in which Danish respondents described their 'others.' On the one hand, these include the big powers that may take the lead in solving international crises, as exemplified on Newsday by the American President Clinton hosting the Danish Prime

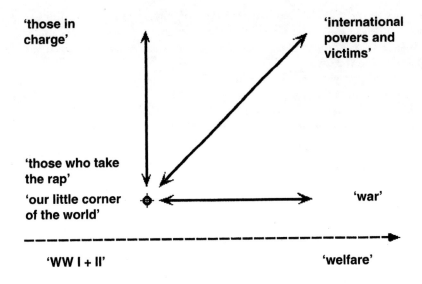

'those in charge'

'international powers and victims'

'those who take the rap'

'our little corner of the world'

'war'

'WW I + II'

'welfare'

Figure 9.3 Danish model

Minister. On the other hand, the 'others' include, for example, the victims of poverty in the Third World. While the Danish respondents could conceive of both problems and solutions with reference to these various agents associated with the identity dimension, they tended not to identify themselves as either victims or problem solvers. These 'others' remain far away, even if they are encountered on television, and whereas the events of the two world wars provided a backdrop to Danes' interpretation of current conflicts in Bosnia, these accounts referred to something in the deep past, far from the sort of recent direct experiences which, for instance, were related by the Belarusian respondents.

India

The two overarching, interrelated super-themes in the Indian context – 'crisis' and 'identity' – may be accounted for, initially, with reference to a configuration of two dimensions in the model – time and power – and specified with reference to their several constituent concepts (Chapter 4). Most urgently, the time dimension, in the form of the violent clashes between Muslim- and Hindu-related groups in late 1992, overwhelmingly informed the Indian respondents' interpretations of the news on the day of the interviews in terms of a crisis. These events had stayed with respondents as an interpretive readiness, and continued to shape their decodings profoundly during the spring of 1993, including news items with no evident link to this problematic. In an even longer and deeper perspective, the respondents formulated their sense of crisis with reference to the power dimension. Questions of power and authority during the crisis of present-day India may ultimately be related to the founding of India through its partition from Pakistan: Who, indeed, is the 'Indian nation' that has been placed in the care of 'the state'?

This question was also implied by the Indian respondents at the individual level: "Who am 'I,' as a citizen and viewer?" Thus, the dimension of identity comes to play a special overarching role in the Indian interview discourses by providing a common denominator for the two super-themes – 'crisis' and 'identity' – even while these, as noted above, were articulated with explicit reference to the power and time dimensions. Like the news programs that they described, a majority of the respondents may have wanted to refrain from naming the main division of Indian society – between its 'religious factions,' Hindu and Muslim. As suggested by a few of the respondents, more than anything else, it is this division that places the identity of the 'Indian nation' in doubt. The current (1993) crisis began in the older foundational crisis that dates from the partition of India and Pakistan in 1947 and which is the origin of the volatile definition of nation and state. Crisis may thus be the permanent condition of the Indian state, as witnessed by the recurring flare-up of ethnic violence and other unrest.

Given this pervasive condition of crisis, it is no wonder that the Indian respondents may think of themselves as 'small people' facing an unresponsive or helpless state apparatus on the power dimension. Their lived crisis is exacerbated by what they referred to variously as opportunism and outright corruption in national politics. Compared to, for example, Belarus, which faces similar problems with its system of government, India may be perceived as a political and cultural experiment that, from the point of view of its citizens, has failed to materialize for as much as fifty years. Furthermore, it is this acute sense of crisis which could be detected behind the Indian respondents' understanding of the place of India on the space dimension: although, within the subject of international politics, they made reference to both friends and enemies, most of their attention was given to potential 'allies' of India, especially to the USA, in countering potential aggressors – particularly Pakistan. In sum, the internal foundational conflict of India was conceived as constitutive of the nation, its international relations, as well as the identity of its citizens, as articulated along the four conceptual dimensions (see Figure 9.4).

Israel

Although Israel faces a constitutive internal, as well as external, crisis which is comparable in several respects to that of India, the historical background of the Israeli crisis, and hence its focal dimensions as referred to by respondents, are rather different (Chapter 5). While the partition of India and Pakistan allocated a significant minority of Muslims to the Indian territory, Israel may be said to have been established according to a principle of exclusion in relation to local

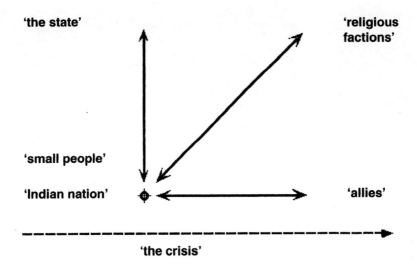

'the state'

'religious factions'

'small people'

'Indian nation'

'allies'

'the crisis'

Figure 9.4 Indian model

non-Jewish cultures. Therefore, the 'others' who threaten 'our' existence may be more easily identifiable in this context. The super-theme of 'them outwitting us' on the identity dimension most importantly comprises Palestinians and other immediate enemies in the Arab world, even if the negatively evaluated 'others' include groups within Israeli society who may also threaten the peace. Thus, as in the Indian case, the identity dimension appears to have special explanatory value for the Israeli respondents' interpretations. In addition, however, these interpretations place a similar emphasis on the space dimension, as follows.

The super-theme of 'gridlock' (see Figure 9.5) might be said to summarize the position that the Israeli viewers find themselves in, being subject to threats and unforeseen repercussions from their surroundings, no matter which solution Israel may attempt. This conundrum also helps to explain why some respondents explicitly thought of themselves as 'the center of the world.' Such a reaction can serve as a self-defense as part of an almost constant alert – what may be termed 'clear and present danger' from the immediate context on the space dimension. Under such circumstances, the news attains direct instrumental value for ordinary citizens.

These circumstances carry implications for the understanding of self, not only in relation to the threatening 'others' outwitting 'us,' but also in relation to the state on the dimension of power and authority. Israeli respondents often articulated a super-theme which drew parallels between the state and the individual or the single family. The implication is that the problems facing the nation as a whole are so massive that the individual problems of its constitutive families pale by comparison. Beyond the concrete argument that, if only the really big problems

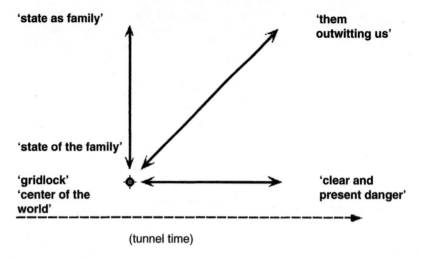

'state as family'

'them
outwitting us'

'state of the family'

'gridlock'
'center of the
world'

'clear and
present danger'

(tunnel time)

Figure 9.5 Israeli model

were solved, families could take care of their own small problems, the respondents introduced a conception of the state as a second-order family. The 'state of the family' could be understood as being ultimately dependent on the functioning of the 'state as family.'

It may be surprising that the Israeli respondents made little reference to historical background along the time dimension given the short specific history of Israel, which might have helped to place contemporary events in context. Whereas the viewers' attention may be so intensely focused on survival and present dangers as to blot out this dimension, it is also possible that, as in the case of India, the crisis is not really experienced as a delimited period or a transition, but rather as one in the sequence of threatening events that is the nation's history. This sense of a compression of time will be referred to as 'tunnel time,' by analogy to 'tunnel vision,' which denotes a detailed awareness of a particular portion of the field of vision to the exclusion of a broader range of visual input. The section on the US later in the chapter also returns to this phenomenon of 'tunnel time'.

Italy

Italy (Chapter 6) has also been affected by a recent national crisis arising from political corruption, although in a different manner from that in, for example, Belarus or India. This crisis was repeatedly introduced in the Italian interviews in relation to quite a diversity of news items and was articulated with reference to super-themes along two dimensions (see Figure 9.6). On the time dimension, the respondents distinguish between the time of the 'old system' and their hopes for the future, which may be summed up as a 'revival' of Italian society.

174

On the power dimension, the hopelessness of this old system was explained with reference to 'bad government and corruption,' whose victims are, by definition, the citizens of the country, but who were often conceived in terms of 'the family.'

The burdens which are placed on individual families, not only because of political corruption, but also in the form of higher taxes, for instance, make up one element of the overarching notion of a 'threat' which could be identified in the Italian interviews. Arguably, such a generalized threat is posed to families by a wide variety of events reported in the news. Threats were perceived most acutely by Italian respondents along the space dimension, as summed up by the super-theme of 'war.' It is worth noting here that compared to another European country such as Denmark, where distant wars also gave rise to a local emotional involvement in global conflicts, the Italian respondents appeared to reemphasize the reality and urgency of hostilities, even if these are somewhat removed in geographical terms (in the case of Bosnia, admittedly closer to Italy than to Denmark). The fact that the highly generalized 'threat' to viewers comprises and collapses not merely armed conflicts around the world, but also rising taxes and other measures taken by political authorities, may suggest a relatively 'introverted' approach to the relevance of news. This is something that could be partly explained by the sense of an ongoing national crisis, and also perhaps by the national culture of news (see Appendix A). For example, compared to Israel, there would seem to be less of a clear and present danger to the Italian nation and citizenship.

Along the identity dimension, it is particularly noteworthy that the Pope was

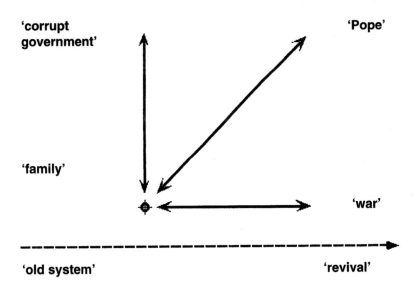

Figure 9.6 Italian model

identified as a positively evaluated 'other,' a potential source of moral rebirth amidst national crisis. Certainly, the 'others' of the Italian respondents might be said to include both the political class that is feared and loathed, and the victims of war and other violence who are to be pitied. However, the Pope could be singled out in the interview discourses as a specific super-theme who represents genuine hope for Italian individuals and families despite their preoccupation with the national crisis. This is in contrast to the cases of Belarus, India, and Israel – countries that are facing even more severe crises – where the super-themes instead place the focus on a negative, threatening 'other.'

Mexico

The configuration of super-themes emerging from the interviews in Mexico suggests a peaceful, almost complacent setting (Chapter 7), something that may be explained by the fact that this study took place before the regional and national conflicts that have been associated with the Chiapas incidents of 1994–95. In the first place, the power dimension (see Figure 9.7) comprises references to various authorities – the 'powers that be' both inside and outside Mexico itself, with regard to national politics and international relations – and, second, to a principle of 'non-intervention' which served to reemphasize that neither individuals nor, in the case of foreign issues, Mexico, could or should do much to affect the course of events. It was such detailed considerations in response to a variety of stories which made the power dimension the most salient one for an understanding of the Mexican respondents' interpretations. The centrality of this dimension is suggested both by the respondents' retelling of individual stories and also, for example,

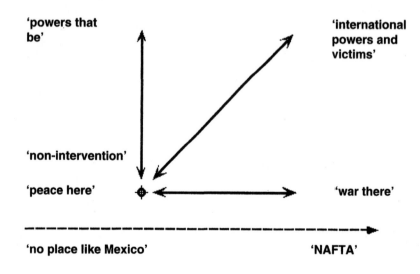

Figure 9.7 Mexican model

by reflections on whether non-intervention in international matters might not be a matter of convenience more than anything else. In addition, the respondents' assessment of the limited use value of television imply that 'action should be taken, but I'm not the one to take it'. As far as the Mexican respondents are concerned, the world as reported in television news may be sufficiently in balance, requiring no further action – at least on the part of viewers as citizens in relation to any political organs.

This conception of 'our' world as being under control, was reasserted by the super-themes which could be associated with the space dimension: there is 'peace here,' but 'war there.' And, the absence of strongly evaluated, negative or positive 'others' along the identity dimension supports the conclusion that the Mexican respondents conceived the world and their place in it as being in a steady state. As was the case with the Danish respondents, the 'others' of the Mexican viewers were of two kinds – the victims of evil, with whom viewers may identify, and the international power(s) which represent(s) the current international order, primarily the United States, and which can be expected to take the necessary action. No sense of urgency, however, was expressed by the Mexican respondents in referring to either potential friends or enemies, or to the distant 'war.'

The respondents' understanding of Mexico's place in the world as unproblematic was summed up in the traditional notion, with a long historical background on the time dimension, that there is 'no place like Mexico.' This notion parallels the reference to 'peace here' on the space dimension. This is not to say that, in the respondents' view, things might not go from good to better. In particular, they referred to the anticipated benefits of the NAFTA trade agreement for the country. Still, as of 1993, there were no indications of the Mexican respondents calling for a transition to a new form of society.

USA

The central interpretive dimension in the United States was the one of power, relating ordinary people like the respondents themselves to various relatively diffuse authorities or powerful interests – 'the powers that be' (Chapter 8). This opposition was the super-theme invoked most frequently among the American respondents. The implication is that the common people have competencies and qualities which may not be given the proper conditions to develop because the authorities will pursue their own selfish interests. This concern was also raised with reference to the two other super-themes in the US: 'human potential' and '(obstacles to) fairness and personal freedom.' These latter super-themes could be said to address the identity of the individual viewer. Along the identity dimension (see Figure 9.8), the American respondents articulated themselves in relation to certain agents and values that might ensure individual freedom in the longer term. Compared to several of the other countries studied, however, the values and agents appeared not to be personified to the same degree. As in the case of the vaguely described authorities on the power dimension, the American respondents made rather few concrete references to the specific representatives or contexts of their preferred values.

Indeed, a unifying orientation behind the super-themes of the US respondents could be identified in the form of the individual's perspective on his or her life chances. The American version of the model as a whole bears witness to a focus at the bottom left-hand corner, what was referred to in the general model (Figure 9.1) as the 'here' of the 'individual.' (However, the individual accomplishments mentioned by respondents were not necessarily their own.) An individual or local focus was also in evidence in the references to the authorities that were mentioned, which were individuals or institutions rather than other nations or transnational agents.

Moreover, the space dimension, as identified in the other six countries, was not instantiated in the American respondents' super-themes. While this might be due, in part, to the nature of the particular news items that they watched and commented on in Newsday, it seems at least equally possible that these respondents, belonging to the one remaining super power, may perceive their country and themselves as 'the center of the world.' In contrast to the Israeli respondents who specifically commented on this perspective of their own place in the world, the place of the US at the center of world events may be so obvious as to require no explicit commentary, being an absence that speaks. This outlook on the world might be dubbed 'tunnel space,' denoting a highly selective form of attention from a centralized point of view, again by analogy to tunnel vision.

A similar absence implying selective attention, already referred to as 'tunnel time' in the case of Israel, could also be identified in the interviews from the US. The American respondents did not introduce any super-themes along the time

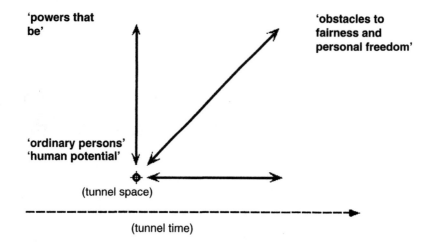

Figure 9.8 USA model

dimension and, thus, did not appear to interpret the news of the day with reference to historical events or the recent past to any important degree. Again, this might be due to the particular news contents of Newsday. However, in this respect, it is more likely that the American respondents – in contrast to those in Israel and the other countries studied – placed little importance on historical change. This is a notion that has often been put forward by journalists, scholars, and other observers of American culture, i.e. that due to the brevity of their own history and experience as a nation and the prolonged period of domestic peace and relative economic prosperity enjoyed in the US, Americans in general have a limited awareness of other cultures and time periods (p. 144). While, for the Israeli respondents, their history may seem to be compressed in the many current threats to their existence, for the American respondents time may appear as a more or less continuous present.

Correlated cultures

At an immediate, substantive level, the interview discourses bear witness to a variety of similarities and differences between the seven countries, both in terms of the place that each country is assigned on an 'international news map' of the world, and in terms of the configurations of super-themes which respondents in different national settings employ in their interpretations of particular TV news stories. Regarding the respondents' 'maps' of the world, it is not surprising to find the United States depicted as a major center which commands attention from a large periphery that includes, for example, Indian respondents looking for an ally and Mexican respondents looking for a trade partner. Conversely, Danish respondents explicitly defined themselves as being on the periphery, referring to the US as a world leader in times of conflict. At the same time, it seems clear that, in their mapping of the world, the respondents will focus on crises close to home which are affecting them directly, either in the region (Belarus, Israel) or within the borders of the country (India, Italy). From each respondent's perspective, then, his or her country may constitute a center, even if explanations for, and solutions to, a current crisis will have to be found in *its* periphery, depending on the nature and severity of the crisis. Equally, the special attention that was given to domestic news, and to national perspectives on foreign news – as witnessed in a number of household interviews, but also in the individual interviews and the news contents of the period studied (Appendix A) – implies a stepwise 'domestication' (Cohen et al. 1996) of the news from the viewer's perspective within a specific cultural setting.

Moreover, structural homologies between the super-themes of the seven countries suggest that news items about rather different events, as received under equally different conditions, may produce comparable responses among the viewing public. The homologies also point to a possible categorization of the seven countries in the present study. Their cultural and national-political context is a necessary constituent of any explanation of how viewers may decode and socially use television news. The participating countries may be classified as either 'cultures of stability' or 'cultures of crisis' – the latter are examined first.

While recognizing the very different origins of the crises affecting Belarus and India, one finds in both cases a transitional, national event in the recent past (sovereignty in Belarus, renewed ethnic violence in India) which has implications for the status of the country as a nation and in relation to other countries in the region. This type of event appears to have thematized both the power dimension and the identity dimension for respondents in these two countries. Whereas a sense of disillusionment with the state was articulated along the power dimension in both contexts, certain negatively evaluated 'others' in the region, associated with the identity dimension, were blamed for the present difficulties in each country. A somewhat related interpretive structure could be identified in Israel, whose crisis may be as foundational as in the case of India and Belarus. In Israel, the respondents pointed to the negatively evaluated 'others' who are 'outwitting us,' even though the main, concrete threat was associated with Israel's neighbors along the space dimension, rather than with representatives of the state along the power dimension. Also in the Italian interviews, a transition – from the old, corrupt system to a possible political revival – was key to several super-themes, although this development may not qualify as a foundational experience of the same order. In addition, the Italian study found the Pope to be a positively evaluated 'other' along the identity dimension, in contrast to the negatively evaluated 'others' in the other 'cultures of crisis,' which might imply that the Italian respondents saw their national crisis as at least soluble.

Compared to these 'cultures of crisis,' that are experiencing hardship and change in different forms and with different intensities, Denmark and Mexico can be said to represent 'cultures of stability', with both enjoying relative, if not equal, peace and prosperity as of 1993 – as witnessed by super-themes along several dimensions. Whereas the Danish respondents repeatedly emphasized their distance from the center of events, Mexican respondents introduced the notion of there being 'no place like Mexico,' simultaneously noting its peacefulness and its principle of non-intervention. In both countries, moreover, the respondents' 'others' were divided, respectively, into the positively evaluated international powers who are supposed to take charge of crises, and the similarly positively evaluated victims who are not 'us,' but who should be pitied and helped. Lastly, the US, while being a 'culture of stability' in present terms, belongs in a category by itself. Here, respondents tended to conceive of crises, change, and hardship in individual rather than institutional, national, or transnational terms. For example, whereas the 'powers that be' were described in Mexico as institutionalized agents, including other countries, in the US 'the powers that be' comprised a more vaguely defined set of obstacles to personal freedom and enterprise.

CONCLUSION

Global theory

In turning to an examination of the relevance of the model for theory development, this section first clarifies the nature of the analysis which generated it, and then reconsiders the research issues that were outlined in Chapter 1 in light of the model. Whereas the model has literally been the outcome of a multitude of analytical operations (as documented in the chapters about the individual countries and in the paragraphs above), the elements and stages of the analysis may be specified. One of the main challenges for qualitative studies of media remains that of explicating the analytical procedures employed and their grounding in the theory of science (see further, Appendix B).

Qualitative research, as practiced in the present audience study, may be characterized as the in-depth analysis of human discourse with constant reference to its context. In reception studies, audience discourses are examined with reference to media discourses as well as to the context of media use. Importantly, the analysis proceeds in an iterative or recursive process which facilitates the reinterpretation and reconceptualization of the individual elements of discourse in several successive stages. The principle of inference which underlies such a qualitative analysis is neither deduction nor induction as traditionally defined, but has been referred to as 'abduction' (Peirce 1992 [1878]; see also Eco 1984; Jensen 1995). Abduction is a form of hypothetical inference which proceeds by theoretical argument and contextual evidence. In the present study, the repeated and comparative analysis of individual interview responses enabled the identification of super-themes in each national setting. A further comparative analysis of interview responses and super-themes from the seven different settings enabled the formulation of the four interpretive dimensions of the model, in part with reference to social theory about the time, space, and social relations of modernity. (This is further addressed below.) Next, a key stage in the process of abduction was the configuration of the four dimensions in the form of 'a model of the world in the head,' which provided a framework in which to reassess the relevance of each dimension and of the various super-themes as the viewers' interpretive repertoires (Potter and Wetherell 1987). Finally, the version of the model that has been proposed for each country was the product of a reexamination of its 'national' super-themes with reference to the full model, and to its configuration in the other six countries.

In sum, this form of research contributes to theory development by taking the individual analytical operations of a concrete empirical study as a basis, step by step, for the broader conceptualizations and models that inform theories of communication and reception. In formulating the model and its constituent concepts, the present study has also been able to draw not only on previous communication theory, but also on both classic and recent social theory, as outlined in Chapter 1. One of the main strengths of qualitative research designs such as this one is that it facilitates an integration of a 'bottom-up' analysis, departing from empirical data, with a 'top-down' analysis, departing from

181

previous theoretical positions. In particular, the model above has drawn on recent social theory as developed, for instance, by Giddens (1984, 1990) on the everyday life and lived culture of modern societies. The dimensions of the model indicate how the audiences of the modern mass media may articulate specific and different understandings of social space, time, authority, and identity, in response to particular media genres and with reference to their cultural context. The empirical research in the seven different cultures has lent substance and texture to some previous general accounts of the role of the media in political and cultural processes (e.g. Thompson 1995), while simultaneously specifying some of the forms that modernization and globalization, as experienced by the public, may take in different settings.

While the empirical evidence thus provides support for the explanatory value of the heuristic model outlined in Figure 9.1 as a macro-level description of cultural differences, the precise status of the model calls for further discussion. As a micro-level, mental model, it might also be seen to serve individual viewers as an operational model – a means of orientation and a readiness to act in relation to world events – what has been labeled here 'a model of the world in the head.' This notion, of course, has a long history both in philosophy, dating at least to Plato's metaphor of the cave, in which shadows hint at a richer, external reality (in *The Republic*), and in communication research, with Lippmann's (1922) account of the 'pictures in the head' of the audience as one early contribution. In recent research, the findings resonate with a growing variety of cognitive theories and empirical studies on how audiences may approach media by analogy to perception and cognition of everyday phenomena outside the media (e.g. Bordwell 1985; Branigan 1992; Grodal 1997; Messaris 1992; 1997; Reeves 1996), including research on the schemata by which information from news media is processed (e.g. Graber 1984).

In the context of discussing the present model, it may suffice to briefly consider the relationship between, on the one hand, such cognitivist and sometimes universalist approaches to media reception and other human experience and, on the other hand, various culturalist and historicist approaches. As suggested by the present findings, empirical research on media and communication must allow for the specificity and variability of culture as a lived experience. One danger, as identified perhaps most famously by Said (1978) in his analysis of 'orientalism,' is that researchers and other observers may impress their particular (Western) worldview on the foreign culture being studied. Another danger is that empirical accounts, by their very discursive construction, may end up naturalizing one perspective on the culture in question, a concern which has been reasserted in anthropology and cultural studies at least since the volume by Clifford and Marcus (1986) on ethnography as a form of discourse.

Nevertheless, there is no way around universalism in research, in the sense of theoretical generalization. Not least, cross-cultural and other specifically comparative research evidently requires some unified, if preliminary, theoretical perspective or discursive position from which the objects of research may be observed and interpreted. Contrary to the assumptions of some radically decon-structionist conceptions of empirical research (e.g. Clough 1992), entailing infinite loops of reflexivity, the meta-analytical or self-reflexive stages of research need to be guided by an explicit, focused purpose if it is to have more than academic relevance. Otherwise, studies are unlikely to make the sort of social or political difference that critical research especially, including its deconstruc-tionist variety, commonly claims for itself.

One way of addressing the duality of media and other cultural forms – being both situated, lived experiences that are organized in 'fuzzy' themes, and a set of more delimited conceptual categories which lend themselves to abstract analy-sis – has been proposed by Kenneth Pike in his distinction between 'emic' and 'etic' modes of understanding. This distinction permeates anthropology, a disci-pline founded on the premise that research may broach the two sides of culture. Pike (1967: chap. 2) extrapolated his categories from the study of linguistic sounds. Linguistics distinguishes between a 'phonetic' approach, which assumes a universal set of sounds as measured, for instance, on acoustic scales, and a 'phonemic' approach that proposes to establish the distinctive set of sounds which constitute a particular language. In a wider sense, Pike suggested the emic–etic distinction would be relevant for the study of forms of human expres-sion other than verbal language. Hence, he matched and differentiated the distinction regarding linguistic sounds through a further set of conceptual pairs, including internal–external, specific–cross-cultural, and relational–absolute units of analysis. In anthropology and other social science, for example, in studies of subcultures, these distinctions have served to remind scholars of the importance of examining the constitutive elements of a society or culture both from the (emic) perspective of its members or participants – the native's point of view – and from the perspective of a(n) (etic) common denominator of theoretical concepts and terms which make possible a comparative analysis of several perspectives either across or within cultures.

The 'model of the world in the head,' as derived from interviews with media audiences in seven cultures, rests on this distinction. At an emic level, the super-themes represent ways of understanding the world which are grounded in the respondents' everyday lives in specific national and cultural settings, as articu-lated in their interview discourses. At an etic level, the dimensions of the model constitute analytical categories which cut across cultures. The model certainly calls for further research, for example, on the theoretical relationship of various super-themes to the interpretive dimensions and on the nature of the emic-etic continuum in practical research. However, the four dimensions of the model have proven relatively robust in the analysis of the present, admittedly small, samples of viewers from radically different cultures. Before turning to some additional implications of the model, the other main substantive findings of the project should be summarized. (Findings about the contents of television news in the seven participating countries during Newsweek, complementing the accounts in the country chapters of how stories on Newsday in various ways informed super-themes, are reported in Appendix A.)

Television and other news media

Survey research in a number of countries regularly measures, first of all, the extent to which different news media are consumed by the public, providing what is probably the most voluminous and readily available evidence on news audiences. Second, survey studies commonly seek to establish which news medium is perceived by the public to be, for example, the most informative or credible, offering a measure of the sorts of gratifications which audiences seek from news. However, a commonsensical response to questions about the relative merits of different news media, underscored by respondents from these seven countries, is that it depends on the particular issue, on the prospective uses of the information, and on the economic basis and organizational structure of each medium, rather than on the medium as such. To exemplify, in the Indian context, TV was referred to as the most credible source, not least because of the visuals, but not unequivocally so in the case of Doordarshan (DD), Indian state television. On the one hand, DD was perceived as an agent of the state; on the other hand, DD escaped the suspicion directed at some other channels that their commercial motives tend to lead to sensationalist news coverage. Similarly, in Israel, the argument for considering TV the more credible medium was that newspapers traditionally express partisan viewpoints. Among the US respondents, the point was reemphasized that television is one among several news media. This was not surprising in view of the versatile American media environment – if several news media are available every day, why choose, except in response to pollsters?

The everyday context helps to explain why people turn to a specific medium at a given point of the day. In Belarus, respondents described radio as offering in the morning what TV provides in the evening, that is, an overview of events, to be followed up in various print media. In both cases, media use was presented as a habit that is to be coordinated with other duties and activities. In Mexico, especially some of the younger respondents noted that TV offers a convenient and cheap means of access to news compared, for instance, to newspapers.

Despite the attention given by respondents to a plurality of news media, television may be conceived as a center of the entire media environment. Italian respondents found that newspapers seem to be increasingly dependent on TV in their coverage. Danish respondents noted that newspapers may now be skimmed rather than read carefully, having been replaced by TV as the main source. Both Danish and Indian respondents, incidentally, predicted that transnational satellite channels such as CNN will set the terms or ideals for news coverage also on national channels in the future. In addition, the individual interviews in all seven countries referred to TV as a source of news more often than any other medium (Appendix A).

Contexts of reception

As in the comparison of news media, the role of newscasts in the immediate context of viewing was a minor topic in the household interviews. No extended observations were conducted, and the following brief account rests on verbal descriptions by household members.

Lull's (1980) typology for categorizing the uses of television in the family remains the most comprehensive framework for research in this area. He identified 'structural' uses, referring to the ways in which TV serves to regulate, structure, and accompany other activities, and 'relational' uses, designating TV as a medium of exchange for interaction within the households, with each type of use having a number of subcategories. Whereas all of these categories are in evidence in the present material to varying degrees, it will be useful to elaborate briefly the typology with reference to the theories of everyday life and society which also informed the model above. First, 'structural' uses concern the role of television in organizing time and space, primarily in the home setting, but frequently with reference to a larger social space or to historical time. Social space surrounds and impinges on the household just as, to a degree, world history shapes and explains family history. Second, 'relational' uses treat television programming as a source of knowledge and as a topic for discussion in the household, but always in the context of particular family structures and cultural traditions. Television viewing – reassembling the family as a social group – provides an occasion for asserting and displaying the prevailing roles of power and competence, both between generations and genders and as an occasion for reconsidering one's social and cultural identity either as an individual or as a family group.

Under the heading of structural uses, Lull (1980) distinguished between 'environmental' and 'regulative' uses. TV creates an environment of background noise, companionship, and entertainment; it also offers a means of regulating family life by punctuating time and activities, including talk patterns. In these respects, the very act of using the medium may be the message. However, the specific social uses – environmental and regulative – of the various television genres may be rather different. In several countries, news was singled out as a genre which calls for particular attention by the household as a unit. Not only was news viewing described as a 'family affair' in Denmark, Israel, Italy, and the US, but many respondents in these countries also ascribed particular importance and seriousness to the news genre, because it gives an occasion for considering some of the larger issues that may ultimately affect the household. In Belarus, India, and Mexico, while respondents similarly attached great importance to news, joint viewing and conversation about stories was not described as a regular feature of daily life. The respondents in Belarus found that there was little time for joint viewing, especially for women working outside the home, whereas the respondents in Mexico noted that other genres such as sports or soap operas would more typically attract joint viewing. In the US, there were some indications that the news served as a background or environment just as often as it would become a focus of attention. These variations in the environmental or regulative uses of television may also suggest differences in the degree to which the medium has been adopted and integrated as a natural part of everyday life, in addition to other cultural differences. For further research, the present findings suggest the importance of examining not merely the social uses of television in general, but the specific uses of genres such as news as it relates to a particular cultural context.

The importance of genre, and of its varied uses in different cultural contexts, also became clear in connection with relational uses of television, which comprise four subcategories. First, 'communication facilitation' – that is, the use of television as an agenda for conversation – was exemplified for the news genre in numerous households in the present data. However, in India little conversation about news was said to take place around the television set, just as in Mexico such conversation was found to take place more often outside the home. Second, TV is an occasion for 'affiliation' or 'avoidance' of contact in the family. As noted, in some countries news viewing was defined as a family affair. Third, TV contributes to 'social learning,' not only by the individual viewer, but in the interaction between parents and children. In Italy, some adult respondents expressed a need to correct the representation of events in the news to their children, while some Mexican respondents noted that it is a duty for the older generation to urge the young to watch and discuss the news. Fourth, interaction around television is an occasion for demonstrating 'competence' or 'dominance' in relation to other members of the household, either through knowledge or argument. This occurred in various guises – for example, in one exchange in an Italian family about the possible dangers for Italians which would arise from an involvement in the Bosnian conflict.

Several other examples underline the importance of the news genre and its current relevance for the 'relational' uses of television. In Belarus, for instance, while news was said to stimulate discussions of topical issues in public life, as a consequence of the drastic reorganization of the Belarusian economy, political topics had recently given way to economic ones as the center of attention. In Denmark, both the events in former Yugoslavia and the upcoming EU referendum attracted special commentary and discussion, being international issues with potential ramifications for Danish viewers. Finally, in Israel, it was interesting to note that some interviews suggested a thin line between conversation in front of the screen and parasocial interaction with figures in the news. One issue for further research is the form and the extent to which different genres attract parasocial interaction. In the context of the proposed model, parasocial interaction may be studied as a 'relational' use across time and space, with implications for the viewer's identity and place in a hierarchy of power, which compares to other relational uses in the immediate viewing context as well as in the viewers' further contexts of action.

News as a social resource

The model which has been developed in the present study (Figure 9.1) is perhaps best understood as a schematic representation of how citizens may orient themselves in a political, economic, and cultural field of action, what the pragmatist tradition in social theory refers to as a predisposition to act (e.g. Bernstein 1991; Joas 1993). A widespread assumption among these respondents, as well as in much public and policy debate and in the normative theories of the press that inform such debates, is that news constitutes a resource for awareness of, and participation in, politics and other aspects of social life. Not only do the news media represent a social obligation, as suggested, for instance, by some Mexican viewers' reference to being suspended between pleasure and duty, but presumably unless one attends to the news regularly a loss of socialization also would follow, even if its precise consequences may be difficult to establish. And unless one participates actively in the reproduction of polity and society with reference to events in the news, one's claim to citizenship may be put into question. Nevertheless, these respondents almost unanimously indicated that the news does not, and could not, lead to much concrete action, particularly when it comes to political and other major social issues. This ambivalence regarding the principles and practice of political communication in some cases created explicit frustration or disillusionment. Polysemy may be a feature not only of media contents, but also of the audience response to, and the social definition of, news (Jensen 1990a).

The conception of news as a specific resource varies with the political and other social contexts in which the respondents find themselves. Cultures of crisis and stability (p. 180) require different news with different forms of use value. On the one hand, respondents in Belarus, India, and Israel referred to news as a necessary means of staying alert to immediate threats, conflicts, and other events affecting the individual viewer. (In addition, as noted in Chapter 6, Italian respondents referred to a generalized threat which was addressed in the family setting, but which was not linked in the interviews to possible courses of further action.) The sense of urgency was most pronounced in India, as an aftermath to news about the recent (1993) ethnic clashes, and in Israel, being in a more or less continuous state of emergency that may require immediate action by each citizen. Furthermore, in Belarus, news was described as having an almost existential importance for viewers. Here, the very regularity of news programming was said to serve as a reassurance in times of change, even if the content of news was found to overshadow any consideration of its form in Belarus. It was also interesting to note in the interviews with Belarusians that, while news as a political resource for audiences in their role as activists and propagandists had been its main use during the Communist era, economic uses of news were now considered of primary importance. However, despite the urgency of events in the news in these 'cultures of crisis,' viewers may find it difficult to apply the information as a resource in institutionalized contexts of

187

action. This was the case, for example, in India, in the context of the most urgent crisis, where several respondents concluded that the news has little use, partly because of the low relevance of the information offered by television, partly because of the powerlessness of viewers in relation to the rest of the social system.

On the other hand, not surprisingly, news was described as having even less direct applicability in the 'cultures of stability' – Denmark, Mexico, and the US – even though the respondents here also noted the importance of generally 'keeping up' with events which might at some point and in some respect affect them. In view of the extent and regularity of news viewing and reading that was also described in these countries, one may detect an implicit contradiction between news consumption as a daily political ritual and the negligible concrete use value of the activity. One reference to such a contradiction emerged in the Mexican viewers' reference to an experience of being suspended between pleasure and duty. This is comparable to the contradiction between the potential and actual relevances of television news which the Indian respondents identified.

That contradiction in the social definition of the news genre is among the policy issues raised by this study. By way of introducing these issues, it should be added that there were also demographic variations between respondents within the countries studied, as examined in much previous research on news audiences – for example, in the ability of different socioeconomic groups to recall information from news media (p. 6). In several countries, viewers with a higher socio-economic status displayed more analytical procedures in interpreting news items even though both the characteristic super-themes and the various other aspects of reception identified above were in evidence across socio-economic groups. Mexican respondents with a higher socio-economic status attached greater importance to international news, whereas those with a lower status expressed a special interest in national news. In addition, female respondents in Mexico did not refer to the importance of 'keeping up'. While further research is needed to explore such relationships between the various demographic and discursive factors shaping reception, some of the present findings have a bearing on policy issues of how audiences may define themselves, and act, as citizens.

Audiencehood and citizenship

Determination in the first instance

An unfortunate consequence of the renewed research interest in reception as a cultural microcosm has been a comparative neglect of the social macrocosm embedding reception and necessarily determining some of its conditions, a tendency which Curran (1990) has labeled "the new revisionism" (but see p. 14). This development has produced a certain alienation between, on the one hand, reception analysis and cultural studies, and, on the other hand, international communication research and political economy – the traditions of research which most consistently have explored the implications of the flow of news in the world. However, a common ground may be developing, as suggested by the recent reconceptualizations of cultural imperialism in terms of longer and deeper processes of modernization and globalization (Golding and Harris 1997), and by the growing number of reception studies that have addressed research problems with specific social and political implications (e.g. Corner et al. 1990; Jhally and Lewis 1992; Schlesinger et al. 1992). At issue in all of these research traditions is the relation between (cultural) agency and (social) structure, as addressed from one perspective by the present study.

Hall (1983) contributed an important specification of the concept of 'determination' in the area of culture. He questioned the widespread, often implicit, notion in a broadly Marxist tradition of social theory that, despite many intervening variables, it is the economic and other material infrastructures of society which produce a determination of culture in the final instance – when all is said and done, money rules and talks. Instead, Hall argued, the technological level of the means of production and the control over the relations of production amount to a determination in the first instance, within which there is some variable scope for a restructuration of everyday social practices and for a rearticulation of cultural forms. It is this field of relative determination which occupies the center of most social and cultural research.

For reception analysis, the concept of determination in the first instance suggests a further analogy between social and content structures. The discursive structures of news and other media content may be understood as determinations which predict, to a degree, the audience experience and social uses of media. Although reception studies have amply demonstrated the activity and creativity of media users, interpretations are clearly far from random, notwithstanding the more radical versions of reception theory proposed, for instance, by Fish (1979). For example, despite the documented ability of audiences to commute between several discursive positions within media texts as well as in real life, apparently audiences are quite able to identify different genres and to approach them with an awareness of their different representations of social reality, their reality status. One finding of this project is the importance of genre characteristics for the respondents' understanding of how television news may be relevant in the immediate context of viewing as well as in the wider social context.

It is against such a background of relative determination in social, as well as discursive, terms that the implications of the present study should be interpreted. In summary, the respondents consistently redefined and reinterpreted the agenda offered by journalists and by political actors appearing on the news, as evidenced in the super-themes. It is also worth noting that the different types of television systems represented in the study (commercial, public service, one/several channels – with varying degrees of state control) did not as such appear to elicit markedly different audience responses despite the expression of varying degrees of frustration or mistrust. Moreover, the findings supporting the models of 'the world in the head' suggest that the varied local cultures manifest themselves in the interpretation of foreign as well as domestic news. Culture shines through. News is potential resource for action in a specific time and place.

This does not entail, however, a celebration of the cultural specificities and critical faculties of audiences. For one thing, the relative attention given to foreign and domestic issues in, and perspectives on, the news in both household and individual interviews, was similar to the focus of news contents in each country during the period studied (see Appendix A). This suggests a correspondence between the available information and the audiences' conception of their context of action, which, in turn, corresponds to the place and status of each country on the scene of world politics. For another thing, the available information and types of news services enable certain kinds of audience activity while discounting others. The concept of determination in the first instance may also redirect the attention of communication theory away from what will by some measure of necessity happen to what could not happen given the preparatory conditions of communication. Most concretely in this study, viewers in Belarus and India have video coverage of world events available much less frequently than viewers in the other countries (Appendix A). More generally, national television systems amount to specific procedures of social communication which tend to excommunicate certain voices and which are inextricably linked to changing political relations of power as witnessed here, for instance, in Italy and Mexico. In addition, the availability of relatively little foreign coverage on television news in the US means that certain world events may never enter the American viewer's agenda.

The audience perspective does not replace other perspectives on the flow of news in the world but, rather, complements them. The availability of a diverse range of information as well as the building of communication infrastructures remain important policy issues in international cooperation. What the audience perspective may contribute by exploring the general public's interests in and uses of information is a complication of the question of who and what the news flow is for.

The melodrama of news

The contradictory conception of news, as discussed in the previous section, helps to explain the viewers' contradictory and unexpected decodings of stories which may not be foreseen by the journalistic institution or by political theory. The super-themes provide an alternative structure of interpretation that articulates the viewers' everyday perspective on the world. One might say the respondents uncover a 'hidden' or 'double' reality underneath what appears to them as an opaque surface of news.

The understanding of news by its audiences as uncovering a hidden reality has been examined in previous research with special reference to tabloid or sensationalist journalism (Gripsrud 1992). The melodramatic qualities of such news can serve to mediate between the political principles of the public events covered and the moral principles of personal life, which are the audience's immediate frame of reference. The super-themes may be the viewers' means of introducing or emphasizing certain melodramatic aspects of television news. Before considering similarities and differences between the content of tabloid journalism and the reception of national television news, the argument concerning sensationalism as a form of melodrama should be laid out. Relying on the work by Peter Brooks (1976) about classic melodrama on the stage and in literature, Gripsrud (1992: 86–9) develops the following argument, which is worth quoting at length:

> Brooks regards the melodrama as 'a sense-making system' (. . .) in the desacralized modern society emerging from the French Revolution. God was no longer the ultimate signified, the meaning behind every phenomenon. Everything was in principle debatable, no meaning was absolutely guaranteed. Melodrama was a textual machine designed to cope with the threatening black hole God left after Him when he returned to His heaven: it was constructed to demonstrate the existence of an underlying universe of absolute forces and values, moral forces and values. The melodramatic is, therefore, an expressionist aesthetic, striving to *externalize* what is underneath the chaotic and uncertain surface of modern existence. (. . .) Melodrama was didactic drama, designed to teach the audience a lesson. Today's popular press also teaches the audience a lesson, every day. It says that what the world (the news) is really about, is *emotions*, fundamental and strong: love, hate, grief, joy, lust and disgust. (. . .) If the world looks incomprehensibly chaotic, it is only on the surface. Underneath, it's the same old story.

Although this study did not perform a detailed analysis of the narrative structures of television news or the modes of addressing the audience in each country, the findings at least hint that there may be less of a melodramatic element in the national television news programs than what is described for prototypical sensationalist news in the quotation above. This is suggested both by the mostly traditional types of news categories – national politics, foreign events, the economy – that are referred to in the country chapters, and by the formats of the programs, some of which have been characterized in rather authoritarian terms, for example, in Belarus and India, where a special effort may be required of viewers if they are to decipher what is the whole point of stories behind a formal, convoluted style of reporting. Previous studies have also found that in the American context, for example, national network news presents a more classic form of 'quality' journalism (e.g. Gans 1979), while

191

local news programs represent a more 'popular' journalism in television (e.g. Altheide 1976).

Even in its own terms, however, regardless of varying degrees of sensation and drama in television newscasts, the reception of television news seems to be characterized by an aspect of melodrama, as defined above. The melodramatic aspect of news reception may be found less in particular personalized or intimate ingredients, as emphasized in tabloid news texts, than in its focus on a simple reality beneath the complex surface of news. As noted by Gripsrud (1992), news can reassure viewers that, amidst the chaos of modern existence, they are still able to relate to a familiar if hidden reality in relevant terms – it is "the same old story." What the super-themes suggest is that a melodramatic interpretation and deconstruction – in terms of such underlying interpretive constructs as authority, conflict, history, and identity – may be a more general feature of the communication of news, beyond its sensationalist varieties, and may be inter- jected by audiences in order to formulate the meaning of stories, thus perhaps compensating for a perceived irrelevance of the 'journalists' story.' The super- themes consistently rearticulate news stories from the point of view of the individual viewer, often with a high emotional investment as expressed for instance, in condemnations of 'the powers that be' or in fears of 'war' approaching, but not necessarily with reference to the private lives of people in the news or other personalized issues.

Although the super-themes and other elements of a melodramatic reception may serve viewers as a helpful interpretive aid, then, such a reception poses a problem for the traditional understanding of news as the citizen's resource in addressing specific issues as part of the political process. This problem has already been indicated in the section on news as resource (p. 187–8) which iden- tified a contradiction between the potential and actual uses of news in political practice. A related problem was noted in the discussion of the fact that many respondents seemed unable to move beyond the abstract super-themes in order to connect their interpretation of the news stories to the issues and agendas of the day. Indeed, the present data contain several specific indications that only a small group of the respondents were able to reflect upon the news, its status as discourse, or its relation to particular ongoing events. Among the Danish respon- dents, only those with a higher education were able to transcend their super-themes; in the US, too, well-educated viewers seemed more likely to link up with the 'journalists' story'. In India, specifically resistant or oppositional decodings were found among the educated, upper-class urban group, in addition to some marginalized minorities; in Israel, only a small group of respondents engaged in aesthetic criticism of the form of news; and Mexican respondents with a higher socioeconomic status were found to offer more reflection and criticism of the news than other groups. Other previous research has also noted specific limitations to the critical faculties of audiences as they attempt to reflect on the status of the news as discourse (Hacker et al. 1991).

CONCLUSION

Mediated action

The contradictory conception of news, as articulated also in the super-themes and the melodramatic aspect of reception, can be traced to a related contradiction between participatory and representative conceptions of democracy. The promise of the political revolutions in Europe and North America, symbolized by the events of 1776 and 1789, was a higher degree of participation by the general population in shaping the conditions of its own existence, in part through the emerging public sphere with the free press as its centerpiece. However, as retold by Habermas (1989 [1962]), for instance, the development of modern political systems has been characterized more by representative forms of democracy and by a press poised between the Scylla of state control and the Charybdis of market forces. Not only is most political communication mediated within bureaucratic social systems organized around a market economy and a representative form of national government, but so are most forms of political action. In a modern context, democracy works at a distance through parties, legislatures, interest groups, and other fora of mediation.

If only for this reason, it is important to recognize the limits to agency and reform in the area of public access to, and political uses of, news media. The news genre is part and parcel of that long historical process which shaped the institutions of modern societies, carrying with it submerged social conflicts and continued cultural contradictions concerning what might be and what actually is. The experience of such ambivalences is among the key features of modernity (e.g. Berman 1982; Giddens 1990; Huyssen 1986). Moreover, one aspect of modernization in recent decades has been an accelerated globalization, affecting the seven countries studied to varying degrees, but being reflected in their news coverage as well as in the very issue of news flow in international debate. Not least in a globalized economy, it is unclear what the actual relationship between news and citizens' action could be. Paraphrasing a title by the sociolinguist, Basil Bernstein (1972), who cautioned against assuming that language reform would entail social reform, it may be well to remember that 'media cannot compensate for society.'

And yet, these respondents, across cultures, join political observers from John Milton in the *Areopagitica* (1644) to Hans Magnus Enzensberger (1972) in suggesting that it could be otherwise, that an alternative proactive conception of media in politics is possible. On the one hand, they approach the news at the level of generalized super-themes, distanced from day-to-day politics, but in a sustained daily attempt to make sense of political information. On the other hand, they imply, and occasionally argue, that under different circumstances such meaningful information might enable audiences to engage in politics more actively as citizens. While the inherent contradictions of the news genre might be said to serve a broadly ideological function, alienating citizens from political practice while holding up to them the potential for participation in principle, there may still be ways of empowering audiences as citizens through institutions

193

of communication policy and education. Interventions in this respect would seem to be a necessary condition of promoting not only a nominally balanced, but also a practically relevant, flow of news in the world. The capacity to reflect upon and appropriate news beyond the abstract melodramatic form of super-themes, and to identify the social fora in which super-themes may come to inform specific procedures for action, is among the requirements for a substantially 'new world information and communication order.' This is especially true if one wants to insist that any such order be open to continuous revision, subject to enhanced public debate.

Giddens (1984) developed his notion of a 'double hermeneutic' that is at work in social science to refer to scientific concepts and procedures for interpreting social reality which may, in turn, affect how social agents reinterpret and restructure that reality. The double hermeneutic is exemplified by ideas ranging from normative theories of the press to psychoanalysis: notions of a free press, and of the unconscious mind, have become part of the working memory of modern humans. A specific double hermeneutic can be said to apply in the case of media being social institutions of reflexivity that are comparable to science and which may, in turn, reorient the actions of their audiences. If audiences are to participate in this double hermeneutic as consenting citizens, an extended definition of the rights of communication as well as of reception would seem to be needed. The issue here is not the specific form of 'media literacy' (e.g. Green 1991; Masterman 1985; Messaris 1992) to be developed in different cultural contexts, but the very importance of reintroducing audiences on the agenda of international communication policy, as supported by more comparative audience studies.

A future for comparative research

Comparison, history, and systematics

Comparative approaches, as employed in the present volume, reflect on foundational issues of methodology, substantive theory, and of a theory of science for communication research (e.g. Gurevitch and Blumler 1990). In methodological terms, this comparative analysis suggests that important aspects of audiences' situated experience and social uses of media are to be tapped through a qualitative mode of inquiry. In terms of the theory of science, which traditionally distinguishes between idiographic approaches to singular cases and nomothetic approaches to lawlike regularities of culture and society, comparative studies provide an opportunity for combining these perspectives, as exemplified by the 'idiographic' super-themes informing the 'nomothetic' models of 'the world in the head'.

Swanson (1992) identified three ways in which comparative empirical research relates to the development of substantive theory. While studies may choose 'the avoidance strategy,' ensuring theoretical consistency by giving up the opportunity for confronting a diversity of research positions with each other, and for applying them to a diversity of empirical contexts, the other options were labeled 'metatheoretical' and 'pretheoretical.' Metatheoretical analysis examines several related studies which, while relying on different methodologies and empirical materials, may arrive at common themes for conceptualizing their shared domain of inquiry. Finally, the pretheoretical strategy, as exemplified by the present study, relies on a preliminary conceptual analysis in order to construct a set of empirical research questions to be addressed in several settings as the basis of a more robust theory development. Whereas all three strategies have their strengths, depending on the purpose of the research, one advantage of the last strategy is that it facilitates a focused empirical design which is likely to yield a delimited, yet fertile, ground for theory building.

In a wider sense, the comparative perspective reflects on the classic distinction between systematics and history in research. The systematics of media and communication research is always a historical construct, building on previous research as well as on a wider cultural consensus about the nature of these phenomena, and the history of media at any given time is written according to the prevailing systematics. Comparative studies, across time as well as across space, may help to keep the systematics of research reflexive and flexible.

History is a special case of comparative research as yet underdeveloped in communications (see Schudson 1991), perhaps due to the manifestly modern qualities of media. Because of the nature of the available evidence, conclusions about the forms of communication in the past must frequently be made on a less than representative basis – or not be made at all. While the scholarly debate concerning the status of history and other humanistic disciplines as sciences has itself a long history (e.g. Popper 1972), in a contemporary context, the comparative, cross-cultural perspective also reactualizes the question of which forms of inference and documentation should be allowed as relevant and legitimate. The present investigation, for one, suggests that certain aspects of communication and reception can only be known by qualitative inquiry: the 'emic' categories of the super-themes and their relation to the 'etic' models do not lend themselves to hypothetico-deductive forms of research, representative samples, standardized categories of analysis, and the quantitative processing of data sets. The alternative would be either willful ignorance or a forcing of alien analytical categories on to, in this case, media experience as situated in cultural contexts, which would jeopardize the validity of such research projects. The 'how' of research depends on the 'what' and the 'why' (Kvale 1987).

Unification in the last instance

The most general implication of the *News of the World* project is a plea for the consolidation of qualitative methodologies in media and communication research, particularly in order to capture what was referred to as the 'emic' qualities of experience within and across cultures. Survey and experimental methods of data collection and analysis are necessary and efficient research tools for the study of many aspects of communication, but they are not suited to documenting and interpreting, for example, the various ways in which audiences engage media in context. While this may be recognized in principle in many quarters of the field, and whereas the argument is regularly made that research debates may overemphasize the qualitative–quantitative distinction for strategic reasons, there is still a widespread tendency not to grant qualitative studies any independent explanatory value, and instead to consider them as pilots for research on representative samples or as interesting illustrations of variation. The qualitative–quantitative divide is, if nothing else, a fact of research practice that is true in its consequences (W. I. Thomas in Rochberg-Halton 1986: 44).

Underlying the assessment of qualitative research as inferior or, at best, subordinate to other scholarly traditions, appears to be the assumption that, in order to contribute to a mature, comprehensive, cumulative field of inquiry, individual studies should rely on similar analytical procedures throughout the several different stages of research, as well as in examining both the institutions, processes, and contexts of communication. This assumption can be summarized as 'unification in the first instance' at the level of elementary data and analytical procedures. An alternative is 'unification in the last instance' at the level of substantive theory, as well as of the theory of science (Jensen 1995: chap. 9). This alternative would allow for multiple methodologies, whose explanatory value would depend on the object of analysis, and whose findings might ideally be interpreted with reference to a unified theoretical framework.

In audience studies, the intermediate stages of the entire communication process – that is, the moments of decoding and of the social uses of media in the immediate context – require in particular qualitative methodologies. Conversely, the early and late stages – for example, the public's exposure to various media, audience assessments of the different media, and the possible long-term effects of media use – remain more suited for quantitative methodologies. The flow of news in the world is one natural candidate for a multi-stage, multi-method project exploring such a possible division of labor in future research.

One additional challenge for qualitative communication research will be to reconsider the findings of its previous studies in an attempt to replicate, confirm, or reject their implications. While this is standard procedure in most other research traditions, qualitative reception studies have rarely, if ever, been replicated – perhaps, in part, because of their roots in culturalist, idiographic forms of scholarship; perhaps also because they have accepted a defensive position of being a less than equal enterprise compared to quantitative audience research. At the present stage, the analytical resources are available in the form of relevant theoretical frameworks, institutional frameworks such as conferences, journals, and other fora of publication and debate, as well as practical aids such as manuals and reference works, both in media research (e.g. Jensen and Jankowski 1991; Lindlof 1995) and in the broader field of social and cultural research (e.g. Denzin and Lincoln 1994; Miles and Huberman 1994). The logical consequence of claiming both independent explanatory value and a critical edge for small, in-depth audience studies, as is increasingly and rightly done, is to begin replicating findings. The super-themes by which news viewers in seven different countries managed to model and orient themselves in the world offer one starting-point.

APPENDIX A

News contents, news sources, and audience agendas

*Klaus Bruhn Jensen and David L. Swanson,
with the News of the World Research Group*

Aims

The *News of the World* project is a qualitative study. However, leading up to the household interviews on Newsday (11 May 1993) that constituted the core of the study, some limited quantitative analyses of television news content during Newsweek (5–11 May 1993) were conducted in order to produce an overview of how the world was presented to viewers in each of the seven participating countries at the time of the study. This 'menu' of news provides a background to interpreting how viewers made their own 'diet' by giving priority to certain news items on Newsday, and by processing these items as more or less relevant information as reflected in the household interviews. Findings from the content analysis contain implications for further research that might be done on a larger, representative scale about general characteristics of news coverage in these countries and about similarities, as well as differences, between the countries. However, it must be emphasized from the outset that the present sample, limited as it is with respect to time period, number of newscasts, and number of respondents, does not justify any such general conclusions.

Similarly, the individual interviews with the members of the households studied – about their preferred sources of news and about their perception of main topics in the news – can be taken as suggestive only. The small number of respondents cannot be regarded as representative of each national population, and their responses offer only a description of news interest and an evaluation of available news sources among the particular households examined in depth. These data sets, then, provide a background and supplement to the household interviews, while suggesting avenues for further comparative research of news texts and their reception and of news reception across cultures.

198

Sampling and data collection

The main evening newscasts on all nationally broadcast television channels in the participating countries were recorded during the week 5–11 May 1993 (Newsweek). Since the goal of the project was to examine events and issues in the news as viewed from the perspective of different national cultures, both local (that is, subnational, such as regional or city) newscasts and transnational satellite news channels such as CNN were excluded. (Transnational news programs do pose an important topic for further research, in part because they offer a test case of how identical newscasts are received in different cultural settings and across language barriers at a time when such transnational media appear to be growing in importance in their viewerships, and as a point of reference for journalists and the public alike for how the news genre may be developing.)

Individual interviews were also conducted with the members of the households that had been recruited (see Appendix B), in most cases also during Newsweek. Respondents were asked, first, to mention some of the current events in the world that were most important to them, and were probed for a total of between two and five events. Second, they were questioned on how they learned about these events – whether from various media or from family, friends, or colleagues. Third, respondents were asked to supply basic demographic information about themselves.

Analysis

The analysis was limited to some basic descriptive statistics of news contents and of the responses from the individual interviews. Regarding contents, the analysis gave special attention to the countries covered in news items, and to the countries originating this coverage. The findings, briefly presented below, are suggestive of the priority given to each of the seven countries in television news coverage elsewhere in the world during the limited period of this study, as well as about the outlook on the world from each participating country through the medium of television. In addition, the analysis noted the extent to which stories included video coverage – a distinctive feature of television as a news medium, and a particular asset for viewers trying to form an impression of cultural contexts of which they will most likely never have first-hand knowledge.

Regarding the small set of individual interview responses, the analysis noted the geographical focus of the respondents' news interest, whether domestic or foreign. It was recognized that their news interest was doubtless influenced to a greater or lesser extent by the geographical focus of the news programs in their home country which they view regularly. The analysis also noted the respondents' references to different sources for learning about news from around the world.

Findings 1: News contents

A first way of describing the newscasts is to note the total number of news items examined, the number of references to different countries in the sample, and the distribution of these references between foreign and domestic. The distinction between foreign and domestic news is notoriously difficult to specify theoretically and to apply in practice, partly because foreign news tends to be covered from the perspective of the culture in which it is presented and will be received. In this sense, to some extent nearly all television news is domestic. Nevertheless, the relative degree of attention given to matters inside and outside each country may suggest differences between the countries in their modes of orienting towards the rest of the world.

The sample consisted of a total of 1,355 news items which appeared in the news programs of the seven countries during Newsweek. In order to assess the relative attention given to foreign and domestic news, as well as the specific attention given to certain individual countries, all news items were coded for references to different countries. The 1,355 news items included 1,705 references to different countries (country references).

First, in respect of the news items broadcast in each country, Table A.1 indicates what percentage of the country references were to the country itself (domestic references) and what percentage concerned other countries (foreign references). At one end of the continuum, the US, Israel, and Italy all had similarly high proportions of domestic references. India was closer to the mean of the sample. At the other end of the continuum, the proportion of foreign references in Belarus was somewhat higher than domestic references, and slightly higher in Mexico. During Newsweek, Denmark's newscasts contained almost equal proportions of foreign and domestic references.

Table A.1 seems to suggest a set of countries with relatively introverted, or inward-looking, news coverage (Israel, Italy, the US) and another set of countries characterized by more extroverted, or outward-looking, coverage (Belarus, Mexico, and, with qualifications, Denmark). While this might be explained by the place of these countries on the scene of international politics, as well as by aspects of the national cultures, more extensive research is needed to examine this implication further.

In general, the results of our analyses were also consistent with previous research showing geographical regionalism to be a distinctive feature of the content of television news (pp. 7–8). With some exceptions noted below, the overall pattern across the seven countries was that, for each country, foreign news coverage concentrated primarily on regional neighbors. In Belarus, for example, 47 percent of foreign news references concerned Eastern European countries, 17 percent concerned Bosnia, and 15 percent concerned Russia; of Denmark's foreign news references, 20 percent concerned the European Union (which at the time was the subject of an upcoming referendum), 20 percent concerned various Western European countries, and 10 percent concerned Bosnia. Nearly

APPENDIX A

Table A.1 References to home country and other countries in national newscasts

	domestic references	*foreign references*	N
Belarus	38%	62%	161
Mexico	45%	55%	326
Denmark	49%	51%	271
India	57%	43%	192
USA	72%	28%	272
Israel	73%	27%	94
Italy	79%	21%	389
Country Average/Total	60%	40%	1705

Note: N = number of country references

half of India's foreign news references had to do with events in Pakistan and other Asian countries, and more than half (52 percent) of Israel's foreign news references concerned Israel's immediate Arab neighbors. In Mexico, 22 percent of the foreign news items focused on the US – a different kind of cultural proximity was reflected in 9 percent of Mexico's foreign news references which related to Spain. No data were available concerning references to other countries in Italian news stories.

One exception to this general pattern was the comparatively high degree of attention given to the US by other countries, regardless of region. For example, the US was the subject of 25 percent of foreign news references in Belarus (but see further pp. 202–3), 12 percent in India, and 10 percent in Denmark.

A second exception was the pattern of foreign news coverage within the US. Similar to television news coverage in Italy and Israel, US television news gave comparatively little attention to foreign events, as Table A.1 indicates. Moreover, the foreign news stories that were broadcast did not reflect a regional emphasis. Instead, 35 percent of foreign news references were to Bosnia and 12 percent to countries in the former Soviet Union. Arguably, this had to do with the perceived interest – and, perhaps, responsibility – of the US, as the remaining super power, for surveillance of major sites of conflict or potential crisis across the world (and the seemingly high probability during Newsweek that US troops would be sent to Bosnia), and, from their television news coverage, it appeared that the other countries in the study also viewed this super power in just the same way. At the center of regionalism, presumably, is the interest of each individual, each social or cultural group, and indeed, each country, in itself, as evidenced by the fact that the large majority of all news

201

items about each country in this study derived from its domestic newscasts. Of course, it remains for future studies to specify the extent and nature of such regions, as compared, for example, to political and economic conceptions of spheres of influence and cultural proximity, and to operationalize these concepts in larger and more reliable samples.

One further element of the analysis concerned the mutual interest that the seven countries took in each other during Newsweek. There were notable variations across the seven countries, which may begin to suggest the place of each, at least during Newsweek, on an international news map. These findings are presented in Figure A.1. That figure confirms the perception of the US as a world leader, with the United States being referred to in eighty-nine cases in foreign newscasts, which means that 31 percent of all references to the US in the sample as a whole originated from newscasts in the other countries.

The two countries that were subjects of the largest number of references in other countries in our sample were the US and Bosnia. These two countries were singled out for an analysis of which countries originated this foreign coverage. (No data were available on this point from Italy.) Figure A.2 indicates that Mexico gave most attention to its great northern neighbor, in keeping with the regionalism already noted. A high proportion of coverage also emerged from Belarus. While this might suggest that Belarus is surveying the country from which many of the trends and terms arise that may affect its modernization and development as a sovereign state, just as the US news media are surveying 'trouble spots' of some political and economic significance, a simpler explanation may be found in the fact that world news on Belarusian TV is

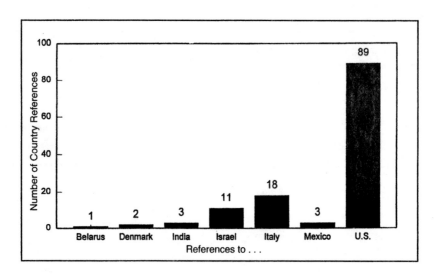

Figure A.1 References to each country in the newscasts of the other countries

Note: (N = 127)

supplied by CNN (see p. 25). The limited coverage of the US in Israel is some-what surprising, given the traditionally close ties between the two nations and the ongoing US involvement in the Middle East. However, this may be explained by the particular week selected for analysis in the current audience study.

Figure A.3 shows the corresponding figures for Bosnia, the only country outside those participating in the study to attract any large measure of coverage. This was due, of course, to the ongoing national and ethnic conflicts in the area which might affect the stability of, and the relations between, the former Eastern and Western blocs. (The comparatively high measure of news interest in Bosnia at that particular time may have made the various national newscasts in this study seem abnormally similar, and is one reason why Newsweek cannot be considered representative of the countries as such.) As much as 36 percent of all stories about Bosnia for the week came from the US, in line with the argument that the US news media serve as an early-warning system for political, and ulti-mately, military decisions and action. The proportional coverage in Belarus (23 percent) and Denmark (21 percent) is explained, in part, by their proximity to Bosnia and, in the case of Denmark, also by its role in the peace-keeping mission there.

A last measure of an international news map is suggested by the number of lead stories (defined as references within stories that were offered first or second in the order of stories within each newscast) about each country in the sample

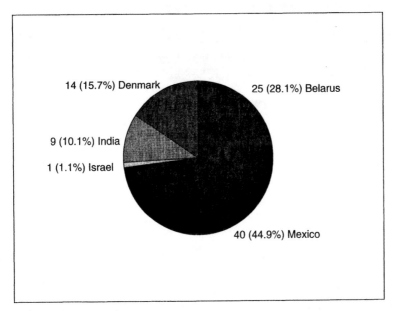

14 (15.7%) Denmark

25 (28.1%) Belarus

9 (10.1%) India

1 (1.1%) Israel

40 (44.9%) Mexico

Figure A.2 Number of news items broadcast by other countries about the US

Note: Data for Italy not available

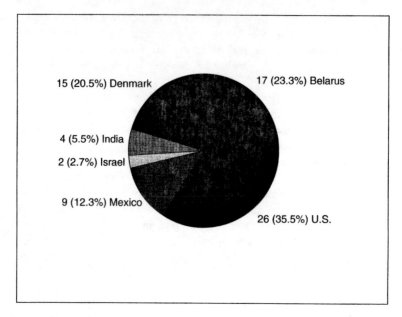

Figure A.3   Number of news items broadcast by each country about Bosnia
Note: Data for Italy not available

as a whole. This analysis, though performed on a small subset of items, points in similar directions as Figure A.2, suggesting a focus of news interest around a few countries during Newsweek, with the US at the center. There were no lead stories about Belarus, Denmark, Israel, Italy, or Mexico in the newscasts of other countries in our sample. The US attracted twelve lead stories from other national newscasts, while two lead stories in other countries dealt with India. Bosnia, again, came in a category by itself, with a total of thirty lead stories in the seven countries studied. Moreover, of all items about Bosnia in US news-casts, 77 percent were lead stories; in Denmark, that proportion was 47 percent. (In India and Israel, no lead stories dealt with Bosnia; two items about Bosnia were lead stories in Belarus, and one in Mexico.)

Finally, the proportion of news items that included video coverage (moving images) was noted for each of the seven countries. While video is a distinctive feature of television as a news medium – a means of getting a more direct impression of the geographical and cultural contexts in question – different economic and technological resources, as well as different concepts of TV news, may account for variations in this respect. The findings are given in Table A.2.

Belarus stands out in Table A.2 with video in only 43 percent of items, while India has a somewhat higher proportion (58 percent), probably reflecting, at least in part, the limited technological and other economic resources of news organizations in these two countries. The Italian news programs offered moving

Table A.2 Video coverage in news items

	% of items with video	% of items without video	N/A	N
Belarus	43%	57%		129
India	58%	42%		143
Israel	71%	29%		82
USA	73%	21%	6%	215
Mexico	90%	9%	1%	247
Denmark	92%	8%		169
Italy	98%	2%		369
Total	81%	18%	1%	1355

Note: N = number of news items

images in practically all items, closely followed by Denmark and Mexico. Given a common understanding of American TV news as both highly visual and dynamic, it may be surprising that the US newscasts, like those in Israel, included video in only a little more than 70 percent of news items (with reservations regarding the cases in which no data were available). Further research is also needed in this respect, not only on more representative samples of news contents, but also about different concepts of TV news around the world, and their historical development.

Findings 2: News sources and audience agendas

A total of 210 individual interviews were conducted during Newsweek (5–11 May 1993) with members of between ten and fifteen households per country that entered into this qualitative reception study. The number of interviews per country varied between twenty-two and thirty-six. By way of introduction, it should be stressed again that these few respondents do not comprise representative samples of their national populations. Instead, the data serve to complement and provide context for the information gained from the in-depth household interviews, suggesting the household members' news interest and their evaluation of the available news sources. In order to present an informative analysis of the individual interview responses, the news topics identified by respondents – both overall and by country – were taken as the unit of analysis. That is, the following analysis concentrates on the individual topics that were mentioned without regard to how many respondents mentioned each topic. Since this approach could not be taken in examining each respondent's assessment of news sources, that element of the findings should be interpreted with particular caution.

The 210 interviews produced 554 responses about news topics, which were defined as any references to events, persons, or issues in response to questions and probes about current events in the world that were considered of most importance. While the responses comprised a wide variety of events and issues, a major proportion of the topics seemed to arise from the respondents' national contexts. However, the events in Bosnia (or the former Yugoslavia) especially stood out, with 40 percent of all respondents referring to this topic. In addition, it was interesting to note references to a highly generalized topic of 'international wars' or 'conflicts in general'. This topic hints at a different conception of news among audiences than within professional journalism, an issue which is examined in detail in the country-by-country chapters.

The analysis noted the distribution of topics between categories of foreign and domestic for the interview responses from each country, paralleling the content analysis presented in Table A.1. These findings are presented in Table A.3.

Table A.3 shows that large proportions of the topics named by respondents in Israel (79 percent), Italy (72 percent), and the US (72 percent) referred to domestic matters. On the other hand, greater attention was given to topics of foreign news especially in Belarus (73 percent), but also in Denmark (63 percent) and in Mexico (59 percent). As can also be seen in Table A.3, the distribution of topics mentioned by Indian respondents between the domestic and foreign categories resembled the average across respondents in the seven countries as a whole.

The analysis also suggested the need for further research on regionalism, in the content of news as well as in the audience agendas of events and issues, with reservations because of the small bases of data regarding each country in this sample. In Belarus, events in the former Soviet Union accounted for 77 percent of foreign topics, Russia itself for 60 percent. In Denmark, Bosnia was referred to in 54 percent of foreign topics, and Eastern Europe altogether in 71 percent.

Table A.3 References to home country and other countries in individual interviews

	% references to home country	*% references to foreign countries*	*N*
Belarus	27%	73%	95
Denmark	37%	63%	73
Mexico	41%	59%	88
India	57%	43%	79
USA	72%	28%	89
Italy	72%	28%	82
Israel	79%	21%	48
Country Average/Total	53%	47%	554

Note: N = number of news topics in interview responses

In Mexico, Bosnia was mentioned in 33 percent of foreign topics, and the US in 15 percent. And, for example, 20 percent of the foreign topics named by Indian respondents referred to the murder of the Sri Lankan President.

A final element of the analysis of news topics, as expressed in the individual interviews, sought to identify to what degree the interest in each of the seven countries came from respondents in the country itself or from respondents in the other countries. The findings are simple, paralleling the content analysis in Figure A.1, and suggesting, once again, an international news map with centers and peripheries. When domestic topics were excluded, only two countries appeared in topics mentioned by respondents in other nations – the US, with fifteen topics; and Israel, with seven topics.

To conclude the quantitative analysis, the individual respondents' descriptions of their sources of news for learning about the topics they mentioned were examined. Since respondents were allowed to name multiple media as well as other people as sources of news, the percentages exceeded 100. (No data were available on this point from Italy.) Across the countries studied, TV was the most frequently mentioned source of news, referred to by an average 92 percent of the respondents. Next came newspapers (66 percent) and radio (40 percent), with family and friends at an almost equally high level (37 percent). Another 12 percent on average referred to colleagues, 11 percent to other sources. However, beyond variations in the sample with regard to the preferred media, it is important to note that the responses suggest that audiences will rely on several rather than just one news medium. Apart from larger studies in various national contexts of the public perception of different news media, the country-by-country chapters in the present volume suggest some of the complementarity of the news media in everyday contexts as well as the specific social uses of each.

Implications

First and foremost, the findings reported in this appendix offer background information on TV news coverage in each of the seven countries participating in the qualitative interview study of viewers, as well as additional information on the news interests and media preferences of members of the households being interviewed. Second, the analysis of this relatively small sample of news contents during a limited time period contains implications for further research – on regionalism, on introverted and extroverted news cultures, on hot spots such as Bosnia, and on the centers and peripheries of an international news map, of which aspects have also been documented in previous studies (pp. 7–9). Third, the analyses brought out what may be important correspondences between these structures of television news contents and the orientation of viewers towards events and issues reported in the news. While it is improbable, prima facie and in the light of the research reviewed in Chapter 1, that television news could be the direct, or even the primary, cause of these viewers' orientation towards events in the world, the empirical question of how television news interacts with other media and genres, as well as with other sources of experience, in shaping the public's frames of understanding and action, calls for a wide spectrum of research methodologies. Chapter 9 further addresses possible strategies of research in the light of findings from the qualitative household interviews which are reported in the rest of this volume.

APPENDIX B

Qualitative interview methodology

Klaus Bruhn Jensen

Aims

The purpose of the qualitative interviews with a small sample of households in the seven countries participating in the *News of the World* project was to contribute to a better understanding of how television viewers in different regions of the world interpret and apply TV news – as part of their everyday life and with a view to their political and cultural contexts of action. While individual interviews, as well as a content analysis of news programs, also entered into the study (as reported in Appendix A), the household interviews constituted its core. The project was conceived, first of all, as a contribution to theory development and to the accumulation of qualitative evidence about processes of media use. Comparative, cross-cultural studies may offer a special opportunity to explore distinctive features of such processes as they relate to particular social, historical, and national settings. Second, the findings may provide insights for policy discussions about the flow of news in the world, which has previously been examined primarily with reference to the production side and to the contents of news.

Sampling

The seven countries – Belarus, Denmark, India, Israel, Italy, Mexico, and the United States – were selected as examples of various political and media systems in different regions of the world. In each country, a sample typically of between ten and fifteen households was recruited, considering as far as possible features such as age, socio-economic status, race and ethnicity, geographical location, and household type (with/without children or live-in relatives, one/several heads of household). Compared to quantitative studies, which generally emphasize large representative samples, it is one of the strengths of qualitative studies that they may examine a small yet highly varied sample in depth. In addition, whereas no random sample was aimed for within the study design that was chosen, close friends and relatives of researchers and interviewers were avoided.

The day on which household interviews were to be conducted, Newsday, was selected so as to avoid weekends and national holidays in all the countries, and to ensure that it did not coincide with any major scheduled or foreseeable events, such as elections or international conferences. It was anticipated, therefore, that Newsday would be a more or less typical day for television news coverage in all the countries involved. (For logistical reasons, in some countries a remainder of the interviews had to be carried out on the following days.)

Data collection

Interviewers, primarily colleagues and graduate students, arrived in the selected households in advance of evening newscasts. (In most cases, the households had been visited once before when the individual interviews, as described in Appendix A, were conducted.) Households were asked to choose the national evening news program they preferred to watch, and the interviewer viewed the program along with members of the household, making occasional notes, regarding comments made and other interaction in the context of viewing, and regarding news items on which questions would later be posed.

Interviews took place immediately after the news program ended, and typically lasted for one to two hours. Audio recordings were made so that transcripts could later be prepared for the purpose of a detailed textual analysis of the interview discourses. The transcripts make up the main data set for the audience analysis, and have been interpreted with reference to the original audio recordings, the interviewer's field notes on the viewing session and interview, and the news programs.

A set of notations is used in quotations from the interview transcripts (see p. xiii). The purpose is, first, to facilitate cross-reference and comparison across respondents and countries. Second, the page references to the individual transcripts will enable further research on the present data. (In cases where names are used to refer to respondents, an alias has been chosen in order to preserve anonymity.)

The interview guide below was translated into the local languages represented in the study, and transcripts and analyses were also first prepared in the local language. Later, in reporting their findings, the participating researchers translated interview quotations and key concepts into English, in collaboration with the editor. Not only would the cost of translating the massive amount of interview texts into English have been prohibitive for a project of this kind, but also important linguistic and conceptual nuances would have been lost by translating data 'in the first instance' (pp. 195–7). One of the main strengths of qualitative research is that it may tap the respondent's categories and worldviews in their everyday form, as experienced and lived. Thus, the varieties of reception were compared and synthesized only 'in the last instance'.

Interview guide

Interviews were intensive and semi-structured. The following questions were posed in all households in all countries, even if not necessarily in this order. Depending on the first responses, interviewers were instructed to probe for additional information, and to cue respondents if necessary.

1   Please tell me about the one story in the news we just watched that was most important to you.
     Probes (optional):

   - To you, what was the main point or event of that story?
   - Did some of you find another story more important?
   - What did you think about when you were watching that particular story?
   - How did you feel about the pictures that were shown in the story?
   - How important is the story to this country?
   - Why do you think television news covers the story?
   - What did you think about when you told me about the story just now?

2   Now I would like you to tell me about another story that was important to you. It should be about an event outside this country.
     Cue: There was a story about . . .
     Probes: as under question 1.
     Extra probe (obligatory): Was this story like any other story which was also in the broadcast, or which you have heard about from another source?

3   Again, I would like you to tell me about a story that was important to you. This time it should be about an event inside this country.
     Cue: There was a story about . . .
     Probes: as under question 1.
     Extra probe (obligatory): Was this story like any other story which was also in the broadcast, or which you have heard about from another source?

4   There was a story about X (selected by interviewer for its topical interest). To you, what was the main point or event of that story?
     Probes: as under question 1.

5   I would like to hear a little about what normally goes on in the room while you are watching the news.
     Probes (optional):

   - Who is normally present?
   - Do you talk, eat, or do other things?

- Do you discuss news stories while watching them? If so, what kind of stories? Who takes part in discussions?

6   After watching the news, people may remember some stories and use the information for various purposes. Do you feel that you can use television news for particular purposes?
Probes (optional):

- in conversation (with whom)?
- for planning your personal economy?
- at work?
- for developing political opinions?
- for consumer information?
- in political activity (political parties, grassroots movements, campaigns, etc.)?

Extra probe (obligatory): Can you use the story about Y? The story about Z? (selected by interviewer for their topical interest).

7   Were there any stories that you had expected to find in the broadcast and missed in their absence?
Probe (optional):

- Have you ever found that a story seemed to be missing in the news?

8   The program we watched tonight is one out of several news media available. In your opinion, how does this program compare with other sources of news?
Probes (optional):

- Compared to other television news programs?
- Compared to other media (newspapers, radio)?
- Do you have any other criticisms of this program?

9   Do you have any further comments on the broadcast or television news in general?

Analysis

The development of systematic procedures of analysis remains one of the main challenges for reception studies and other qualitative research (see further pp. 195–7). In the *News of the World* project, two main analytical approaches were drawn upon: coding for interpretive frames and discourse analysis. In frame analysis, the purpose is to identify and characterize the distinctive, if sometimes overlapping cognitive and emotional categories that individuals employ in constructing an understanding of social reality (e.g. Neuman, Just, and Crigler 1992: chap. 4). In discourse analysis, selected aspects of language use are similarly conceived as indicators of how humans make sense of the world (e.g. Jensen 1986: chap. 10). In each case, the analysis serves to establish the occurrence of particular forms of understanding which may be interpreted with reference to other quantitative as well as qualitative evidence, and with reference to explanatory models and theories of how social institutions and practices may generate such understandings. In view of the exploratory nature of the present study, no standardized procedure was imposed across the national data sets; the categories identified in each national setting are exemplified and substantiated in the respective chapters. The findings provide the background to the comparative analysis in Chapter 9, and they contain implications for further research, both on specific empirical issues and on the complementarity of qualitative and quantitative approaches in media and communication research.

BIBLIOGRAPHY

Abdziralovich, I. (1993) *On the Eternal Way: Analysis of the Belarusian Mentality*, Minsk: Nauka i Technika (in Belarusian).

Adorno, T. and Horkheimer, M. (1977) [1944] "The culture industry: enlightenment as mass deception," in J. Curran, M. Gurevitch, and J. Woollacott (eds) *Mass Communication and Society*, London: Edward Arnold.

Alianza Cívica (1994) "La TV favorece al PRI," *La Jornada*, 15 July, Mexico.

Almond, G. and Verba, S. (1963) *Civic Culture*, Boston: Little, Brown.

Altheide, D. (1976) *Creating Reality*, Beverly Hills CA: Sage.

Anderson, B. (1983) *Imagined Communities*, London: Verso.

Ang, I. (1985) *Watching Dallas*, London: Methuen.

Ang, I. and Hermes, J. (1991) "Gender and/in media consumption," in J. Curran and M. Gurevitch (eds) *Mass Media and Society*, London: Edward Arnold.

Ansolabehere, S. and Iyengar, S. (1995) *Going Negative: How Attack Ads Shrink and Polarize the Electorate*, New York: Free Press.

Asard, E. and Bennett, W. L. (1997) *Democracy and the Marketplace of Ideas: Communication and Government in Sweden and the United States*, New York: Cambridge University Press.

Baacke, D. and Kübler, H. (eds) (1987) *Qualitative Medienforschung: Konzepte und Erprobungen*, Tübingen: Niemeyer.

Baldwin, T. F., Barrett, M., and Bates, B. (1992) "Uses and values for news on cable television," *Journal of Broadcasting and Electronic Media*, 36: 225–233.

Barthes, R. (1973) [1957] *Mythologies*, London: Paladin.

Beniger, J. (1992) "Comparison, Yes, But – The case of technological and cultural change," in J. Blumler, J. McLeod, and K. E. Rosengren (eds) *Comparatively Speaking: Communication and Culture across Time and Space*, Newbury Park CA: Sage.

Bennett, W. L. (1988) *News: The Politics of Illusion*, 2nd edn, New York: Longman.

—— (1992) *The Governing Crisis: Media, Money, and Marketing in American Elections*, New York: St. Martin's Press.

Berelson, B. (1949) "What missing the newspaper means," in P. F. Lazarsfeld and F. M. Stanton (eds) *Communication Research 1948–49*, New York: Duell, Sloan, and Pearce.

Berman, M. (1982) *All That Is Solid Melts into Air: The Experience of Modernity*, London: Verso.

214

Bernstein, B. (1972) "Education cannot compensate for society," in Language and Learning Course Team (eds) *Language in Education*, London: Open University Press.

Bernstein, R. (1991) *The New Constellation*, Cambridge: Polity Press.

Blumler, J. and Katz, E. (eds) (1974) *The Uses of Mass Communications*, Beverly Hills CA: Sage.

Bogart, L. (1989) *Press and Public*, 2nd edn, Hillsdale NJ: Erlbaum.

—— (1995) *Commercial Culture: The Media System and the Public Interest*, New York: Oxford University Press.

Bohmann, K. (1989) *Medios de Comunicacion y Sistemas Informativos en México*, Mexico: CNCA/Alianza Editorial Mexicana.

Bordwell, D. (1985) *Narration in the Fiction Film*, London: Methuen.

Boyd-Barrett, O. and Thussu, D. (1992) *Contra-Flow in Global News*, London: John Libbey.

Branigan, E. (1992) *Narrative Comprehension and Film*, London: Routledge.

Bredegaard, K. and Davidsen-Nielsen, M. (1992) 'The flow must go on,' MA Thesis, Roskilde University, Denmark.

Briller, B. R. (1990) "Zooming in closer on the news audience," *Television Quarterly*, 25(1): 107–16.

Brooks, P. (1976) *The Melodramatic Imagination*, New Haven CT: Yale University Press.

Bryant, J. and Zillmann, D. (eds) (1994) *Media Effects: Advances in Theory and Research*, Hillsdale NJ: Lawrence Erlbaum.

Carey, J. W. (1989) *Communication as Culture*, Boston: Unwin Hyman.

Carlsson, U. (ed.) (1988) *The Nordicom Review*, 1/1988.

Casetti, F. (1995) (ed.) *L'ospite fisso*, Torino: San Paolo.

Caspi, D. and Limor, Y. (1992) *The Mediators: The Mass Media in Israel 1948–1990*, Tel-Aviv: Am Oved (in Hebrew).

Chaffee, S. and Hochheimer, J. (1985) "The beginnings of political communication research in the United States: origins of the 'limited effects' model," in E. Rogers and F. Balle (eds) *The Media Revolution in America and Western Europe*, Norwood NJ: Ablex.

Cheli, E. (1988) "Aspetti sociopsicologici del processo di comprensione," *Problemi dell'informazione* 3.

Chowla, N. L. (1985) "Business by the box," *The Statesman*, 24 November, India.

Clifford, J. and Marcus, G. E. (eds) (1986) *Writing Culture: The Poetics and Politics of Ethnography*, Berkeley: University of California Press.

Clough, P. (1992) *The End(s) of Ethnography*, Newbury Park CA: Sage.

Cohen, A. A. and Wolfsfeld, G. (eds) (1993) *Framing the Intifada: People and Media*, Norwood NJ: Ablex.

Cohen, A., Levy, M., Roeh, I., and Gurevitch, M. (1996) *Global Newsrooms, Local Audiences: A Study of the Eurovision News Exchange*, London: John Libbey.

Cornejo, I. (1994) "Como la ves? El psicodrama aplicado al estudio de la recepcion televisiva," *Cuadernos de Comunicacion y Practicas Sociales*, 6, Mexico: PROIICOM, Iberoamerican University.

Corner, J., Richardson, K., and Fenton, N. (1990) *Nuclear Reactions*, London: John Libbey.

Crigler, A. N. and Jensen, K. B. (1991) "Discourses of politics: talking about public issues in the United States and Denmark," in P. Dahlgren and C. Sparks (eds) *Communication and Citizenship*, London: Routledge.

Crovi, D. (1995) 'TV y Neoliberalismo,' PhD dissertation, Mexican National Autonomous University.

Curran, J. (1990) "The 'new revisionism' in mass communication research: a re-appraisal," *European Journal of Communication*, 5(2–3): 135–64.

Davison, W. P. (1983) "The third-person effect in communication," *Public Opinion Quarterly*, 47: 1–15.

Dearing, J. and Rogers, E. (1996) *Agenda-Setting*, Thousand Oaks CA: Sage.

Delia, J. (1987) "Communication research: a history," in C. Berger and S. Chaffee (eds) *Handbook of Communication Science*, Newbury Park CA: Sage.

Denzin, N. and Lincoln, Y. (eds) (1994) *Handbook of Qualitative Research*, Thousand Oaks CA: Sage.

DeWerth-Pallmeyer, D. (1997) *The Audience in the News*, Mahwah NJ: Erlbaum.

Drotner, K. (1994) "Ethnographic enigmas: 'the everyday' in recent media studies," *Cultural Studies*, 8(2): 341–57.

Eco, U. (1976) *A Theory of Semiotics*, Bloomington IN: Indiana University Press.

—— (1984) *Semiotics and the Philosophy of Language*, London: Macmillan.

Efimova, N. V. (1993) "The Belarusian press on the Chernobyl disaster: the inertia of the totalitarian model of mass communication," in O. Manaev and Y. Pryliuk (eds) *Media in Transition: From Totalitarianism to Democracy*, Kiev: ABRIS.

—— (1994) "The factors of development and restriction of access to electronic mass media," in N. Jankowski and S. Splichal (eds) *Rethinking Access: Theory, Policy and Practice of Access to Electronic Media*, 8th EURICOM Colloquium, 21–25 September 1994, Piran, Slovenia.

—— (1996) "The romance of viewers and state-owned mass media is going through a crisis," *Svaboda*, 26 July (in Russian).

Electronic Media (1995a) "Cable networks' 1994 ratings," 9 January: 62.

—— (1995b) "Season-to-date Nielsen ratings (averages)," 9 January: 48.

Ellis, J. (1982) *Visible Fictions*, London: Routledge.

Enzensberger, H. M. (1972) "Constituents of a theory of the media," in D. McQuail (ed.) *Sociology of Mass Communications*, Harmondsworth UK: Penguin.

Epstein, E. (1973) *News from Nowhere*, New York: Random House.

Ettema, J. and Whitney, D. C. (eds) (1994) *Audiencemaking*, Thousand Oaks CA: Sage.

Fish, S. (1979) *Is There a Text in This Class? The Authority of Interpretive Communities*, Cambridge MA: Harvard University Press.

Fishman, M. (1980) *Manufacturing the News*, Austin: University of Texas Press.

Fiske, J. (1987) *Television Culture*, London: Methuen.

—— (1993) *Power Plays, Power Works*, London: Verso.

—— (1994) *Media Matters*, Minneapolis: University of Minnesota Press.

Foucault, M. (1984) *The History of Sexuality*, Harmondsworth: Penguin.

—— (1986) "Afterword: the subject and power," in H. L. Dreyfus and P. Rabinow (eds) *Michel Foucault: Beyond Structuralism and Hermeneutics*, Sussex: Harvester Press.

Gamson, W. A. (1989) "Media discourse and public opinion on nuclear power," *American Journal of Sociology* 95: 1–37.

—— (1992) *Talking Politics*, Cambridge: Cambridge University Press.

216

Gamson, W. A. and Stuart, D. (1992) "Media discourse as a symbolic contest: the bomb in political cartoons," *Sociological Forum* 7: 55–86.

Gans, H. (1979) *Deciding What's News*, New York: Pantheon Books.

Giddens, A. (1984) *The Constitution of Society*, Berkeley: University of California Press.

—— (1990) *The Consequences of Modernity*, Cambridge: Polity Press.

Gitlin, T. (1978) "Media sociology: the dominant paradigm," *Theory and Society* 6: 205–53.

Glaser, B. G. and Strauss, A. L. (1967) *The Discovery of Grounded Theory: Strategies for Qualitative Research*, Chicago: Aldine.

Golding, P. and Elliott, P. (1979) *Making the News*, London: Longman.

Golding, P. and Harris, P. (eds) (1997) *Beyond Cultural Imperialism*, London: Sage.

González, J. (ed.) (1990) *Estudios sobre las culturas contemporaneas* 4 (10).

Graber, D. A. (1984) *Processing the News: How People Tame the Information Tide*, New York: Longman.

Green, M. (1991) "Media, education, and communities," in K. B. Jensen and N. W. Jankowski (eds) *A Handbook of Qualitative Methodologies for Mass Communication Research*, London: Routledge.

Griffin, M. (1992) "Looking at TV news: strategies for research," *Communication* 13: 121–41.

Gripsrud, J. (1992) "The aesthetics and politics of melodrama," in P. Dahlgren and C. Sparks (eds) *Journalism and Popular Culture*, London: Sage.

—— (1995) *The Dynasty Years*, London: Routledge.

Grodal, T. (1997) *Moving Images*, New York: Oxford University Press.

Grossberg, L., Nelson, C., and Treichler, P. (eds) (1992) *Cultural Studies*, New York: Routledge.

Guizzardi, G. (ed.) (1986) *La narrazione del carisma*, Torino: ERI.

Gurevitch, M. and Blumler, J. G. (1990) "Comparative research: the extending frontier," in D. L. Swanson and D. Nimmo (eds) *New Directions in Political Communication: A Resource Book*, Newbury Park CA: Sage.

Habermas, J. (1989) [1962] *The Structural Transformation of the Public Sphere*, Cambridge MA: MIT Press.

Hacker, K., Coste, T., Kamm, D., and Bybee, C. (1991) "Oppositional readings of network television news: viewer deconstruction," *Discourse and Society*, 2(2): 183–202.

Hall, S. (1975) "La comunicazione strutturata degli avvenimenti. Trattamento televisivo dell'informazione," *Informazione Radio TV* 38.

—— (1983) "The problem of ideology – Marxism without guarantees," in B. Matthews (ed.) *Marx: A Hundred Years On*, London: Lawrence and Wishart.

Hall, S., Hobson, D., Lowe, A., and Willis, P. (eds) (1980) *Culture, Media, Language*, London: Hutchinson.

Halloran, J. (1970) *The Effects of Television*, London: Panther.

Hay, J., Grossberg, L., and Wartella, E. (eds) (1996) *The Audience and Its Landscape*, Boulder CO: Westview Press.

Head, S. W., Sterling, C. H., and Schofield, L. B. (eds) (1994) *Broadcasting in America: A Survey of Electronic Media*, 7th edn, Boston: Houghton-Mifflin.

Hebdige, D. (1979) *Subculture: The Meaning of Style*, London: Methuen.

Heide, M. (1995) *Television Culture and Women's Lives*, Philadelphia: University of Pennsylvania Press.

Hoggart, R. (1957) *The Uses of Literacy*, Harmondsworth UK: Penguin.

Höijer, B. (1990) "Studying viewers' reception of television programs: theoretical and methodological considerations," *European Journal of Communication* 5(1): 29–56.

Horton, D. and Wohl, R. (1956) "Mass communication and parasocial interaction," *Psychiatry*, 19: 215–29.

Hovland, C. (1959) "Reconciling conflicting results derived from experimental and survey studies of attitude change," *American Psychologist* 14: 8–17.

Huyssen, A. (1986) *After the Great Divide: Modernism, Mass Culture, and Postmodernism*, London: Macmillan.

Iyengar, S. (1991) *Is Anyone Responsible? How Television Frames Political Issues*, Chicago: University of Chicago Press.

Iyengar, S. and Kinder, D. R. (1987) *News that Matters: Television and American Opinion*, Chicago: University of Chicago Press.

Jensen, K. B. (1986) *Making Sense of the News*, Aarhus, Denmark: Aarhus University Press.

—— (1987a) "Qualitative audience research: toward an integrative approach to reception," *Critical Studies in Mass Communication*, 4(1): 21–36.

—— (1987b) "News as ideology: economic statistics and political ritual in television network news," *Journal of Communication* 37(1): 8–27.

—— (1988) "News as social resource: a qualitative empirical study of the reception of Danish television news," *European Journal of Communication* 3(3): 275–301.

—— (1990a) "The politics of polysemy: television news, everyday consciousness, and political action," *Media, Culture and Society* 12(1): 57–77.

—— (1990b) "Television futures: a social action methodology for studying interpretive communities," *Critical Studies in Mass Communication* 7(2): 1–18.

—— (1991) "When is meaning? Communication theory, pragmatism, and mass media reception," in J. Anderson (ed.) *Communication Yearbook*, vol. 14, Newbury Park CA: Sage.

—— (1995) *The Social Semiotics of Mass Communication*, London: Sage.

Jensen, K. B. and Jankowski, N. W. (eds) (1991) *A Handbook of Qualitative Methodologies for Mass Communication Research*, London: Routledge.

Jhally, S. and Lewis, J. (1992) *Enlightened Racism: The Cosby Show, Audiences, and the Myth of the American Dream*, Boulder CO: Westview Press.

Joas, H. (1993) *Pragmatism and Social Theory*, Chicago: University of Chicago Press.

Katz, E. (1971) "Television comes to the People of the Book," in I. L. Horowitz (ed.) *The Use and Abuse of Social Science*, New Brunswick NJ: Transaction Books.

Katz, E. and Haas, H. (1994) "Twenty years of television in Israel: are there long-run effects on values and cultural practices?" unpublished manuscript.

Katz, E. and Lazarsfeld, P. (1955) *Personal Influence*, Glencoe IL: Free Press.

Katz, E., Gurevitch, M., and Haas, H. (1973) "On the use of mass media for important things," *American Sociological Review* 38: 164–81.

Keane, J. (1991) *The Media and Democracy*, Cambridge: Polity Press.

Klapper, J. (1960) *The Effects of Mass Communication*, Glencoe IL: Free Press.

Kohut, A. and Toth, R. C. (1994) "Arms and people," *Foreign Affairs* 73(6): 47–91.

Kostenko, N. V. (1993) *Values and Symbols in Mass Media*, Kiev: Naucova Dumca (in Russian).

Kraus, S. and Perloff, R. M. (eds) (1986) *Mass Media and Political Thought*, Beverly Hills CA: Sage.

Krippendorff, S. (1979) "The communication approach to development," in J. A. Lent (ed.) *Third World Mass Media: Issues, Theory, and Research*, Williamsburg VA: Department of Anthropology, College of William and Mary.

Kvale, S. (1987) "Validity in the qualitative research interview," *Methods* 1: 37–72.

Lazarsfeld, P. F., Berelson, B., and Gaudet, H. (1944) *The People's Choice*, New York: Columbia University Press.

Lenin, V. I. (1901) "What to begin with?" in *Complete Works*, vol. 5, Moscow: Politizdat (in Russian).

Levy, M. R. and Windahl, S. (1984) "Audience activity and gratifications: a conceptual clarification and exploration," *Communication Research* 11: 51–78.

Lewis, L. (ed.) (1991) *The Adoring Audience*, London: Routledge.

Liebes, T. (1992) "Decoding TV news: the political discourse of Israeli hawks and doves," *Theory and Society* 21: 357–81.

—— (1997) "Broadcasting in Israel," in H. Newcomb (ed.) *The Encyclopedia of Television*, Austin: University of Texas.

Liebes, T. and Ribak, R. (1991) "A mother's battle against the news: a case study of political socialization," *Discourse and Society* 2: 203–22.

Liebes, T. and Katz, E. (1993) *The Export of Meaning*, Cambridge: Polity Press.

Liebes, T. and Peri, Y. (1998) "Electronic journalism in segmented societies: lessons from the 1996 Israeli elections," *Political Communication* 15(1): 27–43.

Lindlof, T. (ed.) (1987) *Natural Audiences*, Norwood NJ: Ablex.

—— (1995) *Qualitative Communication Research Methods*, Thousand Oaks CA: Sage.

Lippmann, W. (1922) *Public Opinion*, New York: Free Press.

Livingstone, S. and Lunt, Peter (1994) *Talk on Television*, London: Routledge.

Lull, J. (1980) "The social uses of television," *Human Communication Research* 6: 197–209.

—— (1988a) "Critical response: the audience as nuisance," *Critical Studies in Mass Communication* 5: 239–43.

—— (ed.) (1988b) *World Families Watch Television*, Newbury Park CA: Sage.

—— (1988c) "The family and television in world cultures," in J. Lull (ed.) *World Families Watch Television*, Newbury Park CA: Sage.

MacBride, S. (ed.) (1980) *Many Voices, One World*, Paris: UNESCO.

MacGregor, B. (1997) *Live, Direct, and Biased? Making Television News in the Satellite Age*, London: Edward Arnold.

Madan, T. N. (1987) "Secularism in its place," *Journal of Asian Studies* 56(4): 747–59.

Manaev, O. T. (1986) "People's involvement in the mass media sphere," in G. Davidjuk and V. Korobeinikov (eds) *The Effectiveness of Mass Information Media*, Minsk: Nauka i Technika (in Russian).

—— (1991) "Experiences from a content analysis of the alternative press of Belarus," *Sociological Studies* 8: 32–44 (in Russian).

—— (1996) "Media autonomy, diversity vs. unity, and the state in transition: the Belarus experience," *Communicatio* 22(1): 27–42.

219

Mancini, P. (1990) "Selective reception and super themes in decoding television news," paper presented to the conference of the International Communication Association, Dublin, Ireland.

—— (1991) *Guardando il Telegiornale: Per un'etnografia del consumo televisivo*, Torino: Nuova ERI.

Masselos, J. (1993) "The city as represented in crowd action: Bombay, 1893," *Economic and Political Weekly* 28(5): 183–8.

Masterman, L. (1985) *Teaching the Media*, London: Comedia.

Mazzoleni, G. (1992) "Italy," in Euromedia Research Group (eds) *The Media in Western Europe*, London: Sage.

—— (1995) "Towards a videocracy," *European Journal of Communication* 10(3): 291–321.

McClosky, H. and Zaller, J. (1984) *The American Ethos: Public Attitudes toward Capitalism and Democracy*, Cambridge MA: Harvard University Press.

McCombs, M. (1994) "News influence on our pictures of the world," in J. Bryant and D. Zillmann (eds) *Media Effects: Advances in Theory and Research*, Hillsdale NJ: Erlbaum.

McCombs, M. and Shaw, D. L. (1972) "The agenda-setting functions of mass media," *Public Opinion Quarterly* 36: 176–87.

McDonald, D. G. (1990) "Media orientation and television news viewing," *Journalism Quarterly* 6: 11–20.

McQuail, D. (1994) *Mass Communication Theory: An Introduction*, 3rd edn, London: Sage.

Mead, G. H. (1934) *Mind, Self, and Society*, Chicago: University of Chicago Press.

Merritt, D. (1995) *Public Journalism and Public Life*, Hillsdale NJ: Erlbaum.

Messaris, P. (1992) *Visual "Literacy": Image, Mind, and Reality*, Boulder CO: Westview Press.

—— (1997) *Visual Persuasion*, Thousand Oaks CA: Sage.

Meyrowitz, J. (1985) *No Sense of Place*, New York: Oxford University Press.

Miles, M. B. and Huberman, A. M. (1994) *Qualitative Data Analysis*, 2nd edn, London: Sage.

Mitra, A. (1993) *Television and Popular Culture in India: A Study of the Mahabharat*, New Delhi: Sage.

Mitzkevitch, A. (1990) "Mass media and 'perestroika'," *Sociological Studies* 11: 140–7 (in Russian).

Moi, T. (1985) *Sexual/Textual Politics*, London: Methuen.

Molina, G. (1989) 'The making of Mexican TV news,' PhD dissertation, Leicester University, UK.

Monteiro, A. (1993) 'State, subject, and the "text": the construction of meaning in television,' PhD dissertation, Goa University, India.

Monteiro, A. and Jayasankar, K. P. (1994) "The spectator-Indian: an exploratory study on the reception of news," *Cultural Studies* 8(1): 162–82.

—— (forthcoming) "Between the normal and the imaginary: the spectator-self, the other, and satellite television in India," in I. Hagen and J. Wasko (eds), *Consuming Audiences*, Hampton Press.

Moores, S. (1993) *Interpreting Audiences: The Ethnography of Media Consumption*, London: Sage.

Morley, D. (1980a) *The 'Nationwide' Audience*, London: British Film Institute.

—— (1980b) "Texts, readers, subjects," in S. Hall, D. Hobson, A. Lowe, and P. Willis (eds) *Culture, Media, Language*, London: Hutchinson.

—— (1986) *Family Television: Cultural Power and Domestic Leisure*, London: Comedia.

—— (1988) "Domestic relations: the framework of family viewing in Great Britain," in J. Lull (ed.) *World Families Watch Television*, Newbury Park CA: Sage.

—— (1992) "Introduction," in *Television, Audiences, and Cultural Studies*, London: Routledge.

Morley, D. and Silverstone, R. (1991) "Communication and context: ethnographic perspectives on the media audience," in K. B. Jensen and N. W. Jankowski (eds) *A Handbook of Qualitative Methodologies for Mass Communication Research*, London: Routledge.

Morris, M. (1990) "Banality in cultural studies," in P. Mellencamp (ed.) *Logics of Television*, Bloomington: Indiana University Press.

Murdoch, G. (1974) "Political deviance: the press presentation of a militant mass demonstration," in S. Cohen and J. Young (eds) *The Manufacture of News: Social Problems, Deviance, and the Mass Media*, London: Constable.

Nandy, A. (1988) "The politics of secularism and the recovery of religious tolerance," *Alternatives* 13: 177–94.

—— (1993a) "Terrorism – Indian Style," *Seminar*, 401: 35–41.

—— (1993b) "Three propositions," *Seminar*, 402: 15–17.

Neuman, W. R. (1986) *The Paradox of Mass Politics*, Cambridge MA: Harvard University Press.

—— (1991) *The Future of the Mass Audience*, Cambridge: Cambridge University Press.

Neuman, W. R., Just, M. R., and Crigler, A. N. (1992) *Common Knowledge: News and the Construction of Political Meaning*, Chicago: University of Chicago Press.

Newport, F. and Saad, L. (1994) "Confidence in 'institutions'," *The Gallup Poll Monthly* April: 5–6.

Nielsen Media Research (1992) *Nielsen Television Index Special Release: Television Audience 1991*, New York: Nielsen Media Research.

—— (1993) *Nielsen Station Index: Directory, 1992–1993*, New York: Nielsen Media Research.

Nightingale, V. (1996) *Studying Audiences*, London: Routledge.

Nimmo, D. and Combs, J. E. (1990) *Mediated Political Realities*, 2nd edn, New York: Longman.

Noelle-Neumann, E. (1973) "Return to the concept of powerful mass media," in H. Eguchi and K. Sato (eds) *Studies of Broadcasting*, 9, Tokyo: NHK.

Nordenstreng, Kaarle (1972) "Policy for news transmission," in D. McQuail (ed.) *Sociology of Mass Communications*, Harmondsworth UK: Penguin.

Orozco, G. (1988) 'Commercial TV and children's education in Mexico: the interaction of socializing institutions in the production of learning,' PhD dissertation, Harvard University.

—— (ed.) (1992) *Hablan los Televidentes*, Lomas de Santa Fe, Mexico: Universidad Iberoamericana.

—— (1994a) "La autonomia relativa de la audiencia: implicaciones metodologicas para la investigacion de la recepcion," in C. Cervantes and E. Sánchez (eds) *Investigar la*

Comunicacion: Propuestas Iberoamericanas, Mexico: Latin American Association of Communication Research (ALAIC).

—— (1994b) "Farsa, sainete y drama en la compraventa del paquete de medios," *Revista Mexicana de Comunicacion* 34: 46–7.

—— (1994c) "Chiapas: la otra guerra, sus protagonistas y su teleaudiencia," *APUMA* 8: 11–19 (Spain).

—— (1995a) "The dialectic of mediation: audiences' TV viewing strategies," *Mexican Journal of Communication* 2: 93–106.

—— (1995b) "Madres mexicanas frente a la TV," paper presented at the international conference, Estudios de Genero y Comunicacion, Mexico.

Orozco, G. and Viveros, F. (1996) "La oferta de la TV y su percepción por jóvenes de la ciudad de Mexico," *Anuario de Investigacion de la Comunicacion*, 3, Mexico: Coneicc.

Pandey, G. (1993) "Which of us are Hindus?," in G. Pandey (ed.) *Hindus And Others*, New Delhi: Viking.

Park, R. E. (1940) "News as a form of knowledge," *American Journal of Sociology* 45: 669–86.

Patterson, T. E. and McClure, R. D. (1976) *The Unseeing Eye: The Myth of Television Power in National Elections*, New York: Putnam.

Paz, O. (1974) *El Laberinto de la Soledad*, Mexico: Fondo de Cultura Economica.

Peirce, C. S. (1992) "Deduction, induction, and hypothesis," in N. Houser and C. Klosel (eds) *The Essential Peirce*, vol. 1, Bloomington: Indiana University Press.

Petersen, V. G. and Siune, K. (1992) "Denmark," in Euromedia Research Group (eds) *The Media in Western Europe*, London: Sage.

Pike, K. (1967) *Language in Relation to a Unified Theory of the Structure of Human Behavior*, 2nd edn, The Hague: Mouton.

Popkin, S. L. (1991) *The Reasoning Voter: Communication and Persuasion in Presidential Campaigns*, Chicago: University of Chicago Press.

Popper, K. (1972) *Conjectures and Refutations*, London: Routledge and Kegan Paul.

Postman, N. (1985) *Amusing Ourselves to Death*, New York: Viking.

Potter, J. and Wetherell, M. (1987) *Discourse and Social Psychology*, London: Sage.

Press, A. (1991) *Women Watching Television*, Philadelphia: University of Pennsylvania Press.

Radway, J. (1984) *Reading the Romance: Women, Patriarchy, and Popular Literature*, Chapel Hill: University of North Carolina Press.

Reeves, B. (1996) "Hemispheres of scholarship: psychological and other approaches to studying media audiences," in J. Hay, L. Grossberg, and E. Wartella (eds) *The Audience and Its Landscape*, Boulder CO: Westview Press.

Renero, M. (1992) "La mediacion familiar en la construccion de la audiencia," *Cuadernos de Comunicacion y Practicas Sociales*, 4, Mexico: PROIICOM, Iberoamerican University.

Robinson, J. P. and Levy, M. R. (1986) *The Main Source: Learning from Television News*, Beverly Hills CA: Sage.

Rochberg-Halton, E. (1986) *Meaning and Modernity*, Chicago: University of Chicago Press.

Rosengren, K., Wenner, L., and Palmgreen, P. (eds) (1985) *Media Gratifications Research: Current Perspectives*, Beverly Hills CA: Sage.

Rubin, A. (1994) "Media uses and effects: a uses-and-gratifications perspective," in J. Bryant and D. Zillmann (eds) *Media Effects: Advances in Theory and Research*, Hillsdale NJ: Erlbaum.

Rubin, A. M. and Perse, E. M. (1987) "Audience activity and television news gratifications," *Communication Research* 14: 58–84.

Said, E. (1978) *Orientalism*, London: Routledge and Kegan Paul.

Sánchez, E. (1983) 'Capital accumulation, the state, and TV as informal education: case study of Mexico,' PhD dissertation, Stanford University.

—— (1994) "El publico de la prensa: la insoportable levedad de casi no ser," *Anuario de Investigacion de la Comunicacion*, 1, Mexico: Coneicc.

Sandemose, Aksel (1936) *A Fugitive Crosses His Tracks*, New York: Knopf.

Scannell, P. (1988) "Radio times: the temporal arrangements of broadcasting in the modern world," in P. Drummond and R. Paterson (eds) *Television and its Audience*, London: British Film Institute.

Schiller, H. (1969) *Mass Communications and American Empire*, New York: Kelley.

Schlesinger, A., Jr. (1995) "Back to the womb: on the new-old isolationism," *Foreign Affairs* 74(4): 2–8.

Schlesinger, P. (1978) *Putting 'Reality' Together*, London: Constable.

Schlesinger, P., Dobash, R., Dobash, R., and Weaver, C. (1992) *Women Viewing Violence*, London: British Film Institute.

Schudson, M. (1978) *Discovering the News*, New York: Basic Books.

—— (1982) "The politics of narrative form: the emergence of news conventions in print and television," *Daedalus*, Fall 1982.

—— (1991) "Historical approaches to communication studies," in K. B. Jensen and N. W. Jankowski (eds) *A Handbook of Qualitative Methodologies for Mass Communication Research*, London: Routledge.

Semyonov, V. E. (1979) "Social-psychological analysis of mass media, literature, and art," in E. S. Kusmin and V. E. Semenov (eds) *Social Psychology*, Leningrad: LSU (in Russian).

Shaw, D. L. and McCombs, M. E. (eds) (1977) *The Emergence of American Political Issues: The Agenda-Setting Function of the Press*, St. Paul MN: West.

Siebert, F., Peterson, T., and Schramm, W. (1956) *Four Theories of the Press*, Urbana: University of Illinois Press.

Sigal, L. (1973) *Reporters and Officials*, Lexington KY: Heath.

Silverstone, R. (1994) *Television and Everyday Life*, London: Routledge.

Sinclair, J. (1986) "Dependent development and broadcasting: the Mexican formula," *Media, Culture and Society* 8(1).

—— (1990) "Neither West nor Third World: the Mexican TV industry within the NWICO debate," *Media, Culture and Society* 12(3).

Singhal, A. and Rogers, E. M. (1989) *India's Information Revolution*, New Delhi: Sage.

Smith, A. D. (1986) *The Ethnic Origins of Nations*, Oxford: Basil Blackwell.

Sreberny-Mohammadi, A. (1991) "The global and the local in international communications," in J. Curran and M. Gurevitch (eds) *Mass Media and Society*, London: Edward Arnold.

Sreberny-Mohammadi, A. with K. Nordenstreng, R. Stevenson, and F. Ugboajah (eds) (1985) *Foreign News in the Media: International Reporting in 29 Countries*, Paris: UNESCO.

Statham, P. (1996) "Television news and the public sphere in Italy," *European Journal of Communication* 11(4): 511–57.

Stimson, J. A. (1991) *Public Opinion in America: Moods, Cycles and Swings*, Boulder CO: Westwood Press.

Straubhaar, J. D., Heeter, C., Greenberg, B. S., Ferreira, L., Wicks, R. H., and Lau, T. Y. (1992) "What makes news: Western, socialist, and Third World newscasts compared in eight countries," in F. Korzenny and E. Schiff (eds) *International and Intercultural Communication Annual*, 16, Newbury Park CA: Sage.

Swanson, D. (1992) "Managing theoretical diversity in cross-national studies of political communication," in J. Blumler, J. McLeod, and K. E. Rosengren (eds) *Comparatively Speaking: Communication and Culture across Time and Space*, Newbury Park CA: Sage.

Thompson, J. B. (1995) *The Media and Modernity*, Cambridge: Polity Press.

Times Mirror Center for the People and the Press (1994) *The New Political Landscape*, Washington DC: Times Mirror Center for the People and the Press.

Tomlinson, J. (1994) "A phenomenology of globalization? Giddens on global modernity," *European Journal of Communication* 9(2).

Tuchman, G. (1978) *Making News*, New York: Free Press.

Vashkevich, V. R. (1993) "Features of local media in the transition period," in A. Sluca (ed.) *Journalism: Current Problems*, vol. 1, Minsk: BSU (in Russian).

Wallis, R. and Baran, S. (1990) *The Known World of Broadcast News*, London: Routledge.

Webster, J. G. and Phalen, P. F. (1997) *The Mass Audience: Rediscovering the Dominant Model*, Mahwah NJ: Erlbaum.

Williams, R. (1977) *Marxism and Literature*, London: Oxford University Press.

Windahl, S., Signitzer, B., and Olson, J. (1991) *Using Communication Theory*, London: Sage.

Wolton, D. (ed.) (1992) "À la recherche du public," *Hermes*, 11–12.

Wright, C. (1960) "Functional analysis and mass communication," *Public Opinion Quarterly*, 23: 605–20.

INDEX

ABC 145, 146, 151, 152, 153
abduction 181
Abdziralovich, I. 20
Adorno, T. 14
agency 16
agenda-setting 6
Alianza Cívica 126
Almond, G. 144
Aloni, S. 96–7
Altheide, D. 192
analogies between stories in life and on the news 96–7
Anderson, B. 69
Ang, I. 11, 91, 127
Ansolabehere, S. 155
Asard, E. 156
authority 166; Denmark 54–6, *see also* power; powerful interests; state
autonomous images 56–7

Baacke, D. 11
Baran, S. 7
Barthes, R. 14
BBC 79, 80, 81, 82
Belarus 2, 20–38, 166, 167, 168–9, 180, 184, 185, 186, 187, 190, 191, 200–6 *passim*
Belarusian Association of Non-State TV (BANT) 22
Beniger, J. 164
Bennett, W.L. 147, 156
Berelson, B. 10
Berlusconi, S. 104
Berman, M. 193
Bernstein, B. 193
Bernstein, R. 187
bias 92, 154

Biden, J. 152
Blumler, J. 5, 194
Bogart, L. 146
Bohmann, K. 129
Bordwell, D. 182
Bosnia 109–10, 121, 148, 149, 152, 156–7, 200, 202, 203, 204, 206, 207
Boyd-Barrett, O. 9
Branigan, E. 182
Bredegaard, K. 44
Briller, B.R. 154
Brooks, P. 191
Brown, H. 152
Bryant, J. 5

cable television: India 65–6; Israel 89; Mexico 130; United States 146
Carey, J.W. 11
Carlsson, U. 11
Casetti, F. 124
Caspi, D. 89
CBS 130, 145, 146
Chaffee, S. 4
Cheli, E. 106
Chiapas conflict 126, 128
Chowla, N.L. 65
Church, Italy 121–3
Clifford, J. 182
Clinton, B. 148, 151, 152, 153
Clough, P. 183
CNN International 25, 44–5, 80, 81, 130 146
cognitive psychology 147, 182
Cohen, A. 8, 9, 179
Cohen, A.A. 151
Combs, J.E. 147
comparative research 194–7

Head, S.W. 145
health care reform, US 152–3, 156, 162
Hebdige, D. 14
Heide, M. 11
Hermes, J. 91
Hindus 70–2
Hochheimer, J. 4
Hoggart, R. 10
Höijer, B. 15, 56
homosexuals in US armed services 149,
    151, 156, 160, 161, 162
hope 140
Horkheimer, M. 14
Horton, D. 5, 90
Hovland, C. 163
Huberman, A.M. 197
human potential, as super-theme 161–2,
    177
Huyssen, A. 193

identity as interpretive dimension 166–7;
    Belarus 167, 169; India 172; Italy 167,
    175–6; United States 177–8
identity as super-theme, India 61, 66,
    67–8, 69–72, 84, 85, 86, 171
Imevision 129
immediacy 77, 80, 81–2, 86
Independent Institute of Socio-Economic
    and Political Research (IISEPS) 21, 23
India 2, 61–87, 166, 171–2, 180, 184,
    185, 186, 187, 188, 190, 191, 192,
    201–6 passim
influence 4–5
Institutional Revolutionary Party (PRI)
    128
instrumental use of news 9–10
international agencies 8, 9
international events: Belarus 25; Denmark
    47; India 76–7; Mexico 138, 139, see
    also Bosnia; war
interpretation of media contents 10–11,
    105–7; oppositional 14–15
Israel 2, 88–102, 165–6, 172–4, 180, 184,
    185, 186, 187, 201–6 passim
Italy 2–3, 103–25, 167, 174–6, 180, 184,
    185, 186, 201, 204–5, 206
Iyengar, S. 147, 155

Jankowski, N.W. 197
Jayasankar, K.P. 61–87
Jennings, P. 151

Jensen, K.B. 1–19, 29, 39–60, 93, 105,
    106, 127, 163, 164–213
Jhally, S. 11, 189
Joas, H. 187
John Paul II, Pope 121–3, 167, 175–6,
    180
Just, M.R. 4

Katz, E. 4, 5, 12, 88, 90, 92
Keane, J. 90
Kinder, D.R. 147, 155
Klapper, J. 5
Kohut, A. 144
Kostenko, N.V. 28
Kraus, S. 147
Krippendorff, S. 63
Kübler, H. 11
Kvale, S. 195

law and order, India 68–9
Lazarsfeld, P. 4
Lenin, V.I. 21
Levy, M.R. 6, 147, 154
Lewis, J. 11, 189
Lewis, L. 14
Liebes, T. 12, 88–102
Limor, Y. 89
Lincoln, Y. 197
Lindlof, T. 11, 105, 197
Lippmann, W. 182
Livingstone, S. 104, 111
local radio: Denmark 41; Israel 89
local television: Denmark 41; Italy 103;
    United States 146
localization 116–17
lotting system 103
Lugar, R. 152
Lull, J. 11, 12, 14, 19, 46, 104, 127, 154
    185
Lunt, P. 104, 111

MacBride, S. 7
MacGregor, B. 8
Madan, T.N. 63
Magaziner, I. 153
Manaev, O.T. 21, 37
Mancini, P. 19, 103–25
mapping 95–6
Marcus, G.E. 182
Masselos, J. 67
Masterman, L. 194

Mazzoleni, G. 103
McClosky, H. 144
McClure, R.D. 147
McCombs, M. 6, 36, 58, 147
McDonald, D.G. 154
McQuail, D. 9
Mead, G.H. 58, 167
mediation, of political action 193–4
melodrama 190–2
Merritt, D. 154
Messaris, P. 182, 194
metatheoretical analysis 195
Metro channel 66
Mexico 3, 126–43, 166, 176–7, 180, 184,
    185, 186, 188, 192, 201–7 *passim*
Meyrowitz, J. 105
Miles, M.B. 197
Milton, J. 193
Mitzkevitch, A. 21
Molina, G. 126
Monteiro, A. 61–87
Moores, S. 11
morality, India 68
Morley, D. 10–11, 12, 14, 19, 86, 127,
    154
Morris, M. 14
Murdoch, G. 91
Muslims 70–2
Myers, L. 151, 152

Nandy, A. 63, 71, 73, 74, 75
NBC 145, 146, 151, 152, 153
Neuman, W.R. 4, 144–63
newspapers 184, 207; Belarus 25–6;
    Denmark 40–1, 43–4; India 77; Israel
    88, 89, 92; United States 146
Nightingale, V. 11
Nimmo, D. 147
Noelle-Neumann, E. 94
non-interventionism, Mexico 139, 141,
    176–7
Nordenstreng, K. 59
Nunn, S. 151

oppositional interpretation 14–15
Orozco, G. 11, 126–43
the other/others 167; Denmark 170–1;
    India 69–72, 86; Israel 173; Italy 176;
    Mexico 177
ownership of media, Israel 89

Pakistan 73, 74–6
Palmgreen, P. 5
Park, R.E. 166
Patterson, T.E. 147
Paz, O. 140
Peck, F. 151
Peirce, C.S. 181
perestroika 21
Peri, Y. 89
Perloff, R.M. 147
Perse, E.M. 154
personal experience and interpretation of
    news texts 158–9, 163
Petersen, V.G. 41
Phalen, P.F. 145
Pike, K. 183
Pimpinelli, E.A.
Plato 182
pleasure, news watching as 134–5
political action, mediation of 193–4
political cognition 4
politics/politicians: India 83–4; Italy
    113–15, 123
Popkin, S.L. 147
Popper, K. 195
popular culture 13–14
Postman, N. 46
Potter, J. 181
power, of the audience 13–15
power as interpretive dimension 166, 169,
    180; Denmark 170; India 171, 172;
    Italy 175; Mexico 176–7; United States
    177, 178
powerful interests as super-theme 159–60,
    162, 163, *see also* authority; state
press *see* newspapers
Press, A. 11
pretheoretical analysis 195
production, news 8–9
Public Broadcasting System (PBS) 145,
    146
public opinion 4, 39–40
public sector, India 78–9

qualitative research 195–7

radio 184, 207; Belarus 26; Denmark 41,
    44; Israel 89
Radway, J. 11
RAI 103
Rather, D. 152